Acknowledgements

This book would not have been possible without the help and support of many people. I would like to pay particular tribute to the superb editorial team at *Railway Gazette International*: Editor-in-Chief Chris Jackson for giving me the benefit of his encyclopaedic knowledge, for his many helpful suggestions and for reading and correcting my draft text; Senior Editor Nick Kingsley for his keen interest and support and for reading several chapters; Deputy Editor Robert Preston for reading the chapter on Spain; Head of News and Online Andrew Grantham for numerous tips and updates; and Production Editor Izzy Burton for drawing the graphics and other help. Andy Hellawell, Compiler of *Railway Directory* and a former member of the editorial team at *Railway Gazette International*, put in a great deal of time and effort to draw the excellent maps. My deep thanks extend also to Publisher Sheena Rennie for permission to raid the archives and to use the magazine's editorial facilities. I am also grateful to my Commissioning Editor at The History Press, Amy Rigg, for her patience and encouragement, and to Rebecca Newton, Editor, for her meticulous editing.

Special thanks are also due to Professor Rod Smith for contributing the Foreword. Many others, some of whom cannot be mentioned, have contributed photographs and given me their time and expertise. My thanks go to Türker Ahi, Jan Asshauer, Mike Baxter, Andrew Benton, Dailing Hong, David Campione, Didier Delattre, Niki Fong, David Haydock, Alain Hocke, Junyeon Jeong, Liu Jialiang, Igor Kiselev, Ivan Kurtov, Christophe and Jean-Paul Masse, Kazumiki Miura, Christoph Müller, Akihiro Nakamura, Gerald Ollivier, Jerónimo Robledo Morales, Ralf Roman Rossberg, Bodo Schulz, V. Urvantsev, Quintus Vosman, Ivor Warburton and Ian Winfieldale. I am also indebted to my two daughters, Melissa Sharpe and Olivia Wernick, for their encouragement and support. My wonderful wife Kay has been a tower of strength from start to finish, and to her I shall be ever grateful for her many suggestions and much good advice.

Murray Hughes
March 2015

Foreword

The fiftieth anniversary since the opening of the Tokaido Shinkansen allows us to reflect that it was a vitally important turning point in the fortunes of railways worldwide. The title chosen by Murray Hughes for this volume, *The Second Age of Rail*, is truly appropriate. In 1964 railways throughout the world were declining in the face of competition from rapidly expanding car ownership and, indeed, public transport generally was in decline. The boldness of the Japanese, only twenty years on from their defeat and destruction during the Second World War, in conceiving, constructing and operating the Shinkansen was remarkable and was a real renaissance of the railways.

The story is told in this volume of the spread of the high-speed rail idea from its birth in Japan to Western Europe, led by France and then later by Germany. In the last twenty years many other countries have joined the high-speed revolution, notably in the Far East where in the last several years the rise of dedicated high-speed lines in China has been absolutely astonishing. China now has a greater length of high-speed line than the rest of the world combined and will double the total in the next few years. The quality of the service offered on these trains is extremely high, as I have personally experienced on several journeys.

Currently the only high-speed maglev system in the world in commercial use is that connecting Shanghai Airport with the inner suburbs of the city. The story of the development of maglev is well recounted in this book. It is interesting to speculate, but at present unclear, on the reasoning behind the choice in China of conventional steel wheel on steel rail for their extensive high-speed railways as opposed to expanding their embryo maglev system. One key feature is, and the story is well told in this book, that operational speeds on dedicated high-speed lines are now approaching the 300 to 350km/h range. Considerably higher speeds have been reached with prototype and experimental trains, including the superb French efforts which open this volume. However, the damage caused to both train and track by such extremely high-speed running precludes its exploitation in everyday commercial service. A reasonable and economic balance has to be struck between speed and increased maintenance costs caused by speed. If we speculate about the future, one might be tempted to say that something in the order of 350km/h will be an economic ceiling which the steel wheel on steel rail will find difficult to penetrate.

Furthermore, social conditions now are quite different from those which existed at the time of the Shinkansen's inauguration. As well as economic constraints, environmental issues now play a much more important role. These range from the local effects of noise and vibration to global effects caused by energy use and emissions. The electricity which is used to power high-speed trains is generated away from the point of consumption, but if the generation is from fossil fuel, the emissions continue to increase the carbon dioxide in our fragile atmosphere. The global imperatives to produce electricity from sustainable sources will play a significant role in issues of energy use for the railways in the future – and may indeed compromise the railway's present superiority, in terms of emissions, over the automobile.

Paris parade. After its spectacular exploits in April 2007, the V150 train set was displayed on a barge for a cruise along the River Seine. (Christophe Masse)

THE SECOND AGE OF RAIL

A HISTORY OF HIGH-SPEED TRAINS

Murray Hughes

The History Press

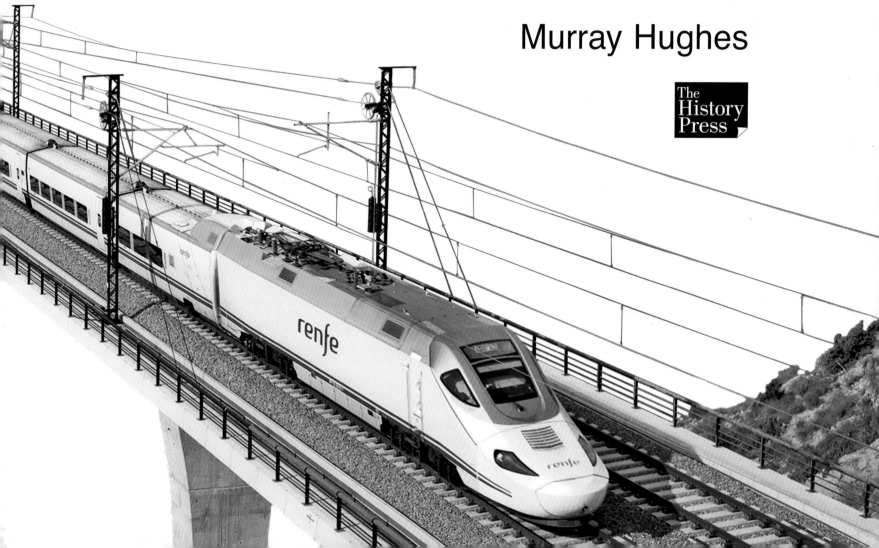

This book is dedicated to

Richard Hope OBE

Editor of *Railway Gazette International* 1970–91

and to

Roger Zeender

Commercial Director for Swiss Federal Railways
in Lausanne when I worked there in 1971

First published 2015

The History Press
The Mill, Brimscombe Port
Stroud, Gloucestershire, GL5 2QG
www.thehistorypress.co.uk

© Murray Hughes, 2015

The right of Murray Hughes to be identified as the Author
of this work has been asserted in accordance with the
Copyright, Designs and Patents Act 1988.

British Library Cataloguing in Publication Data.
A catalogue record for this book is available from the
British Library.

ISBN 978 0 7509 6145 5

Typesetting and origination by The History Press
Printed in Turkey by Imak

Contents

The question of where in the world new high-speed railways will next appear continues to fascinate. A project in the UK has considerable political support but has yet to be enthusiastically embraced by the wider public – the projected opening date is far into the future. Will the USA finally build a modern passenger railway before the oil runs out? To what extent will Middle Eastern countries use some of their oil revenues to build high-speed rail systems? Is Australia too large and its population too small to sustain a high-speed railway? Some answers may be found in the pages of this book.

A most remarkable achievement of the Shinkansen is its unblemished safety record with no fatalities due to train collisions or derailments during its fifty-year life. There have been three major accidents involving high-speed trains in other countries: those at Eschede in Germany, the collision at Wenzhou in China in July 2011, and two years later the derailment at Santiago de Compostela in Spain. It is worth noting that two of these accidents did not occur on dedicated high-speed track but on sections of conventional railway where the protection was more limited. In the case of Wenzhou, the collision happened on a newly built line, but the issue was a software problem which was revealed by a lightning strike.

As we think about the future we might reflect that most professional railway engineers are convinced that the integration of track and train to form a complete system is a vital ingredient of train operation. In recent decades this simple principle has been eroded by efforts to improve the financial performance of railways led by economists and politicians: history has taught us that these groups of people are by no means immune from error.

Professor Roderick A. Smith, FREng, ScD
Future Rail Research Centre, Imperial College, London
Formerly Chief Scientific Advisor, Department for Transport
Past President, Institution of Mechanical Engineers, London
September 2014

Introduction

This book is about the fastest trains in the world.

Today's events are tomorrow's history, and with railways it is no different. The concept of really fast passenger trains on dedicated tracks was pioneered in Japan more than fifty years ago, and the ensuing spread of high-speed railways across the world has been faithfully charted in the pages of *Railway Gazette International* (www.railwaygazette.com). As a member of the editorial team and later as Editor, I was fortunate enough to observe many of these developments at first hand, and the time has come to relate the story to a wider audience than the readers of a professional magazine. This book is the result.

I have endeavoured to recount some of the most significant events and to weave in some technical and political history in a way that is informative and not too dry. It is a truly international tale that entails a journey through Europe, Asia, the Middle East and the USA, a country that remains out of line with much of the world in passenger-train development. Different countries chose diverse ways to create and develop high-speed services, and in most cases governments were involved as the projects were too big to be funded by the private sector. Mistakes were sometimes made, and these too are recounted.

During the second half of the twentieth century rail was often neglected as governments lavished their largesse on motorways and airports. The arrival of high-speed trains has helped to swing opinion back in favour of steel wheels on steel rails. The result is that railways are undergoing a remarkable renaissance that may not have happened had the Shinkansen not demonstrated that rail could be an attractive and effective alternative to

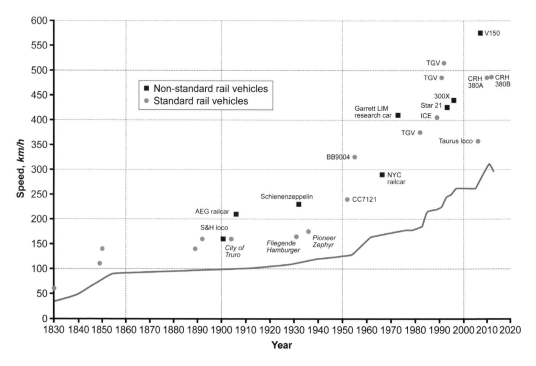

Speeds have risen steadily throughout the history of railways. The red line charts the speed of the world's fastest scheduled trains, measured start-to-stop between two stations; the figure briefly rose above 300km/h in 2009–11 (Chapter 9). The green blobs and blue squares represent individual records by standard and non-standard vehicles respectively.

short-haul flights and private cars for trips of up to 1,000km. Rail's perceived environmental advantage is perhaps another factor.

Far from being outmoded, railways are playing an important role in many national economies. A recent World Bank study in China found that high-speed rail projects generate significant wider economic advantages that accrue in addition to the direct benefits that are measured using conventional cost-benefit analysis. Further studies are expected to support this thesis.

Every two years *Railway Gazette International* publishes a survey of the world's fastest timetabled trains. Thanks to the expertise, persistence and dedication of far-sighted railway engineers and managers, speeds have risen steadily, and this is illustrated in the graph above. The green dots and blue squares represent individual speed records over the 180 years or so that railways have existed. The red line plots the rise in speed of the world's fastest scheduled trains, measured start-to-stop between two stations. You may be surprised to find that today's fastest trains do not run in France or Japan, but in … the answer is in Chapter 9.

In 2014 there were thirteen countries where trains were timetabled at speed maxima of 250km/h to 300km/h, with one attaining 310km/h and two others achieving 320km/h. Proving that this was feasible and safe often demanded special test runs, during which some spectacular one-off records were attained. Yet the challenge is not to clock up a record, but to operate high-speed trains safely and reliably on a day-to-day basis.

Plans for high-speed railways exist in many countries, including Australia, Brazil, Egypt, India, Iran, Malaysia and the Nordic states. Most are not included as they have yet to progress beyond paper. Projects have been dropped in Kazakhstan and Portugal, but many more lines are likely to be completed over the next two decades.

A word about the definition of high speed. The International Union of Railways sets the threshold at 250km/h, which is also adopted here. However, it would be wrong not to mention briefly the superb 200km/h diesel-powered High-Speed Trains in Britain and their successors. Similarly, trains such as Sweden's X2000 and Austria's 230km/h Railjet merit attention but do not feature here for reasons of space. The early development of 200km/h operations was covered in my previous book *Rail 300: The World High Speed Train Race*.

Compiling *The Second Age of Rail* has not been without problems. One difficulty is ascertaining the precise distance between cities over high-speed lines as different sources may cite different figures.

Tomorrow's Eurostar. The e320, Eurostar's 320km/h second-generation train, was unveiled at London's magnificently refurbished St Pancras station on 13 November 2014, twenty years after the first Eurostar trains ran through the Channel Tunnel. It will enter service on the London–Paris and London–Brussels routes in December 2015.

This is partly explained by the quoted length of new lines sometimes including multiple links to and from the conventional network — this is the case in Italy and China. Calculations are not helped by railways publishing so-called 'tariff-km' instead of actual distances. An example is the famous Tokaido Shinkansen, whose length is sometimes misquoted by JR Central as 553km when the actual distance is 515.4km.

Geographical names are generally anglicised in the text, but I have sometimes chosen commonly accepted local names. The maps are derived from *Railway Directory*, published by the *Railway Gazette* group, and these use local spellings throughout. Where there is the possibility of confusion I have shown the local name too: for example Alicante (Alacant) in Spain and Louvain (Leuven) in Belgium.

As the book spans fifty years, I have used the local currency denomination with its historic value and have not converted the figures to current pounds or dollars. For this I beg your indulgence.

The opinions expressed are mine and not those of the *Railway Gazette* group at DVV (UK) Ltd. Any errors are mine, and not those of the countless people who have helped compile this volume.

I invite you to read on.

Murray Hughes
Consultant Editor, *Railway Gazette International*

1

Records Reap Rewards

One Day in Eastern France

Was it fear that gripped the hearts of the passengers, or merely exhilaration? At least one of them was to write about his angst later that day, confessing to the readers of a French newspaper that he was afraid, if only for a few moments. Others were reluctant to reveal their trepidation. Hurtling through the French countryside, cocooned inside a chrome and black projectile on steel wheels, they were no ordinary passengers but the guests of SNCF, French National Railways, who had been invited to take part in an extraordinary event.

Emotions were running high. There was awe, elation, excitement. In the grey-striped first-class seats on the upper deck of car R1, the guests' eyes were all on the screens showing the speed of the train – everyone had long since ceased to look out of the windows where trees, fields and hedges had merged into a greenish-brown blur. Scanning the flickering figures, a journalist clutched the armrests of his seat as the noise mounted and vibrations drummed through the car. Tiny changes in the curvature of the track were magnified. Still the train accelerated, and in car R8 the engineers scanned their computer screens for any telltale sign of trouble. There was none, and the train powered on, faster and faster.

It was 3 April 2007. A few minutes before 10 a.m. that morning a special TGV train had left Paris Est station. On board were VIPs and a group of media chosen to provide maximum coverage of an event that was sure to make headlines across the world. This was nothing less than an attempt to accelerate a train to the improbable speed of 150m a second – or 540km/h. Hence the test train's codename: V150.

A rendezvous had been arranged: the special TGV from Paris was to meet the V150 close to the village of Prény near the town of Metz in Eastern France. Stretching from there towards Paris was the first section of the brand-new *Ligne à Grande Vitesse Est Européen*, France's sixth high-speed railway that was due to enter service just a few weeks later. Part of this pristine infrastructure had been specially fettled for what was about to happen.

In the meantime a second TGV special had left Paris Est at 10.51 a.m., conveying more guests and journalists to Champagne-Ardenne TGV station near the champagne town of Reims. Here a media reception centre had been set up in a temporary building overlooking the tracks where the V150 was due to complete its record-breaking trip.

Near Prény the sixty-two VIPs and journalists chosen as 'live' participants in the adventure had disembarked from the train that had brought them from Paris. They were treated to a private view of another special TGV leaving to 'sweep' the track where the record-breaking attempt was to take place. Shortly afterwards, the five-car V150 train set appeared and drew up imposingly in front of them. Behind the smooth silver nose gleaming in the spring sunshine there was no sign of the standard blue window band of an ordinary TGV. In its place was a deep rippling black and chrome pattern with a tricolour stripe along the bodies of the leading cars. Clearly this was no ordinary TGV. And was it somehow taller than its sister trains?

It was nearly midday, and the visitors were invited to board. Taking their seats on the upper deck of car R1, they could not see the team of engineers and technicians in the laboratory car R8 on whose expertise rested their safety – and the outcome of the record attempt. Among the guests were European Transport Commissioner Jacques Barrot, SNCF President Anne-Marie Idrac and her Chief Executive Guillaume Pepy, together with Hubert du Mesnil, President of Réseau Ferré de France, the organisation that owned the tracks of France's state railway. Accompanying them was Philippe Mellier, the President of Alstom Transport, the company that had built the V150 train, and his boss Patrick Kron, President of Alstom. It was going to be a big day.

Transmission of live TV images began at 12.22 p.m. The timing of the record attempt had been carefully chosen to guarantee maximum coverage, with the V150 due to leave the starting point at precisely 1.01 p.m. so that there would be live images for the lunchtime news bulletins. No fewer than thirteen cameras had been affixed to various parts of the train, and an Aérospatiale Corvette jet aircraft had taken off ready to record the spectacle from the air. Five more cameras had been sited next to the track in the zone where the V150 was expected to reach its maximum speed.

In fact, there were hundreds of cameras in place along the lineside. Weeks of test runs ahead of the record attempt had alerted local people and others to what promised to be a truly spectacular event. The curious and those in the know crowded on to bridges or other vantage points. Some had waited for many weeks. Today they lined the trackside fences to catch a glimpse of railway history in the making.

On board the V150 the countdown had begun. The VIPs were briefed at 12.40 p.m. SNCF Press Officer Philippe Mirville, his excitement barely suppressed, was interviewing key personnel and engineers on board for the live TV programme. Final checks were being made to ensure that all was in order along the track ahead. In the cab, driver Eric Pieczak, Traction Inspector Georges Pinquié and Head of SNCF's Traction Department Claude Maro had completed their own checks. Tension mounted as they waited for the 'off'.

Shortly before 1 p.m. the cameras pan to Daniel Beylot, Head of the V150 Project at SNCF's Rolling Stock Division. All checks and protocols have been completed. The seconds tick away. At last Beylot gives the command that all have been waiting for, and special working no 093.02 is authorised to start. The nose of the sleek streamlined train inches forward and the cameras catch the moment when the wheels start to turn. On board, it is at once obvious that this is no ordinary departure. The acceleration is strong as the hum of the powerful traction motors and electronic equipment grows in intensity.

Starting from Km 264, the train speeds towards the first critical site of the specially prepared track. At Km 255 – the distance is counted from Paris and the train is heading west towards the capital – the train's pantograph has to be lowered to pass through a neutral section in the overhead wires separating the standard 25kV catenary from the test zone where the power has been boosted to no less than 31kV, fed from a substation at Trois Domaines. By 1.05 p.m. Pieczak has raised the pantograph again and the speed recorders are in full flight as they clock the train's unusually rapid progress. By Km 252 the train has reached 200km/h and at Km 246 the figure has shot past 300km/h.

Meteor on rails. The specially configured V150 train set breaks the world rail speed record on 3 April 2007, touching 574.8km/h. (SNCF)

From the cab the driving team glimpses the crowds of well-wishers and photographers as the train rockets under bridges.

The 400km/h barrier is crossed at Km 241. By now the train is streaking through the landscape with a cloud of dust marking its dash through the countryside. The view from a camera on the roof reveals what appears to be an almost continuous arc around the point of contact between the pantograph and overhead wire, but a camera positioned by the leading wheels shows that the ride is rock-steady.

At Km 220 the speed recorders show 500km/h. Seconds pass and loud applause breaks out at 515km/h – the speed of the previous official world record – from now on any speed will qualify for the history books. At 1.10 p.m. the train is roaring through Meuse TGV station, taking the locked points at a staggering 533km/h. But the V150 is steady and still accelerating.

Lineside photographers have just fractions of a second to try and capture the shot of a lifetime as the record-breaker streaks past. More applause breaks out on board as the official target speed of 540km/h is reached. The noise of steel on steel drums through the train as 550km/h is approached and passed. All eyes are on the speed recorders now: 555, 560, 570!

Back in the media centre the figures are appearing on a giant screen, flickering so fast that they are hard to read. They flash up to 573, 574, but no one sees 575. By common consent the figure destined for the history books appears to be 574.6km/h. On board the train Daniel Beylot in car R8 has sent instructions to the cab, and Pieczak has cut the traction and the train is now decelerating, its destination Km 114 and Platform 3 at Champagne-Ardenne TGV station. Still coasting at meteoric speed, it is too early to apply the brakes. Only when the speedometer falls to around 400km/h can dynamic braking be introduced. The train has to be travelling at

Apogée of speed. Crowds of photographers and spectators packed the lineside and bridges as the V150 streaked past on its record-breaking run. (SNCF)

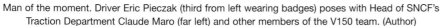

Man of the moment. Driver Eric Pieczak (third from left wearing badges) poses with Head of SNCF's Traction Department Claude Maro (far left) and other members of the V150 team. (Author)

On camera. SNCF President Anne-Marie Idrac gives TV viewers her take on the record at Champagne-Ardenne TGV station. (Author)

no more than 360km/h by Km 166 at Tilloy-et-Bellay where there is a set of unclipped points. With the points safely negotiated, speed continues to fall. At Km 140 the V150 passes Saint-Hilaire-au-Temple, one of the worksites established for the construction teams that had built the new line. Finally, the powerful air-operated disc brakes that will bring the train to a standstill are applied.

Inside the media centre at Champagne-Ardenne station the champagne is already flowing when the V150 draws to a halt in front of an applauding crowd. Moments later, the driving cab door opens

to reveal Pieczak, who climbs down to a barrage of cameras and microphones. Anne-Marie Idrac, wearing a bright orange outfit, appears at the door of the train and disembarks with Mellier, du Mesnil and other guests. They pose for the cameras by the nose of the record breaker as film crews and journalists swarm across the tracks to capture this extraordinary moment in the story of railways.

A press conference is called, and Idrac stresses the human dimension of the technical exploit. I-télé presenter Nathalie Ianetta interviews Jacques

Barrot on live TV and describes him as 'the fastest Commissioner on Earth'. And then comes the official announcement: the V150 has attained an official world record speed of 574.8km/h at Km 193.3 near Passavant-en-Argonne. Yet more applause. Corks pop and glasses clink …

The day was not quite over. Cameras were packed away and final interviews conducted. The V150 slid quietly out of the platform. Its place was soon taken by a TGV reserved for guests returning to Paris. VIPs and media were ushered aboard. As the train hummed westwards, the passengers witnessed one more manoeuvre which the day's organisers had planned. The V150, travelling in the same direction on the adjacent track, appeared alongside. Matching their speed at 320km/h, the future commercial speed on LGV Est-Européen, the two trains streaked towards Paris. It was a final French flourish that rounded off an exceptional day.

★★★

Never before in the long and eventful history of rail travel had a passenger-carrying machine on steel wheels reached such an astonishing speed. And never before had such an event been recorded on live television for instant transmission across the world. This, surely, was the most remarkable thing: the engineers who had planned the event were so confident that speeds of 540km/h and more could be reached safely that they were willing to accept the presence of the world's media on board.

The 'fastest Commissioner on Earth'. European Transport Commissioner Jacques Barrot catches up with the economic news on the way back to Paris. (Author)

One Day in Western France

Back in 1990, when another specially modified TGV had clocked the previous world record near Vendôme on the *Ligne à Grande Vitesse Atlantique*, there had been no live television on board. Instead, the media had been treated to an unforgettable lineside view of what was at that time an equally stunning event. Early in the morning of 18 May that year more than 100 photographers, journalists and TV crew had been whisked by special train from Paris Montparnasse to Vendôme. From there they were taken by bus to a bridge over the tracks of the new line near the point where the record was expected.

A blue-grey haze blurred the outlines of the wooded hills in the distance where the two tracks of the new line from Paris and Vendôme to Tours vanished in a cutting. SNCF had chosen well with its vantage point at Km 167 – it offered an unrestricted view over 4km of long downhill grade where the record attempt would be made. The course of the railway was marked by a long line of electrification masts striding through the fields; in the middle foreground the pale concrete structure of the Naveil viaduct, which carried the new tracks over the River Loir, was picked out by the sun.

The bridge where we were standing had been built to carry the single track of a barely used freight railway from Vendôme to Montoire-sur-le-Loir over the new line; now it was crowded with journalists, some of whom had been following the progress of SNCF's speed trials for months. There had been a long build-up to today's climax of Operation 117, the name SNCF had chosen for the speed trial, again reflecting the speed in metres per second that the engineers hoped to achieve.

A babble of conversation was stilled by the crackle of an announcement over a radio link playing through loudspeakers on the bridge.

The excited voice of a technician on board the test train could be heard: he was saying that TGV Set 325 had been authorised to leave the starting point at Km 123 near Dangeau at 9.51 a.m. Invisible to the watchers on the bridge, the train had begun the record attempt and driver Michel Massinon was applying maximum power on a stretch of track way beyond the distant hill. The commentator's voice relayed the swiftly rising speed figures – by Km 134 the train was hurtling along at 400km/h. Hardly any time elapsed before we heard that it was sweeping through Vendôme station with the speed indicators showing 500km/h.

The pitch of the technician's voice rose as he reeled off the figures. All eyes were on the ribbon of steel that cut across the landscape. Suddenly an aircraft flew over the hill, filming the train somewhere below. And then the train, a tiny speck in the distance, appeared over the hill. The aircraft peeled off to one side. TGV Set 325 was streaking towards the bridge where we stood at well over 500km/h, its three headlights blazing. A V-shaped plume of dust from the freshly ballasted track rose behind as the train tore into the downward gradient. It raced over the Naveil viaduct and stormed beneath us with explosive force. Loud applause broke out as the dust whirlwind settled and the sound of the record-breaking train died away. Reporters gabbled excitedly into their mikes. A helicopter took off with film for Paris. Minutes later the hubbub was broken by an official announcement from SNCF: at 10.06 a.m. precisely Set 325 had touched 515.3km/h; the location was Km 166.8.

Shortly afterwards the media party returned to Vendôme to await the arrival of the record-breaking train which was by now retracing its route. With horn blaring and a deafening squeal of brakes, it arrived to a tumultuous welcome. Out stepped SNCF General Manager Jean Costet and the team of engineers who had made the record possible. Massinon and his colleagues posed for pictures. It was another triumph for SNCF and for French technology.

Many months of research and development had preceded this moment. Staging world records is never undertaken lightly, and at one point it seemed as if the whole idea would be abandoned. Had that been so, there would have been a great deal of chagrin, for the French engineers were rather anxious to win back something they had lost. On 1 May 1988 a German train had eclipsed the previous French-held world record speed. National pride was at stake.

In the late 1980s France had roared ahead in the railway technology stakes. The first *Ligne à Grande Vitesse* between Paris and Lyon had opened in two stages in 1981 and 1983. Spanking new TGVs, finished in a blazing orange livery, were carrying fare-paying passengers in day-to-day service at 260km/h. Before long, in May 1983, SNCF raised the maximum speed to 270km/h to take maximum advantage of the kinetic energy gained on the long downhill grades of the new line.

Before the line opened, SNCF had set out to prove to its future customers that it had truly mastered high-speed technology, and on 26 February 1981 a carefully doctored TGV, Set number 16, attained a world record speed of 380km/h on the new line near the village of Moulins-en-Tonnerrois. This was the start of a new age of railways in France, and far-sighted people could see the potential inherent in the TGV. Among them was President François Mitterrand, who presided at the inauguration of the new line on 22 September 1981. Sensing that political advantage could be gained from providing another chunk of the French population with ultra-fast trains to Paris, he took the opportunity to make it clear that a second TGV line would be built to serve Western France.

The last rail on the second line, known as the LGV Atlantique, was ceremonially welded in place on 2 February 1989. The route formed a Y-shape with the common stem running from Paris to a junction at Courtalain. From there one arm ran west towards Le Mans and the other struck south-west towards Tours. On 20 September that year the Paris–Le Mans section was inaugurated. The second part was due to be opened in September 1990.

Germany was late out of the starting blocks in the race to develop high-speed train technology. Long after French engineers had perfected the first-generation TGVs, the Germans belatedly decided that they had work to do if their railway industry was not to be eclipsed by their rivals across the Rhine. In 1982 funds were made available to develop Germany's own prototype high-speed train, which was branded the Intercity-Experimental.

This was a five-car research unit with two heavy power cars and three trailers. Quickly dubbed the ICE, it emerged in mid-1985, and on 26 November it attained an official German record speed of 317km/h on the long, straight stretch of railway between Hamm and Bielefeld. In the following year, part of Germany's first high-speed line or *Neubaustrecke* between Hannover and Würzburg became available for test runs, and the ICE switched its stamping ground. About this time, officials at Deutsche Bundesbahn, the German Federal Railway, had let it be known that their new toy was capable of 400km/h. Fortune, however, was not smiling on the engineers, and in September 1986 the ICE suffered a derailment. Although the accident happened at only 15km/h, it did nothing for those who were anxious to promote Germany's railway industry with an attempt on a world record. So it was that those who took part in a press trip on 16 November 1986 found that the speed dials went no higher than 345km/h – a disappointing outcome.

Silver streak. TGV Set 325 rockets past Km 166 on 18 May 1990, setting a world rail speed record of 515.3km/h. (SNCF)

All went quiet as the engineering teams retreated out of the public eye. Then, just as the French were completing the first part of LGV Atlantique, the call came for a press visit to Germany. It was April 1988, and DB was in the final stages of testing the Rohrbach–Burgsinn section of its new Hannover–Würzburg line that was due to open on 29 May. On 22 April the ICE, now in a formation of just four cars and all spruced up after a spell in the Minden research centre, was accelerated up to 350km/h. The contact wire tension had been raised from 15 to 21kN for the tests, and higher speeds looked distinctly possible. On 28 April the ICE became the first train in the world to smash through the 400km/h barrier, just touching 401km/h. On the following day the test team took their charge up to 404km/h as a taster for a special event arranged for 1 May.

Three trips were scheduled that day. On the third run, with DB Chairman Dr Rainer Gohlke, Transport Minister Dr Jürgen Warnke and Research Minister Dr Heinz Riesenhuber on board, the train slipped away from Würzburg Hauptbahnhof at 11 a.m. Driver Romano Henning turned up the power and after just 15km his speedometer crept past 400km/h. Shooting out of the Einmalberg Tunnel into the Sinn Valley, the ICE was still accelerating. At 11.12 a.m. the recorders in the laboratory car signalled that the train had reached a new maximum of 406.9km/h. Germany was the proud owner of the world's fastest train.

All this did not go unnoticed in France. As part of the process for testing the new trains for LGV Atlantique, a TGV from the fleet built for the Paris–Lyon line had been modified with the updated technology intended for France's second fleet of high-speed trains. This vehicle emerged in May 1987 as TGV Set 88, and it spent a lot of time dashing up and down the Paris–Lyon route to test its novel traction equipment. With this duty completed, Set 88 returned to the workshop at Bischheim for more treatment. In 1988 the train reappeared, this time in a cut-down formation with only five trailers between the end power cars. This was a clue to the train's new purpose, as was the superior height of the power cars: they had been fitted with larger wheels in the same way that TGV Set 16 had been doctored for the record run in February 1981.

Set 88's immediate task was to check the track, electrification and train control systems on LGV Atlantique. With this job done, Set 88 returned to the Paris–Lyon route for further tests. Here, in December 1988, the test crew powered the train up to 400km/h and beyond. Nine times it broke through the 400km/h threshold, on one trip notching up a speed of 408.4km/h. The record had returned to France – or had it?

The French engineers were thrilled, but no sooner had word got about that a new record was in the bag than Transport Minister Michel Delebarre instructed SNCF to halt the trials. The minister was of the view that now was not the right time to boast about railway speed records – a horrific head-on collision between suburban trains at the Gare de Lyon on 27 June 1988 had killed fifty-six people.

In the wake of the minister's decision TGV Design Engineer François Lacôte and Director of LGV Atlantique Etienne Chambron reportedly clashed with SNCF Deputy General Manager Roger Gérin, who told them: 'You never exceeded 405km/h: do you understand?' Mystery surrounded the speed that Set 88 had really reached. SNCF General Manager Jean Costet and his Chief Rolling Stock Engineer Roger Forray confirmed to me in January 1989 during a demonstration trip for the TGV Atlantique trains that Set 88 had in fact reached 410km/h.

On the same demonstration run, Delebarre confirmed that France was once more the holder of the world rail speed record, but he gave no further details. Instead, he promised a rendezvous in the autumn for what he called 'a good record'. Purdah descended and all publicity about records ceased.

But no one had forgotten Delebarre's promise, and in September 1989 the first rumours surfaced that another record attempt was in the offing. These were officially denied, but reports persisted that a TGV Atlantique set was being specially prepared and that unusual attention was being paid to the track of the Courtalain–Tours branch of LGV Atlantique, which was still one year away from opening. Then came the first sightings of a modified train at the new line's rolling stock depot at Châtillon in the Paris outskirts.

The secret was out. It was one of the fleet for the new line, numbered as Set 325, but between the two power cars were just four instead of the usual ten trailers. Special treatment was immediately obvious: both pantographs had been removed from the leading power car and a smooth fairing covered the other roof equipment. Larger-than-normal wheels had been fitted to the powered axles, adding a few millimetres to the height of the cars, and additional yaw dampers were evident on the bogies.

Hidden from view, many other changes had been made to the power equipment and drive trains. The main transformer had been modified for a higher output and the traction motors uprated. The gear ratio had been changed so that the motors would rotate at 4,000rpm at 400km/h rather than at 300km/h. Alterations had been made to the suspension and adjustments made to the braking equipment. Apart from all that, special monitoring apparatus had been fitted to check the temperature of the motors, axle boxes and other mechanical components. Sensors had been

installed to record the forces exerted on the rails by the wheels of the leading bogie and one of the intermediate bogies.

Out on the test section the ballast had been carefully trimmed to minimise the chances of stones being blown up by the slipstream of an ultra-fast train. Devices to check for movement of the track were put in place, and at the lineside speed counters and noise-measuring equipment were being readied. The tension of the overhead wires was increased from 20 to 27kN and the power supply was upped from 25 to 28kV.

Preliminary trials began on 23 November with a sister train set, and a week later, on 30 November, Set 325 emerged from the Châtillon depot. On the first trip the souped-up train romped up to 380km/h, following this on 1 December with a new record speed of 442.6km/h. The technical team then made further adjustments, and in the following week even higher speeds were attained, with one run clocking 473km/h.

On 5 December the conditions were good for another attempt to push the figure even higher. Cold weather made the air dense, perhaps limiting the speed that could be reached, but a favourable northerly breeze made up for this. The usual practice was to 'sweep' the track with another train before the record attempt, and as soon as the 'all-clear' had been received from the sweeper train, Set 325 was authorised to leave the starting point at Dangeau. Maximum power was applied by driver Michel Boiteau, and this time speed peaked at Km 166 at 482.4km/h, prompting François Lacôte to burst out: 'Perfect, it's perfect.'

SNCF's publicity teams went into action, but at that evening's press conference the media complained bitterly that they had not been forewarned of the record attempt. A decision was taken to stage another run two days later, and among those on board Set 325 when it touched 471.1km/h was Michel Delebarre. Lacôte too was present, and he said after the trip that he believed that 'there is still a margin available at 480km/h; I am sure that 500km/h is not ruled out', adding that 'we are a long, long way from the limits of wheel-rail technology'.

The press wrote up their stories, and Set 325 continued its trials. The results were encouraging, and the test team sent the train back to Châtillon. There it underwent further changes, finally emerging in February 1990 in a fresh guise. Now there were just three intermediate cars, giving a better power-to-weight ratio. The power car wheels had an even larger diameter of 1,090mm, while the exterior had been altered to improve aerodynamic performance. Prominent below the headlight array of the rear car was a spoiler, racing-car style, while at the front end the valance below the nose had been lowered by 100mm. Rubber fairings were fitted between the intermediate cars and the 25kV link along the roofs had been replaced by a flush-mounted cable.

Once more the test teams began to put their charge through its paces. The big day was set to occur on 8 March 1990, but the date came and went with no news. It turned out that the specially manufactured transformer in the rear power car had blown up on 5 March, and SNCF announced that record attempts had been postponed *sine die*.

In due course the damage was repaired, and Set 325 reappeared in early May to resume its test runs. On 4 May it shot past the previous maximum with a new record of 485km/h, breaching the 500km/h barrier five days later. Progress was temporarily halted when some troubles emerged with the pantograph, but on 16 May the record speed was nudged up to 510.8km/h. By now SNCF had regained its confidence, and journalists were once again summoned to Paris for a special event on 18 May. The rest of that day in 1990 is history.

The Search for Perfection

In 2007, all the events of 1989 and 1990 were eclipsed by the V150's stunning exploit. Although seventeen years separated the two records, there were many factors in common. Some of the engineers were involved in both records. Among them was François Lacôte, who by now had left SNCF and was Technical Director at Alstom Transport. Daniel Beylot, in charge of the V150 operation, had also lived through the events of May 1990. The lessons learnt then had been applied and tested many times before the final record attempt in 2007. Planning and preparations had taken more than nineteen months from the moment the formal decision was taken in August 2005 to try for another record. For some, the decision did not come as a surprise, for SNCF was perpetuating a long history of breaking world speed records that dated back to 1955.

At that time a group of French railway engineers had become convinced that the technology of steel wheels on steel rails harboured a huge unexploited potential. The fastest speeds attained by trains in a Europe still weakened by the devastation of the Second World War were typically between 120 and 140km/h. But there was plenty of evidence from tests and experiments in the first half of the twentieth century that much higher speeds were possible.

In the early 1900s, barely two decades after the first electric train had been pioneered in Berlin by the German engineer Werner von Siemens, the *Studiengesellschaft für Elektrische Schnellbahnen* was experimenting with new technology called electric traction. Using a 23km military railway between Zossen and Marienfelde south of Berlin, they quickly found that undreamt of speeds could be attained. In 1901 they accelerated a four-axle Siemens & Halske locomotive up to 162.5km/h, following this with similarly spectacular speed

runs with a pair of electric railcars. During one test a bogie lifted off the track, and when it landed back on the rails it spread them apart – a terrifying moment for those on board. Fortunately, no one was hurt. The line was hastily rebuilt before the tests resumed. When they did, the AEG railcar set a new world record speed on rails of 210.2km/h on 27 October 1903.

As it happened, the complicated three-phase electrification used on the military railway was not practical for commercial operations, and further development ceased. In any case, the better-known technology of the steam locomotive was advancing rapidly, and there were many claims to speed records in the first half of the twentieth century. Steam streamliners appeared in Britain, Germany, France, Belgium, the USA and elsewhere, with mechanical engineers constantly striving for better aerodynamic performance and more efficient use of high-pressure steam. The acme of steam traction was attained on 3 July 1938 when the London & North Eastern Railway's *Mallard* A4 class 4-6-2 locomotive stormed to a world record speed of 202.8km/h down Stoke Bank between Grantham and Peterborough. This magnificent feat has never been surpassed.

During the 1930s German engineers pioneered fast diesel railcars such as the *Fliegende Hamburger*, to say nothing of an extraordinary propeller-powered contraption invented by one Franz Kruckenberg, which was driven at 231km/h in June 1931 between Ludwigslust and Wittenberge. In the USA too there were some heroic speed adventures, with both the Burlington Railroad and the Union Pacific achieving spectacular results with diesel-powered streamliners built for trans-continental journeys. Much later, in July 1966, the New York Central railroad fitted a pair of jet engines to an ordinary Budd railcar. This amazing vehicle thundered up to a speed of 295km/h at

Butler, Indiana, earning its place in the roll call of US railway drama. Many other speed adventures can be traced, but it is not the purpose of this book to describe these exploits, all of which have been amply chronicled by railway historians. So let us return to the lineside on the railway from Bordeaux to Hendaye in March 1955.

At that time there were no computers available to simulate what would happen if machines were pushed beyond their design limits. So we should acknowledge the courage of the engineers involved and pay tribute to their deeply held belief that railway engineering was still far from its technical limits. Two locomotives, the four-axle BB9004 and

the six-axle CC7107, had been chosen for a daring attempt to test the limits of railway technology. Each was matched with a test train consisting of three third-class carriages that had been fitted with some rudimentary aerodynamic improvements such as a rounded 'tail' on the last car.

On 26 March the BB locomotive hauled its three test cars along the long, straight stretch of track at an unprecedented 276km/h. Two days later CC7107 crushed this astonishing achievement with a dynamic sprint that smashed through 300km/h for the first time

in railway history. It was truly spectacular, with linesiders watching in horror as the locomotive's pantograph melted, setting fire to nearby pine trees. And on 29 March the BB locomotive outpaced its sister with another breakneck dash – again with a dangerous firework display and ballast fragments blasted into the air by the slipstream. SNCF proudly

Jet propelled. In 1966 the New York Central railroad mounted a pair of spare GE J47-19 jet engines from the gigantic B-36 bomber aircraft on a Budd diesel railcar. Dubbed the M-497, this extraordinary vehicle roared up to 295km/h at Butler, Indiana, in July that year. (*Railway Gazette* collection)

announced that both locomotives had reached the incredible speed of 331km/h. Many years later this was revealed not to be true, but at the time SNCF was anxious not to favour one locomotive manufacturer over another. In fact, only the BB had reached the maximum speed, the CC having attained a no less creditable 326km/h.

For many years SNCF concealed what had really happened during the final record run. Observant spectators who witnessed the event and saw the state of the track after the final passage of the BB9004 were instructed to keep mum. Eventually, the French magazine *La Vie du Rail* published a photograph showing that BB9004 and its train had seriously bent the rails. This had been caused by a bogie thrashing furiously from side to side as the train hurtled along the track, a phenomenon known as 'hunting'. The wheels had exerted so much lateral force that the rails were moved out of alignment. Miraculously, the train did not derail, and the story of high-speed railways moved on.

Daring deed. In one of railway history's most audacious moments, French electric locomotive BB9004 set sparks and ballast flying when it touched 331km/h in March 1955. So powerful were the forces exerted on the track that the rails were bent out of alignment – but the train did not derail. (*La Vie du Rail*)

The lessons of 1955 were never forgotten. Each successive record, and the work that went into it, gave the French engineers greater knowledge of the science of railway dynamics. This expertise was handed down from test team to test team and from designer to designer. And so it was that the V150 train set in 2007 was honed to perfection, the child of engineers who were still searching for the ultimate technical limits of steel wheels on steel rails.

Before we leave France to explore the development of commercial high speed railways, we must spend a few minutes examining the extraordinary train that had been seen by millions on live TV as it charted one of the most exciting chapters in railway history. The V150 train had been assembled under a €30m programme with the majestic title of *L'Excellence Française de la Très Grande Vitesse Ferroviaire*. Yes, it was an expensive publicity stunt designed to showcase France's railway industry, but it was also a serious attempt to investigate the technology and equipment needed to run trains at ultra high speeds – an investment in the future.

Once the decision to go for the V150 record had been taken, the design team set out to develop a train able to surpass the performance of Set 325 in 1990. The trick was to pack maximum power into a really short train to obtain the best power-to-weight ratio. On the Alstom Transport production line in Belfort at the time were the power cars for the so-called POS (Paris-Ostfrankreich-Süddeutschland) train sets. These were destined to operate international services on LGV Est-Européen from Paris to Germany. It was not a difficult decision to divert a pair of POS power cars from the production line where they could later return to be reconfigured for normal service.

In between the two power cars the design team decided to place three articulated double-deck TGV cars on four bogies. From the very outset of the TGV project in 1972 when SNCF had rolled out a gas turbine-driven prototype, TGVs have always used articulation. The intermediate cars are coupled mechanically by an annular structure that supports the end of each car body on a common bogie. This arrangement reduces the overall weight of the train as fewer bogies are required. It has the added benefit of increasing stability in the event of a derailment as the articulation helps to keep the cars in line. Yes, it did happen; more on this in Chapter 4. The double-deck cars of a standard TGV are normally unpowered, but for the V150 the two articulation bogies in the centre of the three-car set were replaced by powered ones. Not just any powered bogies, of course.

It so happened that Alstom was working on the design of what it saw as the successor to the TGV. Known as the AGV or *Automotrice à Grande Vitesse* – of which more later – this dispensed with the TGV formula of a power car at each end, the traction equipment being distributed along the train. This has several advantages, not least the release of the space occupied by the power cars for seats – an important factor in our commercial age when 'bums on seats' drives railway management policy. Alstom quickly decided that the AGV's powered bogies, each housing two newly developed permanent magnet traction motors, would be ideal for the V150 application. Apart from anything else, this was an unprecedented opportunity to test the new traction equipment to limits that would far surpass anything expected of the train in its commercial life.

So the base formula was settled: two POS power cars and three intermediate double-deck cars, with six out of eight bogies powered. The POS traction motors were uprated from 1,250kW to 1,950kW and the AGV motors from 720kW to 1,000kW, giving a stupendous total output of 19.6MW, this to drive a train weighing just 268 tonnes.

The art of speed. In December 2007 record-breaking locomotive BB9004 was exhibited in the Grand Palais
in Paris to mark seventy years of the national railway, SNCF. (Christophe Masse)

The two power cars left their birthplace in Belfort in July 2006 and were sent to SNCF's Bischheim workshops for modifications. The leading power car, M2, was given a complete exterior makeover to eliminate aerodynamic drag. The pantographs were removed as power would be supplied from the rear power car, M1, using roof-mounted cables along the train. An air-smoothed casing was fitted over the remaining roof equipment and the bi-parting clamshell cover over the coupler in the nose was replaced by a single moulding to give a completely smooth surface at the very tip of the train. A special 35mm thick windscreen in its own frame was fitted flush with the bodywork and the windscreen wiper removed. The fairing below the nose was lowered to cover more of the gap between train and track.

Hidden behind this smooth skin was a specially reinforced nose structure. Inside too, there were changes, with sensors fitted to numerous components to record temperatures and other parameters. Drawing on the experience from 1989 and 1990, improvements were made to the suspension and additional dampers fitted to cope with the higher forces that apply at higher speeds.

The three trailer cars were assembled in the Alstom factory at Aytré near La Rochelle in Western France. Car R8, coupled next to power car M2, was built as a standard second-class vehicle. This was designated as a rolling laboratory into which around 400 sensors would feed critical information to the test team's computers. On the top deck the *Agence d'Essai Ferroviaire*, or Railway Testing Agency, installed banks of equipment to monitor the performance of the power supply and the traction and braking components; at the outer end was a desk for the computers that would keep track of the dynamic performance of the whole train, while at the inner end was a console reserved for the test manager.

Downstairs in R8, space was allocated for the Alstom engineers who would be observing the performance of the AGV traction equipment installed in the centre coach, R4, which would normally have spent its life as a bar-buffet car. Instead, the lower floor of R4 was occupied by the main AGV transformer and two AGV traction blocks, each with a pair of powerful inverters, one for each motor. Marshalled behind R4 came trailer R1, which retained its first-class seating for the guests privileged to take part in the record run.

All the train's wheels were replaced by special wheels with a diameter of 1,092mm instead of the normal 920mm. This was unfortunate as it made the train somewhat higher than would usually be permitted, so much so that it infringed the normal loading gauge – the envelope within which a train must fit to pass safely through bridges and tunnels.

Marriage of the power cars and trailers duly took place at Aytré, and special rubber fairings were fitted between the cars to complete an unbroken aerodynamic profile along the train. After a short trip on the factory's test track, the ensemble had its first outing on 17 December 2006. It then departed for its destination: the workshop at Pantin in the eastern outskirts of Paris, which SNCF had grandly renamed the *Technicentre Est Européen*. Here it was that the fleet of trains destined for use on LGV Est-Européen would be maintained. It would also be home to the V150 throughout the series of trials. The journey to Pantin took two days because the over-height V150 could not follow a direct route as it would have fouled lineside structures along the way. Instead, the train had to undertake a lengthy detour through Western and Northern France.

Once at Pantin, care of the V150 was entrusted to a team of engineers and technicians who had volunteered for the task of ensuring that the train was safe and fit for the long series of trials ahead. They were given the onerous responsibility of checking and maintaining the train after every day of high-speed running. This meant working through the night to ensure the train was in perfect condition again next morning.

By mid-January the train was declared ready for its first sortie on the racetrack, which had been prepared for it to the east. Hopes of a smooth progression towards the ultimate speed trial were quickly dashed when a serious transformer fault occurred, necessitating a full replacement. This delayed the start of trials for a week. Emerging once more from the *Technicentre* on 22 January, the V150 travelled without incident to the test site. This time all went well, and the test team settled into a routine for the next few weeks, gradually pushing up the speed of the tests.

To reach the test site the V150 was hauled by another TGV, Set 4404, which had been adapted to serve as the 'sweeper' train. In addition, every morning began with a special run by a *Mauzin* track recording car to ensure that the rails and other infrastructure components were in perfect condition for that day's trials.

Over the next few weeks the V150 made forty runs where speed rose above 450km/h; the cumulative total of high-speed trials amounted to 200 hours and 3,200km. The previous world record was broken on 12 February when the V150 flew along the track at over 528km/h. On six further occasions the record was smashed again, culminating in a superlative sprint at 559.4km/h on 20 February.

It remained to make the final preparations for the big day set for early April – the final decision on the date would depend not merely on track and train being in perfect condition but also on the weather. Rain would not be good, but wind would be worse, because a strong sidewind could affect the train's stability. Only on 1 April was the final decision taken to attempt the record on 3 April, leaving little time to alert the media.

In fact, the press were well prepared. At the end of March selected journalists had been invited under strict embargo on special trips, which were being staged as part of the build-up to the record. It was during a run on 28 March that the unthinkable occurred – a device protecting an extensometer used to measure the strain exerted in one of the wheels became detached and fell on to the track. The V150 was hurtling along at a fraction over 506km/h, and the device smashed into the ballast and rebounded against the underside of the train, fracturing the main brake pipe in the process. This immediately activated the emergency braking, triggering a full application of the disc brakes, which are normally used only at much lower speeds. As the train slowed, the four discs on each axle of the two trailer bogies began to glow red hot, reaching a temperature that the test team measured at 650°C. The test engineers had calculated that it would take 25km before the train stopped, but in the event zero speed was reached after just 16.8km – a world braking record!

Action shots. Photographers had only fractions of a second to capture the moment when the V150 broke the speed record. The train is seen near Passavant-en-Argonne where it clocked 574.8km/h on 3 April 2007. (Christophe Masse)

In the meantime, the V150 had been adorned with a special vinyl and paint job for the record attempt. Inspiration was drawn from the words of Roger Tallon, the French industrial designer responsible for the original styling of the TGV: 'this is metal which is flowing through space'. Accordingly, a 'jet of chrome' against a black background was chosen to represent the peak of railway technology. The chrome was applied in a swirling wave form to symbolise 'all the energy of the human endeavour' involved in the project. The same distinctive decoration was applied to the invitations that were sent out to the guests and journalists for 3 April, and to all the related publicity.

Out on the track, RFF had been making preparations too. Although the track and infrastructure for LGV Est-Européen was brand new, a few tweaks had to be made. The test section was by no means perfectly straight: it included eleven large-radius curves where adjustments were needed. On railways designed for fast trains the outer rail of the curves is higher than the inner rail – on the same principle that a car racetrack is banked in the corners. Termed 'cant' in railway parlance, the banking was in some cases increased to 130mm.

Along the whole test stretch the ballast was specially profiled to be slightly lower than the concrete sleepers to minimise the risk of flying stones.

The traction power was increased from 25kV to 31kV and the tension in the contact wire raised from the normal 26kN to 40kN. A dedicated radio network was established to guarantee contact between the control centre at Pagny-sur-Moselle and the staff on the train. Even a special weather monitoring station was set up to check the air pressure before each test run. Noise recording, pressure measuring and speed recording devices were prepared at the lineside in the zone where the maximum speed was expected. Road traffic over all the bridges in the test zone was halted whenever a test run at more than 500km/h was scheduled and gendarmes were positioned along the test site to ensure than no one could intrude on to the track.

★★★

The 574.8km/h achieved on 3 April 2007 was a magnificent feat of railway engineering. After the record run, a dozen more trips were made at over 500km/h before the programme named *L'Excellence*

Française de la Très Grande Vitesse Ferroviaire drew to a close. The V150 had been accelerated over the 500km/h threshold on twenty-eight occasions, logging more than 700km at these speeds. The programme had proved beyond all doubt that high-speed railways were now a safe and mature technology with enormous safety margins.

For some time it seemed unlikely that the speed attained by the V150 would be surpassed, but on Christmas Day in 2011 the Chinese unveiled a train designed to research railway technology in the realm of 500km/h. And on 3 December 2010 Chinese Railways had accelerated what they claimed was an unmodified CRH380A production train set up to 486.1km/h in a brazen attempt to show off the country's technical prowess just two days before a major congress on high-speed railways in Beijing. China has the world's most ambitious high-speed railway construction programme, but before we explore what is happening there we need to see how the engineers of many countries first amassed a vast array of knowledge about high-speed trains – much of which found its way to China. That expertise originated in Japan, and Tokyo is our next destination.

2

Bullet Trains in Business

A National High-Speed Network

At 6 a.m. on 1 October 1964, President of Japanese National Railways Reisuke Ishida cut a ceremonial ribbon and watched the inaugural blue-and-ivory bullet train glide out of Tokyo Central bound for Shin-Ōsaka, 515km away to the west. Also present was Tokyo Governor Ryotaro Azuma, who predicted that 'the opening of this Shinkansen, linking centres of culture in the east and west of our country in four hours, will bring with it great benefits in all fields, including economy, industry, culture and tourism'. He could not have known just how prophetic that was, nor that Japan's high-speed rail concept would be copied across the world.

At that time, construction of what became the world's premier inter-city railway was a bold adventure. Never before had regular trains travelled at such sustained high speeds as on the pristine railway known as the Tokaido Shinkansen – Tokaido is the name of the densely populated plain between Japan's central mountains and the Pacific Ocean, and Shinkansen means 'New Trunk Line'. The 'bullet train' sobriquet derived from the train's distinctive nose, and the term still applies, even though today's trains bear little resemblance to the original.

Proposals to build a new railway from Tokyo to Osaka date from the 1930s. One suggestion envisaged a line stretching nearly 1,200km from Tokyo to Shimonoseki at the western tip of Honshu. A start was made on excavating the tunnels, but the Second World War forced abandonment.

By the early 1950s, Japan's economy was recovering strongly, and the old Tokaido main line was struggling to handle around 120 trains a day in each direction. The line served a belt of cities such as Nagoya and the historic capital Kyoto. Industry was thriving, and Japanese National Railways (JNR) was electrifying its main lines, with the Tokyo–Osaka route under wires by 1956. Two years later *Kodama* limited express EMUs were launched between Tokyo and Osaka, cutting forty minutes off the timing to complete the trip in 6 hours 50 minutes. The booming economy was stoking demand for travel, and it was an obvious step to revive plans for a new railway.

Japan's national network had been built to 1,067mm gauge, as chosen for the country's first railway that opened in 1872 between Tokyo and Yokohama. It had been designed by Edmund Morel, an Englishman engaged in railway work in New Zealand, where the narrow gauge suited the local topography. When the idea of a new railway surfaced, far-sighted engineers saw an opportunity for faster and physically larger trains by opting for the same 1,435mm 'standard' gauge adopted by railways in other countries.

Although the idea of a different gauge met stiff resistance, it had a powerful advocate in Shinji Sogo, appointed as the fourth president of JNR in 1955. Sogo was a passionate man convinced that standard gauge would transform the prospects for Japan's railways, but he had a serious fight on his hands. His arguments eventually won the day, and today his name survives as the political father of the Shinkansen.

Sogo's campaign won over the Ministry of Transport, which decided in December 1958, in preference to further quadrupling of the narrow-gauge main line, to sanction a new route with a gauge of 1,435mm. There were suggestions that the trains could run at the fantastic speed of 250km/h, slashing the Tokyo–Osaka trip to just 3 hours. With this politically attractive prospect in mind, the government okayed a groundbreaking ceremony on 20 April 1959.

The Shinkansen was conceived as a package of technology that elevated railway engineering to another plane. There were no level crossings – a huge safety and operating headache on the narrow-gauge network – and there would be no sharp curves or steep gradients; minimum curve radius was set at 2,500m and the steepest grade at 2 per cent. The double-track route would be electrified at 25kV 60Hz, while segregation by gauge would preclude knock-on delays from late-running trains on the conventional network. Centralised traffic control would keep operating staff informed of the status of trains along the whole route.

Particularly significant was the decision to adopt automatic train protection and automatic train control using coded track circuits. As drivers would not react quickly enough to signal aspects at 200km/h, there would be no lineside signals. Instead, the speed maximum would be displayed in the cab, and an over-enthusiastic driver would find the brakes being applied automatically if the limit was exceeded.

FINDING THE FUNDS

Much of the ¥190 billion cost was covered through long-term borrowing from the government, plus bonds issued by JNR and funds from JNR's internal reserves. Just under 10 per cent, however, took the form of a loan from the World Bank, which insisted on what it termed 'sound engineering'. A team from the Bank travelled to Japan in May 1960, and a year later, on 2 May, Vice-President Sir William A.B. Iliff and Shinji Sogo signed Loan 0281 for US$80 million with an interest rate of 5.75 per cent and a term of twenty years – the bankers having been convinced that the Shinkansen technology was indeed 'sound'.

The World Bank insisted on other conditions too. Maximum speed was fixed at 200km/h, not the 250km/h originally envisaged. This was a great disappointment to some of JNR's engineers, but at least the project was going ahead – and it was fully funded, another condition being a government guarantee that the scheme would actually be finished.

Tests with two prototype trains began in 1962, and speeds were gradually raised until a test crew accelerated one of them up to 256km/h in March 1963. An account by Shuichiro Yamanouchi, then a JNR manager, claims that the speed was attained for just a few seconds and that a subsequent inspection revealed that the rails were bent. He commented that perhaps it was a good thing that the World Bank had insisted on a 200km/h limit...

Drawing on their experience with narrow-gauge EMUs, JNR's engineers calculated that spreading traction equipment along the train would keep the axle load to less than 16 tonnes. An initial batch of 360 'Series 0' cars formed a launch fleet of lightweight twelve-car trains. Each pair of cars formed an electrical unit fed by its own pantograph, with a 180kW DC traction motor driving each axle. Inside, passengers found spacious saloons with seats in rows of 2+3 or 2+2 in Green Car, the Japanese first class. Two cars had a buffet, although this facility – and the later addition of dining cars – were subsequently withdrawn as passengers could easily buy *bento* lunch boxes at stations or on the trains.

Construction took little more than five years. The opening date was set in stone as the line had to be ready for the Tokyo Olympic Games starting on 10 October 1964. By July that year the ribbon of steel was complete, and in the following month JNR put on a limited service to identify teething troubles. It also staged a publicity run for local media, generating reports about a helicopter trailing behind as it struggled to film the streaking train below.

The inaugural ribbon on 1 October should have been cut by Shinji Sogo, but Sogo, together with his Chief Engineer Hideo Shima – the technical father of the Shinkansen – had felt obliged to resign in 1963 because the project's cost had escalated far beyond the original estimate: the final price was ¥380 billion. In the event, Sogo was replaced by Reisuke Ishida, whose enthusiasm for the Shinkansen was reportedly somewhat muted.

As it turned out, some relaxation of the speed limit had proved possible, and the maximum speed on the launch date was 210km/h, sufficient to permit the limited-stop *Hikari* trains to reach

End of the beginning. In a scene reminiscent of the launch of Shinkansen services in October 1964, Japanese officials bid goodbye to the last operational Series 0 – the original type of bullet train – on its farewell run from Shin-Ōsaka to Hakata on 14 December 2008. (Kazumiki Miura)

Osaka in 4 hours and the all-stations *Kodama* trains in 5 hours. It was soon clear that faster timings were feasible, and around a year later the *Hikari* schedule was cut to 3 hours 10 minutes with *Kodama* services accelerated to complete the trip in 4 hours. For the first time, the average speed of an inter-city rail journey exceeded 160km/h – the magic figure of 100mph in imperial units.

A BUMPY RIDE

To begin with, it was not a smooth ride, literally. The track had not settled sufficiently on some of the embankments, meaning that there was a hump where the bridges were higher than the approach tracks. This obliged the civil engineers to impose numerous speed restrictions. The snag was soon rectified, but JNR then had to deal with overhead wire problems and snow sticking to the underfloor equipment, later falling off as chunks of ice that damaged both track and train. Pressure sealing was another issue: when trains entered tunnels, passengers felt a pulse in their ears, so remedial work was needed on the door and gangway seals.

More serious was the question of noise as the bullet trains roared across steel-truss bridges or viaducts in heavily built-up areas. In some cases the track was laid directly on the bridge girders, meaning that noise was generated not only by the wheel-on-rail contact but also from vibration of the bridge. Lineside residents were understandably unhappy, and train noise became a government agenda item.

The noise row and the huge expense of the new railway were temporarily overshadowed by its instant success. Despite a pricey Super Express supplement levied on top of the ordinary fare, passengers were willing to pay for speed. After just three months, JNR's managers recorded the 11 millionth passenger, and by 1967 ticket sales showed there had been 100 million trips along Japan's new rail artery.

The dream of a profitable high-speed railway was a reality, and this helped to shape the government's attitude. When JNR posited an extension from Shin-Ōsaka to Okayama, the answer was in the affirmative, allowing work to start in 1967 on the 164km Sanyo Shinkansen. The extension offered the chance to enhance the original specification and, mindful of the potential for higher speeds, the engineers chose generous parameters such as a 4,000m curve radius and 60kg/m rails.

JNR also took the opportunity to iron out the early problems. Access for track maintenance was a critical issue, and on the Sanyo line concrete slabs replaced ballasted track on viaducts and in tunnels – the higher capital cost was offset by cheaper maintenance. Concrete structures with better noise attenuation replaced the steel-truss bridges.

In 1969 the Ministry of Transport signed off a second extension. This ran from Okayama to Hakata on Kyushu and entailed boring a long tunnel under the strait between the two islands. As on the New Sanyo line, higher standards were chosen with a view to jacking up the speed. The Okayama extension opened in March 1972, followed in 1975 by the 398km to Hakata. Tokyo and Hakata were now linked by a high-speed line stretching for 1,069km.

So impressed was the government with the Tokaido Shinkansen that in 1970 it passed legislation mandating construction of a national network. The Nationwide Shinkansen Railways Construction & Improvement Act (NSRCIA) envisaged completion of 7,200km of new railway by 1985. One objective was to stimulate regional development. As Tokyo's governor had predicted, a high-speed railway would generate both business and leisure activity. But building so much new railway was hugely ambitious, and it was no surprise that the 1985 target proved unattainable.

In 1971 detailed plans for three more Shinkansen routes were signed off: the Tohoku Shinkansen from Tokyo to Morioka in northern Honshu, the Joetsu Shinkansen from Tokyo through the central mountains to the rice-growing and sake centre of Niigata on the Sea of Japan coast, plus a high-speed link to Tokyo's then new Narita Airport. Construction of the first two began at once, with work on the 84km airport link starting in 1974; this was later abandoned in the face of opposition from furious lineside residents, already incensed about jet aircraft zooming in and out of their backyard.

SETBACKS SLOW PROGRESS

Just as JNR was preparing to celebrate the opening of the Sanyo extension, the economic indicators blinked red as the 1973–74 oil crisis plunged the world into recession. Japan was not spared from the financial storm, and the hefty cost of Shinkansen projects suddenly became an unaffordable drain on the national budget. All this coincided with the worst of the noise furore, and the government forced JNR to revise its plans and to erect high sound barriers where the new lines passed through urban areas.

Despite all this, no one could deny the Shinkansen's success. Passengers flocked to ride the trains, and JNR began adding four extra cars to each train to handle the extra business; it was also replacing the original fleet, which was becoming worn out after thirteen years of intensive use. Economic growth along the Tokaido corridor was phenomenal, and cities in other parts of Japan were keen to secure similar benefits.

Of particular note was the remarkable safety record. There were reported derailments in 1966 and 1973, and an over-run near Gifu in 1967 was attributed to wheel-slide. These were all minor accidents, and the really significant statistic is that there has never been a derailment or collision causing serious injury or death in the fifty years of operation.

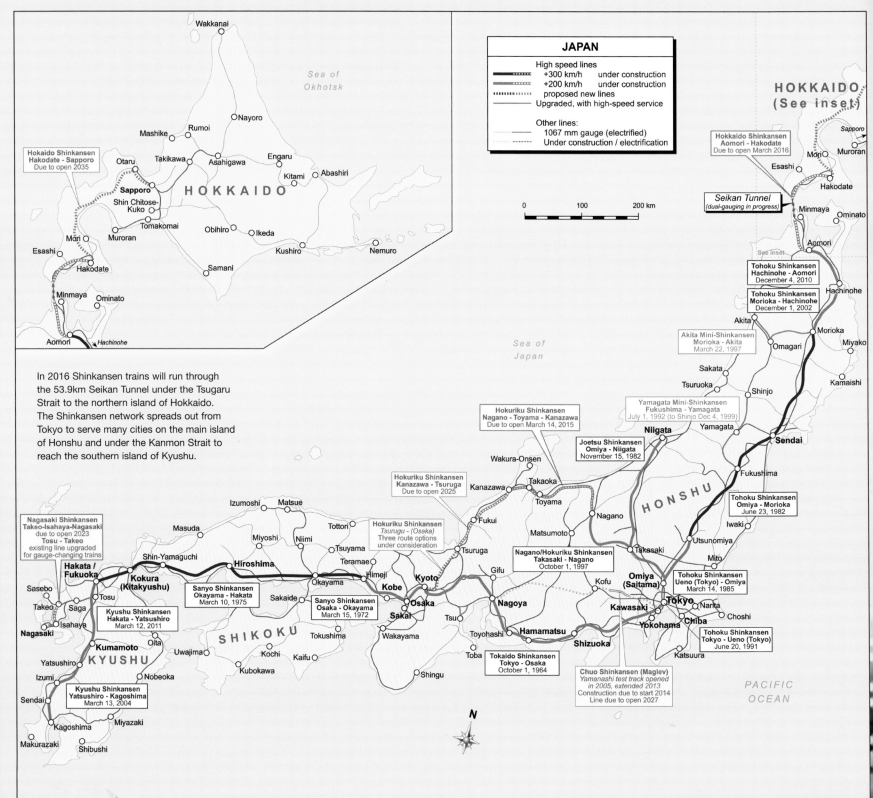

JAPAN

High speed lines

+300 km/h — under construction
+200 km/h — under construction
proposed new lines
Upgraded, with high-speed service

Other lines:
1067 mm gauge (electrified)
Under construction / electrification

0   100   200 km

Sea of Okhotsk

Wakkanai
Nayoro
Mashike
Rumoi
Takikawa
Asahigawa
Engaru
Kitami
Abashiri
Otaru
Sapporo
Shin Chitose-Kuko
Tomakomai
Obihiro
Ikeda
Kushiro
Nemuro
Samani

Hokaido Shinkansen
Hakodate - Sapporo
Due to open 2035

H O K K A I D O

Esashi
Mori
Muroran
Hakodate
Minmaya
Ominato
Aomori
→ *Hachinohe*

HOKKAIDO
(See inset)

Sapporo
Mori
Muroran
Esashi
Hakodate

Hokkaido Shinkansen
Aomori - Hakodate
Due to open March 2016

Seikan Tunnel
(dual-gauging in progress)

Minmaya
Ominato
See inset
Aomori

Tohoku Shinkansen
Hachinohe - Aomori
December 4, 2010

Hachinohe

Tohoku Shinkansen
Morioka - Hachinohe
December 1, 2002

Akita
Omagari
Morioka
Miyako
Kamaishi

Akita Mini-Shinkansen
Morioka - Akita
March 22, 1997

Sakata
Tsuruoka
Shinjo

Yamagata Mini-Shinkansen
Fukushima - Yamagata
July 1, 1992 (to Shinjo Dec 4, 1999)

Yamagata

Sea of Japan

In 2016 Shinkansen trains will run through
the 53.9km Seikan Tunnel under the Tsugaru
Strait to the northern island of Hokkaido.
The Shinkansen network spreads out from
Tokyo to serve many cities on the main island
of Honshu and under the Kanmon Strait to
reach the southern island of Kyushu.

Niigata
Sendai
Fukushima
Iwaki

Tohoku Shinkansen
Omiya - Morioka
June 23, 1982

Joetsu Shinkansen
Omiya - Niigata
November 15, 1982

Hokuriku Shinkansen
Nagano - Toyama - Kanazawa
Due to open March 14, 2015

Wakura-Onsen
Takaoka
Kanazawa
Toyama
Nagano

Hokuriku Shinkansen
Kanazawa - Tsuruga
Due to open 2025

Fukui
Matsumoto
Takasaki
Utsunomiya
Mito

Hokuriku Shinkansen
Tsurugu - (Osaka)
Three route options
under consideration

Izumoshi
Matsue
Tottori
Tsuyama
Teramae
Tsuruga

Nagano/Hokuriku Shinkansen
Takasaki - Nagano
October 1, 1997

Masuda
Miyoshi
Niimi

Gifu
Kofu
Omiya (Saitama)

Tohoku Shinkansen
Ueno (Tokyo) - Omiya
March 14, 1985

H O N S H U

Tohoku Shinkansen
Omiya - Morioka
June 23, 1982

Nagasaki Shinkansen
Takeo-Isahaya-Nagasaki
due to open 2023
Tosu - Takeo
existing line upgraded
for gauge-changing trains

Shin-Yamaguchi
Hiroshima
Okayama
Himeji
Kobe
Kyoto
Osaka
Sakai
Nagoya
Kawasaki
Tokyo
Narita
Choshi

Hakata / Fukuoka
Kokura (Kitakyushu)
Tosu
Saga
Sasebo
Takeo
Isahaya
Nagasaki

Sanyo Shinkansen
Okayama - Hakata
March 10, 1975

Sakaide
Tsu
Hamamatsu
Shizuoka
Yokohama
Chiba

Sanyo Shinkansen
Osaka - Okayama
March 15, 1972

Kyushu Shinkansen
Hakata - Yatsushiro
March 12, 2011

Oita
Tokushima
Wakayama
Toyohashi

S H I K O K U

Uwajima
Kochi
Kaifu
Kubokawa
Shingu
Toba

Tohoku Shinkansen
Tokyo - Ueno (Tokyo)
June 20, 1991

Kumamoto
K Y U S H U

Tokaido Shinkansen
Tokyo - Osaka
October 1, 1964

Chuo Shinkansen (Maglev)
*Yamanashi test track opened
in 2005, extended 2013*
Construction due to start 2014
Line due to open 2027

Yatsushiro
Izumi
Sendai
Nobeoka

Kyushu Shinkansen
Yatsushiro - Kagoshima
March 13, 2004

Kagoshima
Miyazaki
Makurazaki
Shibushi

P A C I F I C
O C E A N

Katsuura

N

© Railway Gazette 2014
Cartography by Andy Hellawell

THE SECOND
AGE OF RAIL

The Shinkansen offered speed, safety and comfort. New trains on near perfect track offered the smoothest of rides, and the Shinkansen's reputation spread to Europe and North America. Taking the bullet train became a 'must' for tourists visiting the Land of the Rising Sun.

The 1970 NSRCIA continued to form the basis of a long-term strategy, and in 1973 plans for five more lines were approved in principle:

- a Tohoku extension from Morioka to Aomori;
- the Hokuriku Shinkansen from Takasaki to Nagano and ultimately Osaka via Kanazawa;
- a line through the Seikan Tunnel from Aomori to Sapporo on Hokkaido;
- a line from Hakata to Kagoshima on Kyushu;
- a branch off the Kyushu line to Nagasaki

Although the plans had government backing, the cost of building so many lines at once was prohibitive, especially when JNR's finances were spiralling out of control. The exception was the money-spinning Tokaido Shinkansen, which was raking in sufficient cash for the World Bank loan to be paid off in 1981. But the government was desperately worried about the mounting cost of the rest of the railway, and in 1982 the cabinet put planning of new Shinkansen lines on hold.

In 1964 JNR's accounts showed a deficit of ¥30 billion, and by 1980 the annual loss had snowballed to ¥2.5 trillion. Long-term debts were a staggering ¥25 trillion. All that was bad enough, but the colossal bill for the Tohoku and Joetsu Shinkansen was another concern, especially as both projects were funded mainly by state loans that would add to the debt mountain.

The Joetsu line presented the formidable challenge of crossing Japan's central mountains, forcing nearly 40 per cent of the alignment to run in tunnel. Nasty geological surprises delayed the

tunnelling and hiked up the price, while on open sections special measures such as hot water track sprays were needed to cope with heavy snowfall and temperatures that could dip to -20°C. Progress was slow, and the prospect of recouping the cost looked slim.

During the planning and construction phase, both the Joetsu and the Tohoku Shinkansen were badly affected by the noise problem, meaning that no work was permitted on the 30km approach through the suburbs from Omiya to central Tokyo. Not until 1978 did JNR cut a deal with local government, allowing work to start in June 1980. Even then, the route stopped north of the centre at Ueno as building through the city to meet the Tokaido Shinkansen at Tokyo Central was fraught with difficulties, not least the reluctance of landowners to release their valuable property.

Before ordering trains for the Joetsu and Tohoku Shinkansen, JNR had nursed hopes of pushing up the speed limit to 260km/h, and a six-car Series 961 prototype packed enough punch to sustain this speed over the long Tohoku route. It was followed by a less powerful Series 962, and the two trains underwent trials that culminated in Series 961 scorching the track at 319km/h on 7 December 1979.

An order was placed for 432 Series 200 cars for the Tohoku and Joetsu routes. Incorporating lessons from the prototypes, Series 200 had thyristor control and aluminium instead of steel bodyshells. Outwardly a cream and green clone of the Tokaido's Series 0, the trains featured snowploughs for the trip through the mountains, plus filters to prevent snow penetrating sensitive equipment. Some sets sported a more pointed nose, heralding a series of design changes to cut aerodynamic drag, but the permitted speed remained at 210km/h.

The Tohoku Shinkansen finally opened to Morioka on 23 June 1982, with the Joetsu Shinkansen following on 15 November. It was far from ideal as the trains terminated at Omiya, obliging passengers to change into narrow-gauge trains for the final leg to Ueno. Only in March 1985 did Shinkansen trains finally reach Ueno, where they terminated at deep-level underground platforms.

Work on the last 3.6km from Ueno to Tokyo Central had begun in 1981. It was a tough assignment. A steeply graded tunnel took the line up to the surface near Okachimachi, from where a viaduct would carry Tohoku and Joetsu Shinkansen trains to Central. The cost was an astronomical ¥100 billion, and with around half the work completed, the project was halted in 1983.

THE END OF JNR

In the same year, Prime Minister Yasushiro Nakasone decided that JNR was a truly intractable problem. Apart from its disastrous finances, the railway was plagued by lamentable industrial relations. JNR was state-owned, and frequent strikes inflamed anti-government sentiment. Drastic action was needed – it was time to say *sayonara* to JNR.

A long and messy battle with railway management culminated in 1987 with the national railway split into six geographical entities that owned the tracks and ran passenger trains; a seventh company was granted rights to run freight over the passenger routes. Initially, the seven Japan Rail Group companies remained in state ownership, but there was a clear intention to privatise the three operating on Honshu: JR East, JR Central and JR West. These three were handed responsibility for Shinkansen operations on their territory.

The package included arrangements to deal with JNR's long-term debt. This was placed with the state-owned JNR Settlement Corporation, which held all the shares in the JR companies. Construction of new Shinkansen lines was assumed by Japan Railway Construction Corp (JRCC), which since 1964 had shared construction responsibility with JNR.

By this time, thanks in part to inverted L-shaped lineside sound barriers, JNR was winning the noise battle. This was vital, as the Shinkansen faced competition from airlines eager to snatch a share of the lucrative inter-city market. A new Kansai Airport was due to open in the early 1990s to serve the Osaka region, and JNR wanted to act before its market slipped away. On 14 March 1985 JNR shaved 2 minutes off the Tokyo Shin-Ōsaka *Hikari* timing which had been stuck at 3 hours 10 minutes for two decades. On the same day, the speed limit for six *Yamabiko* services on the Tohoku Shinkansen was raised to 240km/h. Significantly, this did not trigger an outcry.

Even more significantly, on 28 April 1986, a judge ruled in favour of JNR at the end of a twelve-year legal battle to try and force trains to slow down as they passed through Nagoya. Under the terms of this landmark deal, JNR agreed to try and cut noise measured 25m from the lineside to less than 75dB(A); in return it understood that demands for speed reductions in built-up areas would be dropped. On 1 November 1986 speed on the Tokaido and Sanyo Shinkansen was raised to 220km/h. The 3-hour barrier for trips between Tokyo and Osaka was finally breached, with a headline timing of 2 hours 56 minutes.

Other obstacles were crumbling too. In August 1986 agreement was reached to resume work on the Ueno–Central link, and contractors moved on site in 1987. No one expected rapid progress, but nor did they expect a tunnel to collapse in January 1989, causing subsidence along Tokyo streets…

Meanwhile, regional politicians were anxious to share in the development bonanza that was evident along the Tokaido Shinkansen, and they lobbied to resume construction of the national network. This, plus resolution of the noise issue and the prospect of a positive outcome to JNR's problems, led to the freeze on Shinkansen projects being overturned in January 1987. A deal to resume construction was brokered in 1989, with capital costs shared between government, prefectures and the new JR companies.

JR East Conquers the North

The division of JNR spawned a fierce rivalry between JR Central and JR East. JR East ran the teeming Tokyo commuter network and the Tohoku and Joetsu Shinkansen. JR Central was the proud operator of the profitable Tokaido Shinkansen and twelve narrow-gauge routes in the Nagoya and Shizuoka region. For services beyond Shin-Ōsaka to Hakata, JR Central co-operated with JR West, and the two companies framed an informal alliance around their common interests.

Each company fostered a strong market focus. JR East's fiefdom included cities in northern Honshu not served by the Shinkansen such as Yamagata and Akita. While extending the Tohoku Shinkansen from Morioka to Hachinohe and Aomori would ultimately attract more traffic, the airlines held the upper hand for travel to other destinations. A trip by rail simply took too long: a Tokyo-bound passenger from Yamagata had to take a narrow-gauge train to Fukushima and then change to the Tohoku Shinkansen. Cost ruled out building a new line to Fukushima, so JR East devised something cheaper.

MINI-SHINKANSEN

By converting the 88km narrow-gauge track between Fukushima and Yamagata to standard gauge, Shinkansen trains could travel over the existing route. As it was not practical to rebuild the bridges and other structures to take the Shinkansen stock, JR East ordered a fleet of twelve small-profile 'mini-Shinkansen' trains. These six-car Series 400 sets had all the attributes of their Series 200 sisters, but were physically smaller. The idea was to run a Series 400 coupled to a Series 200 from Tokyo to Fukushima, where the former would detach and continue over the re-gauged route to Yamagata while the latter ran north to Morioka.

The first Series 400 began tests in November 1990, and the train later sprinted up to a record 345km/h – surprisingly high given its expected duties. Decked out in silver-grey, the Series 400 entered service on the Tokyo–Yamagata run on 1 July 1992.

In the meantime, the long-awaited dream of access to the centre of Tokyo had come true. On 20 June 1991 a JR East Shinkansen train finally entered Tokyo Central, offering a direct connection to the Tokaido Shinkansen. Two decades later, the four terminal tracks were handling around 300 trains a day, with arriving trains cleaned and turned round in 12 minutes.

In the early 1990s the JR companies gained fresh confidence. Inter-company rivalry was hotting up, and all three Shinkansen operators faced the prospect of airlines siphoning away their traffic. Not surprisingly, the shape of another generation of Shinkansen stock was being sketched out.

JR East had had an ulterior motive in the Series 400 tests – it was collecting data for a project called 'Superior Train for the Advanced Railway' (STAR21). Unveiling the nine-car STAR21 research train in March 1992, JR East had drawn on aerospace technology to achieve an astonishingly low axle load of just 10.5 tonnes. Articulation between some cars cut the number of bogies, and other innovations included hollow axles. Air-smoothing skirts concealed novel bogie designs, and the traction equipment exploited advances in power electronics: variable-voltage and variable-frequency control fed power to asynchronous three-phase motors.

Fresh from the assembly shop, STAR21 was turned over to the test crews, who set about exploring the potential of their rolling laboratory. In late 1993 the onboard personnel were given the all-clear to push their charge to the limit, and JR East management was informed on 21 December that the train had touched 425km/h on the Tsubame-Sanjo–Niigata section of the Joetsu Shinkansen. Clearly, the 240km/h commercial limit could be raised, but two questions remained: could it be done on a day-to-day basis and would it infringe the noise limits?

Stellar performer. JR East's experimental Star 21 train set attained 425.1km/h on the Joetsu Shinkansen on 21 December 1993. (Kazumiki Miura)

Mini-Shinkansen (1). JR East developed the Series 400 as the first type of 'Mini-Shinkansen' train. Its small profile enabled it to run off the Shinkansen to reach the city of Yamagata over a line converted from 1,067mm to 1,435mm gauge. One of the fleet negotiates a snowy mountain pass near the hot-spring resort of Yonezawa between Fukushima and Yamagata on 17 April 2010. (Kazumiki Miura)

OLYMPIC INCENTIVE

JR East needed new trains for the Hokuriku Shinkansen, the first section of which ran from Takasaki on the Joetsu Shinkansen to Karuizawa. Construction of a 260km/h alignment had been authorised in 1989, and two years later, when Nagano was picked to host the 1998 Winter Olympics, the government signed off an extension beyond Karuizawa to Nagano.

The route demanded a specific type of train. First, the 30km from Takasaki to Karuizawa featured a 3 per cent ruling grade to ascend the 660m of the Usui Pass. Second, Karuizawa marked the boundary where the national power supply switched from 50Hz to 60Hz, so the Hokuriku stock had to accept both frequencies and pack enough power to conquer the steep grade.

Feeding in the knowledge gained from STAR21, JR East worked with Hitachi, Kawasaki and Nippon Sharyo to develop two prototype E2 train sets, and on 15 May 1995 the first of these eight-car trains was unveiled at JR East's Sendai workshop, home to its Shinkansen fleet.

The E2 had six motored cars with a driving trailer at each end; there were 630 ordinary class and 51 Green Car seats. Finished in dark blue and white, the low-profile aluminium cars were crowned by high shields surrounding the two pantographs. At high speed the noise generated by the protruding pantograph arm and head slicing through the air can be considerable, and the shields helped to contain the noise. The train's tare weight was 366 tonnes and the highest axle load was below 13 tonnes.

JR East envisaged that the E2 could inject more speed into the Tohoku service, where its 275km/h ability could be exploited to good effect. Before this could happen, JR East needed to prove that the E2 would generate no more noise or vibration at 275km/h than the Series 200 at 240km/h.

Olympic runner. One of JR East's E2 fleet approaches Omiya to the north of Tokyo in March 2013.
These trains were used to ferry visitors between Tokyo and Nagano for the 1998 Winter Olympic Games. (Kazumiki Miura)

SECOND MINI-SHINKANSEN

In January 1992 the company announced plans to convert the 127km Tazawako line from Morioka to Akita into a second mini-Shinkansen. For this it needed another small-profile train. So the E2 acquired a smaller sister, the E3, which local media inspected at Sendai on 6 April 1995. The two trains shared some components and the same 275km/h top speed.

Akita was 125km from Morioka, itself 535km from Tokyo. While converting the Morioka–Akita line to 1,435mm gauge was relatively simple, eliminating the curves and grades was out of the question. This meant that little time could be gained, so speeding up the Tohoku part of the trip was vital for a competitive timing. Trials were focused on determining noise and vibration levels, and the results were encouraging enough for JR East to promise a Tokyo–Akita journey time of under 4 hours.

On 22 March 1997 JR East President Masatake Matsuda and Akita Governor Kikuji Sasaki were on the platform at Akita to send off the first *Komachi* Mini-Shinkansen service to Tokyo at 6.12 a.m. In Tokyo JR East Chairman Shuichiro Yamanouchi and Transport Minister Makoto Koga flagged away the return working at 6.50 a.m. The trains ran at 270km/h on the Tohoku Shinkansen, and three of the thirteen daily *Komachi* services covered the 660km in 3 hours 49 minutes. Within a year, the accelerated service generated a 30 per cent traffic uplift.

Mini-Shinkansen (2). Splashing its vivid colours against the green landscape near Kaminoyamaonsen one day in July 2014, JR East's Series E3 is another Mini-Shinkansen design built to link Tokyo with Akita. E3 trains part company with the Tohoku Shinkansen at Morioka. (Kazumiki Miura)

NORTHERN NETWORK GROWS

The Hokuriku Shinkansen, renamed the Nagano Shinkansen because of the Olympic Games in Nagano and because the prospect of reaching the Hokuriku region appeared to be rapidly receding during the 1990s recession, opened on 1 October 1997. The Tokyo–Nagano trip time was halved to just over 1 hour 20 minutes, and in February 1998 Olympic Games visitors sped to the snow in a fleet of nineteen E2 sets marketed as *Asama*, the name of a mountain near Karuizawa. After a year JR East Chairman Yamanouchi proclaimed that traffic to Nagano had shot up by 30 per cent.

Next target on JR East's speed-up map was the city of Shinjo, which could be reached by converting the 70km line beyond Yamagata to a Mini-Shinkansen. When this opened on 4 December 1999, 30 minutes were lopped off the journey from Tokyo to give a 3-hour-30-minute schedule. Replacement of the Series 200 fleet was meanwhile under way, with orders placed for nine more E2s and seven more E4s (p38) for delivery by 2000.

In 1991 and 1995 the government endorsed work starting on two segments of the Morioka–Aomori extension of the Tohoku Shinkansen to Hachinohe, and in 1998 it signed off the remaining section from there to Aomori. It was a formidable project – as much as 120km of the 179km would run in tunnel.

Train control equipment had advanced significantly since 1964, and JR took the opportunity between Morioka and Hachinohe to introduce the Shinkansen's first digital automatic train control using train position data. This permitted a smoother braking profile and shorter headways, at the same time offering savings in lineside kit. The same system later replaced the ageing train control equipment on other parts of the Tohoku and Joetsu Shinkansen.

A batch of E2-1000 sets with various enhancements and no 50Hz capability was ordered for the Hachinohe route. Launched in December 2002 under the *Hayate* brand, within a year they were carrying 50 per cent more people than the Morioka–Hachinohe narrow-gauge trains.

Aomori is around 670km from Tokyo, and if the limit on the Tohoku Shinkansen remained at 275km/h, JR East calculated that it would take at least 3 hours 15 minutes. Anxious to take market share from the voracious airlines, which held 57 per cent of this market, JR needed to undercut 3 hours. This could only be done by running even faster, but exceeding 275km/h with Series E2 was a non-starter because of the noise rules. JR East therefore instructed its research department to investigate rolling stock that could attain 360km/h – faster than any other trains in the world.

After more tests with the E2 and E3, JR East ordered two prototypes, an eight-car Series 954 known as Fastech 360S and her six-car mini-Shinkansen sister, classed as Series 955 or Fastech 360Z; the S stood for Shinkansen and the Z for *Zairaisen*, Japanese for a conventional railway.

As Takashi Endo, then Director General of the company's R&D Centre, wrote in 2005, 'a jump from 275km/h to 360km/h cannot be accomplished in a day'. Working out how to guarantee comfort at ultra high speed and to deaden noise and vibration was not easy. The research team came up with active suspension to allow faster speeds through curves, plus a host of changes to limit exterior train noise at source. Apart from various shrouds and fairings, this extended to covering grab handle recesses and fitting honeycomb panels in the body to absorb wheel-rail noise bouncing off lineside sound barriers.

All ears? The yellow panels protruding above the roof of this Fastech 360 prototype are a form of experimental aerodynamic brake. JR East used the two Fastech 360 prototypes to develop Series E5 and E6 for the Tohoku and Joetsu Shinkansen. (Kazumiki Miura)

Fastech 360S took to the rails in June 2005. The 400km/h mark was soon passed, and on 10 March 2006 Fastech 360Z joined her sister at Sendai. Further trials followed, including passing tests with a closing speed of 720km/h.

Finished in 'pearl white' and 'East green', both trains had exceptionally long noses stretching to 13 and 16m. This was the outcome of research to reduce the 'sonic boom' effect in tunnels – when a train enters a tunnel at high speed, it can generate a compression wave that propagates through the tunnel at the speed of sound. This resulting boom can be mitigated by a long nose and by special structures at the tunnel portals.

The most striking feature of the Fastech design was bright yellow 'ears' raised from the roof as an experimental form of aerodynamic emergency brake. Another braking enhancement was a device that squirted a jet of ceramic powder on to the rails to increase adhesion during emergency stops. These improvements meant that a train could be brought to a stand from 360km/h in a distance of 4km.

At the conclusion of trials with the Fastech twins, JR East announced in July 2007 that it would build a ten-car train with a maximum speed of 320km/h as the forerunner of a fleet for the long haul to Aomori. Many Fastech features would be

Turquoise streak. The attractive livery of a JR East Series E5 contrasts with the snowy landscape at Iwate-Numakunai, north of Morioka, on 14 March 2012. The train has a maximum speed of 320km/h. (Kazumiki Miura)

Cherries and crimson. A small-profile JR East Series E6 is framed by cherry blossom in May 2013 near Kakunodate on the Mini-Shinkansen route between Morioka and Akita. (Kazumiki Miura)

NATURE INTERVENES

From 5 March 2011 timings for the 675km trip from Tokyo to Shin-Aomori were due to be cut to 3 hours 5 minutes using the first of fifty-nine Series E5 *Hayabusa* trains operating at 300km/h, but less than a week later the Great East Japan Earthquake intervened – the Tohoku Shinkansen was damaged at 1,200 sites over the 500km between Omiya and Iwate-Numakunai. Astonishingly, JR East restored services just forty-nine days later on 29 April, albeit at reduced speed. The speed-up had to wait until 16 March 2013, when *Hayabusa* services were authorised to streak over the Utsunomiya–Morioka section at 320km/h, reaching Shin-Aomori in 2 hours 59 minutes. The same timetable change saw seven-car E6 *Super Komachi* train sets start to take over the Tokyo–Akita mini-Shinkansen route from the ageing E3s, although initially their speed was limited to 300km/h.

incorporated – although not the 'ears' – but it was clear that 360km/h was off the immediate agenda. Nevertheless, JR East said it would 'investigate the possibility of further staged increases in train speed'.

The wraps were taken off the 'pre-mass production' Series E5 in Sendai on 17 June 2009; its distinctively shaped nose was finished in 'Takiwa green'. Outwardly similar, but sporting a crimson and white livery devised by builder Kawasaki and renowned industrial designer Ken Okuyama, the small-profile E6 went on show at Sendai on 9 July 2010. Together, the two types were destined to become the mainstay of Tohoku Shinkansen services, which were extended from Hachinohe to Shin-Aomori on 4 December 2010. The Tohoku Shinkansen was finally complete.

'Gran class'. JR East's E5 breaks with tradition by offering luxury accommodation in addition to Green Car (first class) and 'ordinary' seating; there are just eighteen Gran Class seats in one car. (Kazumiki Miura)

The E5 marked another new departure. For the first time, a Shinkansen train featured luxury accommodation, with one car designated 'Gran Class'. Working with Hitachi, JR East sought 'an extraordinary experience' for its premium passengers, whom it saw as business travellers and 'wealthy seniors' – doubtless a reflection of Japan's ageing population. Inspired by aircraft and modern hotel interiors, Gran Class offers just eighteen reclining leather seats. Passengers are cosseted with footlights, reading lights, power outlets, blankets, slippers, eyeshades, cocktail trays and light meals and drinks. And the air-conditioning has 'anti-odour and anti-bacteria functions', as one JR East publicity handout put it.

HOKKAIDO IN SIGHT

In 2003 there was a significant change in the arrangements for building Shinkansen lines with the establishment of Japan Railway Construction Transport & Technology (JRTT). This merged the former JRCC and the Corporation for Advanced Transport & Technology into a single organisation. JRTT was charged with preparing detailed plans and with handling civil engineering, track laying, signalling, telecoms and electrification. Two-thirds of the construction cost would be met by national government, with the rest contributed by local governments. The completed line is leased to the JR company concerned, which provides the rolling stock.

A deal between the government and the ruling coalition parties on 16 December 2004 secured more money for Shinkansen schemes, releasing around ¥220 billion in the 2005–06 financial year. Extending the Shinkansen to Hakodate and Sapporo on Hokkaido was a firm national commitment, and from Aomori only a short hop remains to the Tsugaru Strait between Honshu and Hokkaido. The extra funds allowed work to start

Blue streak. The E7 entered service with JR East in March 2014 on the Nagano Shinkansen. As the line speed limit is 260km/h, the design does not feature the extreme aerodynamic nose of its E5 and E6 cousins. (Kazumiki Miura)

in 2005 on the first part of the 149km Hokkaido Shinkansen from Shin-Aomori to Hakodate.

At the core of this project was the 53.9km Seikan Tunnel under the Strait. Completed in 1988, it had Shinkansen dimensions but was laid with narrow-gauge tracks. So the first step entailed installing three-rail track to accept both narrow-gauge and Shinkansen trains. As two-thirds of the ¥470 billion cost of the Hokkaido Shinkansen was coming from government coffers, it was appropriate for Transport Minister Kazuo Kitagawa to join JR Hokkaido Chairman Shinchi Sakamoto at a start-of-work ceremony at Shin-Hakodate on 22 May 2005. The payback will be a Tokyo–Hakodate journey time of 4 hours

10 minutes when the line opens in March 2016. JR East will deploy some of its E5 fleet, which will share duties with four ten-car Series H5 trains ordered by JR Hokkaido for ¥18 billion from Hitachi and Kawasaki.

The funding top-up also channelled money to the Nagano Shinkansen. Rosier economic prospects meant that the line would after all reach Hokuriku, and the name reverted to Hokuriku Shinkansen. Work had commenced over the 162km between Nagano and Toyama in March 1998, and the extra cash bought a further section to Kanazawa. Contractors have meanwhile commenced work on the coastal section from Kanazawa to Tsuruga, but this will not open until 2024/25.

Commuters on Two Decks

As popularity of the Shinkansen rose, JR East faced heavy demand for seats from commuters in towns such as Utsunomiya, 109km distant from Tokyo, and Takasaki, 105km away. Standing

Upstairs and downstairs. To provide more seats on heavily used commuter services over the Joetsu and Tohoku Shinkansen, JR East developed the double-deck E1 and E4 designs. Here a pair of E4s approaches Omiya, just north of Tokyo, in January 2013. (Kazumiki Miura)

room only on high-speed trains is not a formula that thrills impatient commuters, so JR East looked at ways to up capacity – so up it went.

Cramming traction and other equipment into compartments at the car ends, the rolling stock team devised an all double-deck 240km/h train dubbed MAX (Multi-Amenity eXpress); the blander official designation was Series E1. This enormous box on wheels packed 1,235 seats into twelve steel-bodied cars. The upper deck on four cars was particularly cosy, with seats arranged 3+3. Starting in July 1994, a pair of MAX sets was deployed on short-distance peak-hour trips, filling in with off-peak runs to Sendai and Morioka.

The E1 did the job of providing seats, but the trains failed to earn their keep outside the peak. JR East therefore conceived a shorter train for peak-hour commuting, which could run profitably at other times of day. Three eight-car double-deckers were ordered, each with 817 seats, some of them with 3+3 seating as on the original MAX. To achieve the desired flexibility, the 240km/h Series E4 could be coupled with the Series 400, E2 and E3.

Styling and aerodynamics experts strove to blend a long nose with the bulbous cross-section of the E4's double-deck aluminium car body, but Tokyo commuters must have remarked on the extraordinary shape when the inaugural E4 pulled into Tokyo Central on 1 December 1997.

The 228km from Nagano to Kanazawa opened on 14 March 2015. For this route, JR East had ordered a fleet of seventeen Series E7 sets. As the Hokuriku line enters JR West territory east of Toyama, the order was placed jointly with JR West, which contracted for ten more trains designated W7. Line speed was no more than 260km/h, so the extreme aerodynamic form of the E5 and

E6 was not required, and the twelve-car E7 rolled out by suppliers Kawasaki and JR East subsidiary J-TREC in December 2013 had a more conventional appearance. Like its E2 precursor, the E7 can take power at 50Hz and 60Hz as it crosses the frequency boundary at Karuizawa.

As on the E5, JR East and JR West opted to include Gran Class. They made much of the inte-

rior styling, which is inspired by the concept of *wa*, or harmony. The first E7 sets were launched on *Asama* services between Tokyo and Nagano on 15 March 2014, a day that also marked the replacement of the last E3 sets by Series E6, which could run with their E5 sisters at 320km/h on the Tohoku Shinkansen, permitting a further cut in timings to Akita.

JR Central Masters the Market

As owner of the golden goose called the Tokaido Shinkansen, JR Central was in a powerful position. Among its board members was Yoshiyuki Kasai, who had managed JNR's employee issues during the 1987 break-up. Kasai became President of JR Central in 1995, driving the company towards a stock market listing. Kasai was very conscious that the formula of the JNR break-up meant that the Tokaido Shinkansen was effectively subsidising the costs of the Joetsu and Tohoku Shinkansen, and this did nothing to generate *wa* between JR Central and JR East.

Freed from government constraints, JR Central set out to capitalise on the Tokaido Shinkansen's track record – in 1989 the line carried 112 million passengers. JR West, meanwhile, introduced another speed-up, nudging up the maximum on the Sanyo Shinkansen to 230km/h and trimming 10 minutes off the Osaka–Hakata timing.

To exploit the 220km/h maximum on the Tokaido Shinkansen from 1986, JNR began replacing Series 0, which had been through several iterations after the original fleet. The sixteen-car Series 100 took over selected *Hikari* services from 1985. Its hallmarks were a more pointed nose and a pair of mid-train double-deckers, one offering upper-deck dining and the other a Green Car saloon upstairs and private compartments downstairs – hire of which attracted a supplementary fare.

The Series 100's more powerful traction motors meant that the end cars and the double-deckers could be trailers. Thyristor control, faster acceleration and better braking were other attributes, and six rather than eight pantographs achieved a slight reduction in aerodynamic noise. Several versions of the Series 100 followed, but there were no radical technical changes.

On JNR's drawing board before the break-up was a train for the Hokuriku Shinkansen. This formed the basis for the first Shinkansen train to be designed by JR Central, and tests with a prototype Series 300 *Super Hikari* for the Tokaido Shinkansen commenced in 1990 between Kyoto and Maibara. The sixteen-car Series 300 introduced air-sprung bolster-less bogies with smaller wheels and eddy-current disc brakes. Five pantographs, of which only two were raised at one time, were screened in turrets. Four asynchronous induction motors were fitted to each of ten motored cars, giving a continuous output of 12MW. Low-profile aluminium bodies trimmed weight and air resistance, with further weight saved thanks to lighter seats. All this brought the mass of an individual car down to about 40 tonnes. Gone were the diner and private compartments – what counted on the business-led railway was the number of seats.

The Series 300 was a vital tool in JR Central's bid to outperform the airlines. Its new toy could cruise at 270km/h, and on 14 March 1992 it launched ultra-fast *Nozomi* services that dashed between Tokyo and Shin-Ōsaka in 2 hours 30 minutes. This started with two round trips a day, but within a year the Series 300 fleet was big enough for JR Central to advertise an hourly *Nozomi*, with fourteen trains continuing to Hakata and one to Hiroshima.

Series 300 swansong. The lightweight sixteen-car Series 300 was the first Shinkansen train to be designed by JR Central for the Tokaido Shinkansen after the break-up of Japanese National Railways. Already emblazoned with 'last run 2012.3.16', a Series 300 set is dwarfed by Tokyo's skyscrapers near central Tokyo a few days before the fleet was withdrawn. (Kazumiki Miura)

JR WEST STRIDES AHEAD

JR West had been similarly active. On 7 April 1992, in Kobe, it rolled out its own research train. When the wraps came off, they revealed a rocket-shape with the name WIN350 (West Innovation 350) emblazoned on the violet bodyside. Deep hoods enclosed the wing-shaped pantographs, and bodyside skirts and inter-car fairings smoothed the longitudinal profile. JR West claimed that the six-car train's novel bogies were 40 per cent lighter than conventional designs and announced that the train could be fitted with active suspension.

From its base at Hakata, WIN350 underwent testing that reached a climax on 8 August 1992. As the train flashed along the track between Ogori and Shin-Shimonoseki, the cab speedometer registered 350.4km/h.

Straight to the point. When introduced in March 1997, the aerodynamically superb Series 500 claimed the crown for the fastest scheduled service in the world, achieving a start-to-stop average of 261.9km/h between Hiroshima and Kokura. Here an eight-car formation rolls over slab track on a bridge near Shinkurashiki, between Okayama and Fukuyama on the Sanyo Shinkansen. (Kazumiki Miura)

No shrinking violet. JR West's WIN350 research train was used to refine lightweight construction and aerodynamic performance at high speed. Note the huge shields intended to cut aerodynamic noise round the pantographs. (Kazumiki Miura)

WIN350 was the forerunner of JR West's Series 500 Shinkansen fleet, and in 1994 JR West Managing Director Toshiyuki Umehara wrote that 'we have now mastered all necessary technologies for 300km/h running'. The Series 500 was Japan's first train to be conceived at the outset to carry passengers at 300km/h. Distinguished by a 15m-long nose occupying more than half the length of the leading car, the ultra-streamlined Series 500 had a bubble-shaped cab resembling a jet fighter's cockpit. Revealed to the public on 27 December 1995, the Series 500 had what JR West termed a 'maximum performance speed' of 320km/h. Its slim profile was explained by the body cross-section measuring just $10.2m^2$, even less than the $11.1m^2$ of JR Central's Series 300. All axles of the sixteen cars were driven by body-mounted asynchronous motors, giving continuous installed power of 18.2MW. Three cars offered a total of 200 Green Car seats, with 1,124 economy seats in the other thirteen.

The Series 500 represented JR West's bid for a bigger slice of the market over the Sanyo Shinkansen, which brought in 40 per cent of company revenue. JR Central could cite 80 per cent of the rail-air market between the capital and Shin-Ōsaka, but JR West had just 60 per cent on the leg to Hakata. The train first wowed the passengers on 22 March 1997, its Shin-Ōsaka–Hakata timing being just 2 hours 17 minutes, including three intermediate calls. Timed at 44 minutes over the 192km between Hiroshima and Kokura, the Series 500 achieved a start-to-stop average of 261.9km/h. It was not just the first train in Japan to carry passengers at 300km/h, but the fastest publicly timetabled train in the world.

Nine Series 500 sets were built, some destined for *Nozomi* diagrams from Tokyo to Hakata from 29 November 1997. The Series 300 was cascaded to *Hikari* services, and these in turn displaced Series 100 sets that were relegated to slower *Kodama* workings. At the bottom of the cascade was the Series 0. The last of around 3,200 Series 0 cars was built in 1986, and the final unit was pulled out of service with JR West after a ceremonial farewell run between Shin-Ōsaka and Hakata on 14 December 2008.

TOWARDS THE ULTIMATE TRAIN

Like the other JR companies, JR Central could not rest on its laurels. In the early 1990s its R&D teams conceived yet another experimental streamliner, originally as a testbed for the future Chuo Shinkansen – of which more in the next chapter. The 300X started commissioning trials in January 1995 between Shizuoka and Hamamatsu,

Record holder. JR Central's Series 300X test train was powered up to 443km/h between Maibara and Kyoto in July 1996. The pantograph shields protrude high above the roofline. (Kazumiki Miura)

after which it was prepared for ultra-high-speed tests based at Maibara. Testing was only possible at night as there were no spare daytime paths – and with a new train there was always the chance of something going wrong.

A 'cusp'-shaped nose at one end contrasted with a more conventional rounded shape at the other, and bath-shaped shielding round the pantograph deflected fast-moving air away from the pan head. Four body-mounted asynchronous motors drove the axles on each of the six cars, making 12MW available for short-term bursts of speed. On 26 July 1996 the test crew watched triumphantly as the driver coaxed the 300X up to 443km/h between Maibara and Kyoto, setting a Japanese record for a steel-wheeled train set.

Both JR Central and JR West moved swiftly along the privatisation path. In October 1996 JR West was listed on six Japanese stock exchanges, and a year later JR Central followed suit. External pressure was starting to tell, too, with air fares liberalised and fresh airline competitors. Under Kasai's leadership, JR Central's quest for lower costs and higher returns rose up the agenda, driving decisions on rolling stock design. JR Central and JR West pooled their expertise and together sketched out the fundamentals of the next generation of Tokaido-Sanyo stock, the Series 700. Its new features were tested on a prototype called Series N300.

The last of sixty-one Series 300 sets, each priced at around ¥4 billion, took to the rails in 1998. A similar price tag was expected for Series 700, for which the design brief was lower running costs plus enhanced comfort and a quieter interior. The formation had twelve motored cars and four trailers, with a single-arm current collector on two cars. Bodyshells of hollow aluminium profiles filled with resin foam muffled external noise, and advanced electronics eliminated underfloor noise sources that could irritate passengers. Computer-controlled secondary suspension with 'semi-active' dampers adjusting to variations in the

force between bogie and car body were fitted to smooth the ride, while inter-car dampers restricted lateral and longitudinal movements. Each end car featured an 8.5m long 'aerostream' nose.

The prototype began tests at Hamamatsu, about midway between Shizuoka and Nagoya, on 3 October 1997, and JR Central promptly ordered seventeen sets, deciding to extend the nose to 9.2m. Given that the curve radii on the Tokaido Shinkansen dictated a 270km/h limit, the top speed

was set at 285km/h, which could be exploited on the Sanyo extension. On 13 March 1999 the first *Nozomi* diagrammed for a Series 700 departed Tokyo Central for Hakata, where it was due to arrive 4 hours 57 minutes later.

A batch of nine eight-car variants for *Hikari Rail Star* services on the Sanyo Shinkansen came next. Launched on 11 March 2000, they incorporated JR West's individual touches such as four-seat compartments in one car and 'office seats' in

Peak of perfection. JR Central refined the design of its Series 700 with two derivatives, the N700 and the N700A, each improving performance and comfort. From 2015 the N700A is expected to run at 285km/h on the Tokaido Shinkansen, where Mt Fuji is visible on a fine day. (Kazumiki Miura)

three others. A 'silence car' had special seat-back ticket holders so that ticket inspectors need not disturb passengers. Pleased with passengers' reactions, JR West added three trains to the order and signed a contract for another twelve with sixteen cars.

The Series 700 ticked all the right boxes, but JR Central believed that it had not yet found the ultimate lightweight high-speed train. An enhanced prototype called the N700 completed a test programme in 2006, and JR Central announced that refinements such as a 1 per cent passive body tilt – a first for the Shinkansen – inter-car fairings, a superior nose design and smoother bodysides had achieved a 19 per cent saving in energy consumption compared with the Series 700, this despite fourteen instead of twelve powered cars and a rating upped from 13.2MW to nearly 17.1MW. Remarkably, the axle load had been cut to just 11.4 tonnes, and the weight per seat is just 0.48 tonnes.

In summer 2006 JR Central announced that it would buy forty-two Series N700 sets for ¥200 billion, with JR West purchasing another twelve for ¥60 billion. The N700 fleet was pressed into *Nozomi* service from 1 July 2007, cruising on the Tokaido Shinkansen at 270km/h and on the Sanyo at 300km/h.

The final Series 700 development was the N700A. Appearing in the 2013 timetable, it 'employs the fruits of JR Central's proprietary technological development harvested since the creation of the Series N700', according to the company. These included high-performance wheel-mounted disc brakes, a bogie vibration detection system, vestibule-mounted security cameras and what must surely be the ultimate enhancement: 'toilet seats with a warm water washing function'.

From 2015 the N700A is expected to run on the Tokaido Shinkansen at 285km/h, taking full advantage of advances in braking technology and the latest version of digital ATC that was first installed between Tokyo and Shin-Ōsaka in 2004/05.

Dealing with Earthquakes

Visitors to Japan are often struck by the imposing scale of the Shinkansen viaducts. The reason is that Japan lies in a zone of tectonic activity, and structures must withstand the effects of an earthquake. Given the potential for damage, seismographs have been installed parallel to the Shinkansen routes to detect the P (primary) wave that precedes the secondary wave of an earthquake. If a P wave is detected, the equipment triggers a command to cut the power supply so that trains are halted before the main quake arrives.

The value of this measure has been shown several times. In March 2011 the Great East Japan Earthquake devastated large areas of north-east Japan, and even though several Shinkansen trains were in the area, all were halted and no passengers were killed. On 23 October 2004 *Toki* 325 derailed at around 200km/h on the Joetsu Shinkansen near Nagaoka during the Niigata-Chuetsu earthquake, but no one was seriously hurt. Earlier still, on 17 January 1995, four sections of the Sanyo Shinkansen sustained serious damage when a quake wrought havoc in the Kobe region, but on that occasion the quake occurred early in the morning before trains were running.

SECOND TOKYO TERMINAL

Throughout this period of sustained rolling-stock development, work continued to enhance the infrastructure. Capacity was at a premium, and the timetable featured eleven peak-hour departures from Tokyo Central, in addition to which empty stock moved to and from the depot at Shinagawa, 9km to the south-west. The bottleneck was uncorked by building a second terminal at Shinagawa, where four out of fifteen trains approaching Tokyo in the peak hour could terminate. The new terminus opened on 1 October 2003, allowing a timetable recast with up to fifteen trains an hour each way. It also triggered a surge in commercial property development around the station.

KYUSHU CONNECTED

Further west, the Shinkansen connecting the Sanyo terminus at Hakata with Kagoshima-Chuo on Kyushu was under construction. Together with a branch from Tosu to Nagasaki, this route had been approved in 1973, but not until 1991 did the transport ministry instruct JRCC to commence work on the 128km southern section from Kagoshima-Chuo to Shin-Yatsushiro. This opened on 13 March 2004 using five six-car Series 800 *Tsubame* train sets ordered by JR Kyushu, but the line was isolated from the rest of the Shinkansen network. Until opening of the missing section on 12 March 2011, the 121km gap to Hakata was filled by narrow-gauge *Relay Tsubame* trains making cross-platform interchange at Shin-Yatsushiro. With the missing link in place, an unbroken route now runs from Tokyo Central to Kagoshima-Chuo, a distance of 1,317.8km.

The journey from Shin-Ōsaka to Kagoshima-Chuo takes around 4 hours, with *Mizuho* services offering a fastest timing of 3 hours 44 minutes. These duties fall to a fleet of twenty-nine N700-7000 and

N700-8000 train sets, which are 300km/h eight-car derivatives of the N700. JR West bought nineteen and JR Kyushu ten; all axles are powered and there is no tilt as they do not venture on to the Tokaido Shinkansen.

Doctor Yellow

Specially built Series 700 trains are used by JR West and JR Central to inspect the Shinkansen infrastructure. Earlier versions assembled from Series 0 cars had checked the state of the track and catenary for nearly a quarter of a century. Finished in canary coloured paint, they were famously called 'Doctor Yellow', and their replacements, classified as Series 923 and with a much enhanced capability, earned the same moniker.

JR Central and JR West use several 'Doctor Yellow' high-speed track and overhead line inspection trains derived from the Series 700 to determine what maintenance work is required on the Tokaido and Sanyo Shinkansen. An inspection train passes Shinagawa, south of central Tokyo, on 7 May 2014. (Kazumiki Miura)

Limited stop. JR West and JR Kyushu deploy eight-car versions of the N700 design on the fastest *Mizuho* services between Shin-Ōsaka and Kyushu. JR West operates the N700-7000 and JR Kyushu uses the almost identical N700-8000, one of which is seen at Shin-Tamana near Kumamoto on Kyushu in March 2012. (Kazumiki Miura)

Kyushu Shinkansen. In March 2004 JR Kyushu launched operations on the isolated section of line between Kagoshima-Chuo and Shin-Yatsushiro using Series 800 train sets. One of the small fleet awaits its next duty in Kumamoto depot. (Kazumiki Miura)

GAUGE-CHANGING TRAIN

An alternative to the *Relay Tsubame* could have been a gauge-changing train. A three-car gauge-changing prototype was tested in 1998–99 and then shipped to the USA for endurance trials at the Association of American Railroads' test track in Colorado. A second prototype followed in 2007, but developing a train able to roll on Shinkansen tracks at full speed and also negotiate sharply curved 1,067mm gauge routes is no simple matter. In 2013–14 the Railway Technical Research Institute teamed up with JR Kyushu to develop a third gauge-convertible prototype, which was unveiled in early 2014.

It is due to clock up 600,000km of tests on the Kyushu Shinkansen and narrow-gauge lines. If it works, this train could radically change Japan's railway geography.

The Kyushu Shinkansen remains a work in progress. Construction of a branch from Shin-Tosu, around 25km south of Hakata, to Nagasaki began between Takeo-Onsen and Isahaya (45.7km) in 2008, and in June 2012 Transport Minister Yuichiro Hata announced construction over the 21km from Isahaya to Nagasaki. Even when this is finished in 2022/23, it will be isolated from the main network, so gauge-changing trains may yet be needed.

Hata also firmed up plans to complete the 211km Hokkaido Shinkansen from Shin-Hakodate to Sapporo, although this will take another twenty-three years. It will then be possible to travel by Shinkansen from Kagoshima in southern Kyushu to Hokkaido. En route the traveller will glide over the hallowed tracks that in 1964 launched high-speed rail travel. Nor is there any fear of arriving late, for the Shinkansen's punctuality is the envy of every other rail operator. The annual average delay per train on the Tokaido Shinkansen is just 30 seconds, according to statistics published in 2013.

Table I. Shinkansen service names

Kodama –	*Echo*
Hikari –	*Light*
Hikari Rail Star	
Nozomi –	*Hope*
Toki –	*Crested ibis* [no longer used]
Hayate –	*Rushing wind*
Tanigawa –	*A mountain*
Hayabusa –	*Falcon*
Komachi –	*Beautiful girl*
Yamabiko –	*Mountain echo*
Nasuno –	*The upland Nasu region*
Tsubasa –	*Wings*
Asama –	*A volcano*
Asahi –	*Morning sun* [no longer used]
Aoba –	*Green leaves* [no longer used]
Mizuho –	*Fresh ears of rice*
Sakura –	*Cherry blossom*
Tsubame –	*Swallow*

Game changer? If Japan's third prototype gauge-changing train is successful, it could revolutionise access to cities off the standard-gauge Shinkansen network. The train was unveiled in 2014. (JRTT)

3

Powerful Forces Keep Maglev Afloat

The Chuo Shinkansen is one of Japan's most ambitious infrastructure projects. Its purpose is to provide an alternative route from Tokyo to Osaka to relieve the busy Tokaido Shinkansen, which handled a peak of 151 million trips in 2007. Not only is the Tokaido Shinkansen congested, but the fifty-year-old route also needs a serious makeover to keep it in tip-top condition. In April 2013 JR Central launched a ten-year ¥731 billion programme to renovate the infrastructure, but a third consideration has moved up the agenda. In the wake of the Great East Japan Earthquake, the prospect of the Tokaido Shinkansen being crippled by an earthquake or other catastrophic event is very real. This could wreak terrible damage on Japan's economy, so an inland route to Osaka is now seen as a vital insurance policy.

However, it seems that the line will differ fundamentally from every other Shinkansen. Instead of using the finely honed engineering of steel wheels on steel rails, it will rely on maglev technology, with 500km/h trains floating on a magnetic field inside a U-shaped trough. This flies in the face of hard-won experience, but there are powerful forces at work that are keen to trumpet Japan's advanced technological status.

Before we examine the Chuo project, it is instructive to glance at the history of maglev. The world's only commercial high-speed maglev operation is in China, where an elevated guideway strides for 31km across the urban landscape from Shanghai's international airport to Pudong – some considerable distance from the city centre. At Pudong passengers can change to the metro to reach the centre, or if they have a few moments to spare, they can divert to explore the rather quaint maglev museum adjacent to the terminus. Vehicles on the Shanghai maglev line streak along at a maximum of 430km/h, but only for 1 hour 45 minutes in the morning and the same in the afternoon. At other times the rather more sedate pace of 300km/h is not exceeded – if you are using electricity to levitate a vehicle as well as propel it, the power bill can be expensive.

In the days when maglev was little more than a boffin's dream, rival systems emerged in Germany and Japan. In 1971 Japan Air Lines (JAL) began to experiment with a system that was initially based

Magnetic pull. The only commercial high-speed maglev operation in the world links Shanghai Airport with Pudong station in the suburbs of the city. To save energy, speed is normally 300km/h, but 430km/h is permitted for short periods every morning and afternoon. (Author)

on the same electromagnetic technology as in Germany, which has vehicles that sit astride a steel guideway. The sides of the vehicles wrap around the guideway, and electromagnets mounted on 'bogies' protrude down and under the guideway. When the magnets are energised, they are attracted upwards towards the guideway, so levitating the vehicle.

A gap of up to 15mm is maintained between the vehicle and the guideway, and a linear motor is then used to propel the vehicle horizontally. This system is used in Shanghai.

The original German maglev vehicle was the brainchild of Messerschmitt-Bölkow-Blohm, which in time merged its research with that of

Krauss-Maffei. Other companies were quick to leap on the bandwagon, and most of them ended up in a consortium that later morphed into Transrapid International, whose principal stakeholders were Siemens and ThyssenKrupp. Once the principle of levitation by magnet had been demonstrated, successive transport ministers agonised about the

Points to note. The enormous structures required to shift vehicles from one 'track' to another are the Achilles heel of maglev technology as they take a long time to move. These points are outside Pudong station in Shanghai. (Author)

location of a test facility, and the choice eventually fell on a remote area of moorland in the Emsland near the village of Lathen in Lower Saxony. Sponsored by the Federal Ministry of Research & Technology, a 31.5km guideway was built in two stages in the mid-1980s to test the performance of experimental Transrapid vehicles. A visit in 1984 revealed one of maglev's Achilles heels: it took up to 20 seconds to move a large chunk of the guideway to one side to allow a vehicle to switch from one 'track' to another – far longer than changing a set of points on a conventional railway.

Later, visitors could pay for the pleasure of being levitated and whisked around the test loop in one of the Transrapid vehicles, but the crucial step from test site to commercial application remained mired in controversy. Politicians blew hot and cold about where to build a demonstration route – lines were proposed from Hamburg to Hannover, Essen to Bonn or Mannheim, Hamburg to Berlin, and even Hamburg to Munich. Meantime, Transrapid extolled the virtues of its progeny to anyone who would listen, and proposals sprung up elsewhere, including one from Disneyland to Orlando Airport in Florida. None progressed beyond the status of a line on a map, although the Hamburg–Berlin proposal and a link between Munich Airport and the city both reached the formal planning stage before they too were abandoned.

On 2 July 2000 Chinese Premier Zhu Rongji was treated to a trip at 400km/h in the Emsland, after which he professed to suffering from 'a little dizziness'. In the following year, on 23 January, Transrapid International, Siemens and Thyssen Transrapid signed a DM1.29 billion deal with Shanghai Maglev Transportation Development Co to build the Shanghai shuttle. A start-of-work ceremony was staged on 1 March and the contractors got to work. In an astonishingly short time they had erected the guideway, and on

31 December 2002 German Chancellor Gerhard Schröder and Chinese Premier Zhu Rongji met to cut a ceremonial ribbon marking the maiden departure of a commercial high-speed maglev train. And in October 2003 the first fare-paying passengers whizzed to and from Shanghai Airport on a magnetic cushion.

CATASTROPHE STRIKES

Back in Germany, the promoters hankered after a domestic maglev route, but a decision never came. Tests continued in the Emsland, but trials came to an abrupt halt on 22 September 2006 when the automatically driven Transrapid 08 collided at around 170km/h with a rubber-tyred maintenance vehicle. There were thirty-one people on board, and two staff on the maintenance vehicle. The leading maglev car was almost completely destroyed and twenty-three people died, while ten more were seriously injured. Investigations found that human error was to blame – control staff had inadvertently authorised Transrapid 08 to operate when the maintenance vehicle was still on the guideway.

Various transport experts had previously expressed concern about the lack of crashworthiness of maglev vehicles, but supporters had argued that a collision between maglev vehicles was all but impossible because the track is only energised in the immediate vicinity of a vehicle. What they had not foreseen was a collision with a non-levitating vehicle.

Sporadic tests went on, but passengers were no longer permitted on demonstration trips. Transrapid International affirmed in April 2008 that 'this is not the end of the Transrapid maglev technology', but the words returned to haunt the company the following December when the Economics Minister of Lower Saxony Walter Hirche announced that testing would cease on 30 June 2009. In August 2013 *Eisenbahn Magazin* published a photograph of a vehicle removing electrical equipment from the

Emsland guideway, and its reporter suggested that the concrete beams and piers would be dismantled shortly afterwards so that the site could once again become a 'green meadow'.

Back to Japan. JAL completed a 1.3km experimental guideway near Tokyo in 1977 with a view to building a maglev link between Tokyo and Narita Airport, then under construction. In 1974 JNR began its own investigations, and a 7km guideway was erected at Miyazaki on Kyushu. In contrast to JAL, JNR opted for the electrodynamic system. In this case the lifting force is generated by currents induced in coils in the guideway by the vehicle moving over them. However, the lifting forces are only powerful enough to support a vehicle once it is moving relatively fast, so the vehicle has to 'taxi' on rubber-tyred wheels before 'lift-off' is obtained. For some reason, maglev promoters are always rather coy about their vehicles having wheels, and a low-speed system in Berlin called the M-Bahn, now long dismantled, was fitted with 'vertical guide rollers'.

Another problem is the need for a very strong magnetic field. The choice fell on superconducting magnets, a technique briefly tried in Germany in the 1970s. Superconductivity is the state of having no electrical resistance, which can be obtained in certain metals by lowering their temperature to something approaching absolute zero. In this state a powerful magnetic field can be created. But keeping the magnets cool is a serious challenge, and JNR used cryostats that took the temperature down to -269°C thanks to liquid helium. This becomes a gas as it warms up, and initially it had to be recovered and re-liquefied between trips until on-board refrigeration could be perfected.

By 1976/77 JNR was experimenting with an unmanned test car, and on 21 December 1979 an image of the ML-500 maglev vehicle was splashed across newspapers when it romped up to 517km/h. At that stage the guideway was T-shaped, somewhat impractical for commercial vehicles, so JNR rebuilt it as a U-shape, housing the levitation coils in the floor and the propulsion and guidance coils in the sidewalls.

The break-up of JNR in 1987 interrupted the development programme, and maglev research became the responsibility of the Railway Technical Research Institute (RTRI). Further test vehicles were built, this time with seats. In October 1991 one of them was destroyed by fire, but a replacement reached 431km/h in unmanned mode in 1994.

JAL had meanwhile lost interest, leaving the JR Group with a clear run to develop the technology with RTRI. By this time the potential of the Miyazaki guideway had been exhausted, and in 1989 a decision was taken to build a much longer installation. The chosen location was in Yamanashi Prefecture, about 90km west of Tokyo, not far from Mount Fuji. The site had been carefully picked so that it could later form part of the future Chuo Shinkansen. The original plan called for a 42.8km test track, but in the event only 18.3km were built as a so-called 'priority section'.

To visit the Yamanashi guideway, it is possible to travel by train from central Tokyo to the town of Otsuki by taking a Chuo line narrow-gauge express towards Kofu. From Otsuki a local train runs to Tanokula, the nearest station to the test site's visitor centre. Here there is a reception building overlooking the guideway where it crosses the Chuo Expressway on the Ogatayama bridge, but much of the rest of the alignment is hidden in tunnel.

My first visit was in 1997, when I found myself accompanied by Jolene Molitoris, then Federal Railroad Administrator in the USA. A great maglev enthusiast, she had hoped to ride the first maglev car on the guideway, and of course, so had I. Our hopes were dashed when we found that our Japanese hosts were reluctant to let us even board the vehicle while it was at a standstill. After some persistence, they agreed to a brief inspection. Before being allowed inside, we were asked to deposit our credit cards in the visitor centre (and other items susceptible to influence by strong magnetic fields). We were then politely escorted on board.

The first set of maglev vehicles had arrived at the depot at the Tokyo end of the Yamanashi site in July 1995, but not until December 1996 was all the equipment assembled and checked. Around ten days were spent testing in the depot, moving the vehicles over short distances. The MLX01 three-car set then ventured out on to the guideway, where it was hauled in unpowered mode by a maintenance tractor.

At low speeds, the vehicles ride on their rubber tyres, with levitation achieved at around 150 to 200km/h. Once levitated, the gap between vehicle and guideway is maintained at about 100mm, and the landing wheels and horizontal guide wheels are retracted. After the hauled tests, the linear motor was switched on, and checks were made to ensure that the train's position was correctly detected by inductive loop. On 11 March 1997, the day of my visit, the vehicles notched up their first 1,000km of trials.

The initial vehicles had different front ends: the 'double cusp' type and the 'aero-wedge' type. Boarding was through a sealed gangway

Superconducting streamliner. The MLX-01 maglev test vehicles featured a 'double cusp' nose at one end. A five-car formation is parked in the 'double track' guideway in front of the visitors' viewing platform at Otsuki on the Yamanashi test site. (*Railway Gazette* collection)

incorporating magnetic shields that was aligned with the car doorway, which opened vertically. The magnetic shields were designed to keep magnetic fields below 20 gauss, and shields on the vehicles were fitted in the bodyshell insulation.

Inside the passenger saloon the seats were arranged in a 2+2 layout with a pitch of 880mm. Overhead luggage lockers and seat belts were evidence of aircraft practice, as were the tiny windows measuring 400mm deep by 300mm wide. General Manager of the test centre Dr Akio Seki assured me that the seat belts would not be needed on commercial maglev trains.

There was no driver's cab as the train control function is carried out from the ground. A small crew compartment resides in the leading car behind the levitation bogie, and here it was possible to view the guideway ahead thanks to a screen linked to a camera in the nose.

Of special interest were the four braking mechanisms. Aerodynamic brakes folded up from the roof above each levitation bogie. On the MLX01 train there were three single brake panels and one twin panel looking like a pair of ears at one end. Deceleration was also achieved by reversing the current in the guideway coils to provide a form of regenerative braking, while a rheostatic guideway brake saw the linear motor used as a generator, with kinetic energy consumed in resistances. Finally, disc brakes of carbon resin and carbon fibre composites were fitted to the undercarriage for application when the train 'landed'.

Three years of tests were planned. The first twelve months were to be used for 'basic running' trials, with the second year devoted to 'general function tests' that were to include the two sets of vehicles passing at high speed. The third year was assigned for endurance trials, after which an evaluation committee was to rule on the feasibility of the technology for commercial application.

The test site was officially opened on 3 April 1997, and levitated running trials began on 30 May. On that day MLX01 made nineteen runs, levitating on nine occasions during which it ran 14km in levitated mode for periods of 24 to 53 seconds. On 3 October it attained 451km/h, a new world record for a manned maglev train.

More records fell later that year, when a programme of ultra-high-speed trials began. A speed of 531km/h was twice reached on 12 December, once in unmanned mode, and once with a test team aboard. But there was more to come. On 18 December the unmanned test train reached 542km/h, and an attempt to reach 550km/h was planned for the following day. This had to be abandoned because of a transformer failure, but this was quickly rectified and trials resumed on 24 December. This time MLX01 was accelerated to 545km/h, and later that day it twice broke the 550km/h barrier with 550.8km/h attained in the Takagawa tunnel at 12 p.m. and 12.37 p.m. respectively.

By this time a second set of experimental vehicles was available – MLX01-3, MLX01-4, MLX01-121 and MLX01-21 arrived on 25–26 October 1997. This presaged another sequence of high-speed trials, this time with both trains running at the same time. The second train was commissioned on 16 May 1998, when Transport Minister Takao Fujii joined a run that reached 450km/h.

On 14 April 1999 a five-car MLX01 formation with a test team on board achieved a world record speed of 552km/h on two occasions. On each trip

Awaiting lift-off. The aircraft-like interior of one of the superconducting maglev test vehicles at the Yamanashi guideway in 1999. During the trip the vehicle attained a speed of 452km/h. (Author)

the maximum velocity was sustained for 3 seconds. More passing trials followed, and a closing speed for two manned trains of over 1,000km/h was achieved on 16 November 1999: one three-car train was travelling at 546km/h and the other at 457km/h.

In October 1999 the World Congress on Railway Research (WCRR) was held in Tokyo, and many delegates seized the chance to take part in a programme of demonstration rides. It was not my first maglev trip as I had travelled on the rather bumpy and jerky maglev people-mover between Birmingham International and Birmingham Airport before it was dismantled in 1995. The Japanese project was altogether more serious. In contrast to the low-speed British scheme, it enjoyed high-level political backing and the support of JR Central's powerful leadership.

On 22 October 1999 a party of WCRR officials and delegates assembled at the test centre at 10.30 a.m. After a briefing by Dr Seki, we were ushered aboard the MLX01 'B' set of three vehicles. This time no one was asked to hand over their credit cards as shields had been fitted to limit the magnetic field inside the cars to 10 gauss.

We took our seats in the aircraft-like interior, and the faces of fellow delegates revealed fascination and excitement as at 11.05 a.m. MLX01 moved slowly away from its dock. We eased out on to the 'main line', traversing a set of large and complex points. We halted in the Takagawa tunnel just outside the test centre as the vehicle was positioned for the first run. All aboard were watching the screen showing the picture from the camera in the nose. The view then switched to the other end of the train, with the portal of the tunnel we had just entered clearly visible.

At 11.10 a.m. we rolled back into the daylight and past the test centre. There was a distinct rumble from the tyres below as we gathered speed.

The levitation magnets hoisted the vehicle off the guideway as the speedometer showed 162km/h, prompting a burst of applause as the wheel rumble died away. We had lift-off!

There was some aerodynamic noise as we quickly powered up to 300km/h before decelerating again and 'landing' at about 125km/h. We came to a stand near the Tokyo end of the guideway. Here we reversed direction again for the day's main test run.

Those aboard included Jolene Molitoris, Chief Executive of the International Union of Railways Philippe Roumeguère, and Francois Lacôte, who as SNCF's Head of Research had masterminded the TGV speed record in May 1990.

This was not another world record attempt, but we were not disappointed. Once again MLX01 began to move, and this time the acceleration pinned us to our seats. All eyes were on the speedometer mounted on the end partition wall. The green figures flashed past 200km/h to 250, 300, 350 and 400. Still we accelerated. Just 85 seconds after we started the figure of 450km/h was reached and held before we briefly touched 452km/h. Applause erupted from the delegates, and with 450km/h still on the screen, there was a rush to be photographed in front of it.

There was no lack of sensation. Apart from a considerable amount of aerodynamic noise, there was quite noticeable vibration in the peak speed range, and a strong humming noise was evident. Dr Seki said that the interior noise level was typically 83 to 84dB, which one of my companions later said was too loud for passengers to remain comfortable for long periods.

We quickly slowed down, landed and halted at the 'Kofu' end of the guideway. Another short trip during which we reached 400km/h took us back to the test centre where MLX01 was prepared for its next run, due to depart at 11.27 a.m.. We were among the first 6,500 people to ride Japan's maglev train.

I made a second trip to Yamanashi on 28 November 2000, when the vehicle again reached 452km/h. This time the ride was noticeably worse, with intense vibrations above 400km/h. So much so, in fact, that it was practically impossible to hold a camera steady to photograph the digital speedometer. Perhaps I was unlucky, but it seemed obvious that much more development was required to reach the point where maglev would offer an acceptable ride.

The Yamanashi research teams continued their work, and in July 2002 two more vehicles were delivered. They incorporated significant changes. One, designated MLX01-901, introduced a third nose design with a very long taper intended to improve aerodynamic performance. The nose was so long that only sixteen seats could be accommodated in the car, although the length of the vehicle was a full 28m. The other new vehicle was MLX01-22, a sixty-eight-seat intermediate car with a bodyshell altered so that the lower part matched the shape of the levitation bogies to reduce aerodynamic drag. Changes had also been made to simplify bogie maintenance and improve reliability. The infrastructure too was modified, with levitation and guidance coils contained in the guideway sidewalls.

The new vehicles were successfully integrated with their older sisters, and on 2 December 2003 the manned MLX01 vehicle was pushed up to a phenomenal 581km/h. Asked later if this could be exceeded, Dr Seki replied that this was the safety limit for back-up systems needed if 'quenching', or loss of the magnetic field, were to occur. Side wheels would be deployed to prevent the vehicle striking the guideway sidewalls, but above this speed there would be insufficient time to deploy the wheels before the risk of contact.

The next milestone was a test with two vehicles passing at a closing speed of 1,026km/h in

November 2004. Encouraged by this technical success, JR Central began to promote the Chuo Shinkansen more actively, announcing in 2007 that it believed the first stage from Tokyo to Nagoya could be built for ¥5,000 billion by 2025; meanwhile it would allocate ¥300 billion a year for maglev research. In December 2008 the Ministry of Land, Infrastructure, Transport & Tourism asked JR Central to prepare four reports covering capacity and demand, rolling stock, construction costs and other items. Three different alignments were meanwhile being costed, and this work concluded in favour of a route from Tokyo Shinagawa to Nagoya with four intermediate stations and a 25km tunnel through the Southern Alps.

Nearly commercial. A seven-vehicle formation of the latest superconducting 'L0' maglev vehicles sits in the U-shaped guideway of the Yamanashi test section. JR Central may extend the guideway further so that visitors to the 2020 Olympic and Paralympic Games in Tokyo can sample a maglev ride. (Kazumiki Miura)

In May 2011, just two months after the Great East Japan Earthquake, the Council for Transport Policy produced a report for government stating that the country needed the Chuo Shinkansen and that JR Central should be assigned responsibility to build and operate it using maglev technology. On 26 May the transport minister gave details of a programme for the project, and on the following day JR Central was instructed to go ahead. The company committed to bear the construction cost, now standing at ¥5,400 billion, and promptly set to work.

The next step was to lengthen the guideway to the original planned length of 42.8km, and in September 2011 the priority section was closed for modifications and to allow work on an extension at each end. In November 2012 the first of fourteen more test vehicles built to an updated design arrived on site, and trials with a five-car 'L0' train began in June 2013. (The 'L' stood for linear and the 0 reflected the Series 0 of the first Shinkansen trains.) The end car had a 15m-long nose, leaving room for twenty-four seats.

Full-scale trials resumed on 29 August. The following month JR Central announced more details of the 286km Chuo Shinkansen route and published a draft environmental impact assessment. Completion as far as Nagoya was now envisaged in 2027, with Osaka not reached until 2045. If the line is built, and assuming a speed of 500km/h, Nagoya will be just 40 minutes away from Tokyo, while Osaka would be reached in another 20. However, it would hardly be a scenic ride as much of the route would run in tunnel.

Asked for technical details of the guideway extensions, and the differences from the priority section, JR Central pleaded that information was confidential. It did, however, concede that an outstanding concern was energy consumption, failing to deny reports that, in terms of energy consumed per seat, each maglev trip would require about three times as much as a train on the Tokaido Shinkansen.

Uncertainty also surrounds the arrangements for intermediate stations. The planned peak capacity in each direction is 10,000 passengers/hour, requiring a 1,000-seat train every 6 minutes. Yet, as a correspondent to *Railway Gazette International* pointed out, scheduling stops at intermediate stations with trains routed into passing loops would jeopardise this because of the length of time taken to operate points routing the stopping service in and out of the loops.

Route details were made public just a few days before the announcement that Tokyo would be the host city for the 2020 Olympic Games. The 1964 debut of the Tokaido Shinkansen a few days before the Games of that year had clearly not been forgotten, and JR Central at once came under pressure to complete the Chuo Shinkansen by 2020. JR Central President Yoshiomi Yamada explained to the media in Japan that the scale of the work precluded an earlier completion date. But Chairman Yoshiyuki Kasai, in London for an event at the Japanese embassy, offered the prospect of completing another short segment of guideway as far as the planned station at Kofu, around 5km west of the end of the test section near Sakaigawa. He expected that many Olympic visitors would relish the chance of a ride at 500km/h and the chance to 'experience superconducting maglev technology'. Whether they will have that opportunity remains to be seen, but JR Central is wasting no time: start of work ceremonies were held at the Shinagawa and Nagoya station sites on 17 December 2014.

Journalists around the world have consistently been mesmerised by the idea of 'frictionless' travel, whether on hovertrains blasting around on air cushions or vehicles floating on magnetic fields, and there is no doubt that they will keep a close eye on what happens with the Chuo Shinkansen. In the meantime, it is worth reflecting that the genesis of maglev technology in the early 1970s coincided with the early development of high-speed trains on steel wheels in Europe. Since then, thousands of kilometres of high-speed railways have been built in many countries, but the Shanghai shuttle is so far the only live commercial application of research into high-speed travel using magnetic levitation.

4

TGV Takes the Lead

Not everyone has heard of the TGB or *Très Grande Bibliothèque*, the unofficial name of the French national library commissioned on Bastille Day in 1988 by former French President François Mitterrand. The letters TGV, in contrast, standing for *Train à Grande Vitesse*, have become a household word, not just in France, but across the world.

Mitterrand took office in 1981, the year when the first part of France's initial TGV line between Paris and Lyon opened, and Mitterrand himself rode the inaugural train, duly identified by cabside tricolour flashes, on 22 September. On the return trip the Presidential TGV called at Mâcon-Loché and at a parkway station crisply named Le Creusot-Montchanin-Montceau-les-Mines (reflecting the names of the three towns it serves). Here the President announced that he had asked national operator SNCF to study a second TGV route from Paris to Western France. It was no secret that he would do so, as Transport Minister Charles Fiterman, one of four communist ministers in Mitterrand's administration, had indicated that his policy would favour new railways rather than motorways – in marked contrast to previous governments.

The rationale for the Paris–Lyon line, or *Ligne à Grande Vitesse* (LGV) Paris–Sud-Est, to give it its official title, was the inability of the old Paris–Lyon–Méditerranée (PLM) main line to cope with traffic that had more than doubled to 12 million trips a year in the two decades to 1976. Two sections of double track on what was essentially a four-track artery formed bottlenecks where trains were easily delayed. SNCF wanted to quadruple the two sections, but the job was so expensive that SNCF had to return to the drawing board.

What had happened in Japan was instructive, and SNCF's planners and engineers foresaw the need to embrace a future where trains would run at similar speeds. The 1955 trials in the Landes had suggested that this was feasible, and the formula of a separate new line for passenger traffic only – à la Shinkansen – was attractive, as it could be shorter than the old route and would release space on the PLM tracks for freight. With no need to make allowances for heavy freight, construction costs could be kept low by having no tunnels and accepting gradients as steep as 3.5 per cent that would present no obstacle to high-powered train sets of the kind that SNCF had been studying since the late 1960s.

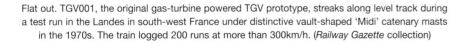

Flat out. TGV001, the original gas-turbine powered TGV prototype, streaks along level track during a test run in the Landes in south-west France under distinctive vault-shaped 'Midi' catenary masts in the 1970s. The train logged 200 runs at more than 300km/h. (*Railway Gazette* collection)

SNCF had amassed a good deal of knowledge about lightweight trains, including two builds of *turbotrain*, and since 1967 the electrically hauled premium-fare express named *Le Capitole* had attained 200km/h on a daily basis over part of the Paris–Toulouse main line. It was time to take the next step and, with its supplier Alsthom, SNCF conceived an experimental high-speed train set driven by gas turbines.

Outshopped in April 1972 at Alsthom's Belfort factory, the five-car articulated TGV001 gave SNCF the opportunity to gain practical experience of high-speed running. The train's angular aesthetics and aerodynamic form were largely the handiwork of industrial designer Jacques Cooper, whose signature achievements included designs for German car maker Porsche. Turned out in a brilliant orange livery that commanded attention, TGV001 also served the admirable purpose of introducing policymakers to the enticing possibilities of high-speed rail travel. During this phase of experimentation, the TGV001 test crew logged over 200 runs at more than 300km/h, with a maximum of 318km/h clocked on 8 December 1972.

The appeal of gas turbines was their low mass compared with diesel engines, but the penchant for this form of traction came to an abrupt halt with the 1973–74 oil crisis. It was clear that the future of railways would not involve gas-guzzling machines from the aerospace industry but would rely on electricity that could be sourced from any primary fuel.

Accordingly, SNCF commissioned another test vehicle to confirm the feasibility of high-speed running under electric power. Dubbed *Zébulon*, it afforded SNCF the opportunity to test long-wheelbase bogies and a drive system with the traction motors mounted in the body to limit the unsprung mass – and hence the forces exerted on the track.

In the late 1960s and throughout the early 1970s SNCF conducted a long campaign to promote its high-speed line concept to sceptical government officials, and this eventually bore fruit with President Giscard d'Estaing's government authorising the LGV Paris–Sud-Est in 1976. SNCF moved swiftly to acquire the necessary land, and work began in earnest in October that year. The line was funded entirely by loans, placing the onus for success firmly with the railway.

The design followed Japanese precepts of large radius curves, cab signalling and no level crossings, but the steep gradients were a new departure. Much of the line cut through open countryside and, as the accompanying SNCF press officer said at the time, you could identify the route by the new tractors, reflecting the handsome pay-offs farmers received for their land.

While high-speed operations originated in Japan, they differed fundamentally from those in France. The Japanese Shinkansen is isolated by gauge, whereas in France the high-speed lines form an integral part of the national network. This means that there is no need to build costly infrastructure through densely populated suburbs to reach city centres – so avoiding the long delay suffered by the Tohoku and Joetsu Shinkansen in progressing beyond Omiya into Tokyo.

Compatibility with the existing network also meant that trains could fan out to a range of destinations beyond the high-speed line, so giving a much larger chunk of the population access to superspeed trains. Right from the start, French TGVs continued beyond Lyon to St Etienne, Besançon and Geneva. Many other destinations were added later, including Marseille, Chambéry, Annecy and Montpellier in 1982, Lausanne in 1984 – which required a small batch of TGVs to be equipped to accept the Swiss 15kV 16.7Hz power supply – and Nice and Bern in 1987.

Taking the best technical concepts from TGV001 and *Zébulon*, two pre-production and eighty-five series-built trains were ordered from industry giants Alsthom and Francorail. In contrast to Shinkansen trains, the power equipment was concentrated in the end cars, whose static axle load, at the insistence of SNCF's civil engineers, could not exceed 17 tonnes. Between the power cars were eight low-profile articulated trailers, with one powered bogie at each end of the rake to ensure that enough power was available to climb the steep grades from a standing start. Drive from the body-mounted DC motors giving the train a continuous rating of 6.35MW was through a complicated tripod transmission. As the new line was to be wired at 25kV 50Hz and the conventional lines at each end were electrified at 1.5kV DC, the power cars had to accept both voltages.

On 11 July 1978 the first pre-production train was shown off to a curious media, and less than a month later it attained its design speed of 260km/h on a test run between Strasbourg and Mulhouse. Like TGV001, it was decked out in bright orange and attracted huge publicity, which SNCF sought to milk as it began to promote its future service. Those seeking the luxury of France's long-distance expresses of the 1960s were, however, disappointed – the TGV had no frills and the 368-seat (later reduced during refurbishment to 345 or 351) interior with a rather spartan bar in one car was best described as functional. This was in line with a policy of spreading the benefits of speed to everyone, exemplified in SNCF's phrase '*la démocratisation de la vitesse*'. A few sets were turned out with all first-class accommodation for premium business runs, but the formula did not survive and they were converted to two-class trains. All TGV travel required compulsory seat reservation.

Veteran colours. A pair of 35-year-old Paris–Sud-Est TGVs displaced from their original stamping ground by more modern trains heads for Paris-Nord near Montagny-Sainte-Félicite in the Picardy region in May 2014. The set nearest the camera has been refurbished and sports SNCF's latest livery. (Christophe Masse)

More publicity ensued from the 380km/h world-record run on 26 February 1981, and media excitement grew as preparations were made for opening the new railway. After the presidential launch, the southern two-thirds of LGV Paris–Sud-Est opened for business on 27 September 1981. Within a year, the line speed was raised from 260 to 270km/h, and the second part of the route was inaugurated by Fiterman on 22 September 1983. Three days later the first fare-paying punters raced over the 427km from the capital to Lyon in just 2 hours at an average speed of 213.5km/h, immediately confirming France's position at the top of the league for the world's fastest station-to-station timings. The 2 hours compared with around 3 hours 50 minutes by the fastest *rapides* in 1980.

WESTWARD BOUND

France's second LGV, on whose southern branch TGV Set 325 swept into the history books in May 1990, marked an important milestone – the LGV Atlantique was the first railway in the world where trains ran from the outset at 300km/h. In fact, 300km/h had been the design speed for LGV Paris–Sud-Est, but SNCF had opted for prudence at the debut of its high-speed venture.

In developing plans for LGV Atlantique, SNCF foresaw a promising business and leisure market right along the Atlantic seaboard. The tranche of services over the western arm would serve Brittany and the north-west and those routed via the south-western branch would link Bordeaux and the south-west to the capital. Destinations served from the Paris terminus at Montparnasse, rebuilt to handle the new trains, included Brest, Nantes and the Spanish border at Hendaye.

To gain access to Montparnasse, SNCF made use of an abandoned alignment from Chartres to Paris – which had to be partly covered over to placate lineside householders – meaning that TGVs could run at high speed to within a few kilometres of the terminus. Elsewhere, SNCF was less fortunate, encountering vociferous opposition from landowners, especially from winegrowers near the Vouvray vineyards. This led to a splendid farce that entailed vibrating bottles of wine to simulate passing trains. Legend has it that the tasters could not distinguish the vibrated wine from the still variety, but SNCF was taking no chances and quickly offered to bury the railway in a tunnel past the vineyards.

More opposition from communities along the route was stirred up by local politicians seeking to gain advantage from their negative stance, but when the result of a public enquiry was announced on 5 August 1983, the project was declared to be in the public interest. The government eventually agreed to contribute 30 per cent of the construction cost, and formal approval was granted in May 1984.

In 1984 a fleet of seventy-three trains (later increased to ninety-five) was ordered from the same two suppliers that had assembled the Sud-Est train sets. Lessons had been learnt from day-to-day operation of a large fleet of TGVs – the Sud-Est fleet had been augmented to a total of 109 sets – and these were incorporated into the design of the Atlantique fleet. Improvements included secondary air suspension instead of coil springs, a modification made to all the Sud-Est fleet in 1986–90.

A ceremony marrying the first power cars to their rake of trailers was staged at Alsthom's Belfort plant on 14 April 1988. Finished in pure white with a blue window band, the train presented a sober image compared with the brash orange of its Sud-Est antecedents. From the third set onward, the livery switched to silver and blue, a formula chosen by industrial designer Roger Tallon, whose input to the TGV Atlantique styling has stood the test of time.

Technology had advanced dramatically since the late 1970s, and the biggest change was the choice of self-commutating three-phase synchronous traction motors. These had significantly more muscle than the DC motors on the Sud-Est fleet, with eight motors producing a continuous output of 8.8MW, enough for sustained operation with ten trailers at 300km/h. The success of the technology package, which included the large-scale use of microprocessors to automate routine tasks, can be judged from the 1990 world record described in Chapter 1.

Seating 485 passengers, the trains were longer, more powerful and cheaper to run than the first-generation TGVs, and interior comfort was much enhanced, with little touches of luxury that included snug 'semi-compartments' in two first-class cars.

Prime Minister Michel Rocard opened the western arm of LGV Atlantique on 20 September 1989, and Mitterrand did the honours for the south-western arm on 28 September 1990, although he was obliged to travel to the ceremony in Poitiers by helicopter as angry farmers protesting about low prices for their produce were using the tactic of delaying trains to make their point.

The city of Tours could now be reached in just over 1 hour from Paris, and thanks to the ability to run at 220km/h over long sections of conventional line, TGVs to Bordeaux were timed to undercut the 3-hour barrier by 2 minutes. There were some teething troubles persuading the 'Tornad' train computers to talk to each other when pairs of trains ran in multiple, but these were soon dealt with and forgotten. The TGV concept was on a roll.

Indeed, it had truly caught on. By the time the second part of LGV Atlantique was commissioned, other LGV projects were moving rapidly towards fruition. In 1984, just one year after the full opening of the LGV Paris–Sud-Est, all expenses, including interest payments for the trains and financial charges and debt repayments for infrastructure, were being covered by operating revenue, allowing a start to be made on repaying capital costs. In the twelve months to September 1984, the original LGV carried 15 million passengers.

THE EUROPEAN DIMENSION

The new line and its overnight success had focused interest across Europe on the concept of high-speed rail travel, and in July 1983 the French, German and Belgian transport ministers met in Paris, where they set up a working party to examine a high-speed line from Paris to Brussels and Cologne. The report submitted a year later came up with a reference alignment and a recommendation to discard maglev technology as too expensive and incompatible with other rail services. Further reports were commissioned, and a link to Amsterdam was added to the brief.

On 28 January 1986 the ministers reconvened in Brussels, on this occasion being joined by their opposite number from Luxembourg and a Dutch delegation. They agreed in principle to the Paris–Brussels–Cologne project. The French were also looking seriously at a bypass round the east of Paris that would join the northern route with LGV Sud-Est and give access to LGV Atlantique, paving the way for truly fast inter-regional services such as Lille–Lyon and Lille–Bordeaux. It would include stations in the Paris suburbs, at Roissy-Charles de Gaulle Airport and the planned Disneyland site in Marne-la-Vallée; a link to a proposed high-speed route to Eastern France was also on the cards.

Meanwhile, another factor was complicating the equation. This was the Channel Tunnel, which had the potential to double the rate of return on the French section of the putative line from Paris. The problem was the fickleness of les Anglais, who had encouraged everyone to make plans for the Channel Tunnel in the 1970s before promptly abandoning it in January 1975.

Precisely eleven years later, some of the doubts were dispelled. On 20 January 1986 Mitterrand met British Prime Minister Margaret Thatcher in Lille to announce the selection of France-Manche Channel Tunnel Group as the winner of a competition to build a 'fixed link' between the two countries. Despite the unlikely combination of a left-wing president and a right-wing prime minister, momentum for the tunnel was rapidly building up, and on 12 February Mitterrand visited Canterbury Cathedral for the signing of the Treaty of Canterbury. This opened the way for signature of a private sector concession – a sine qua non for Mrs Thatcher – to build and operate

the tunnel. The Concession Agreement was inked on 14 March 1986, and the treaty was ratified in Paris by Thatcher and Mitterrand on 29 July 1987.

On 9 October 1987 the French government granted outline approval for LGV Nord and an extension of LGV Paris–Sud-Est as far as Valence. Also in the announcement were details of the 102km Paris bypass with links to all three LGVs, although access to and from LGV Atlantique required use of part of the old Grande Ceinture belt line round Paris. It became known as LGV Interconnexion, and a decision to proceed was announced on 9 December 1987.

The French go-ahead added momentum to the international element of the project, and on 26 October 1987 the transport ministers were joined in Brussels by their opposite number from Britain to endorse the Paris–Amsterdam scheme. The British minister, however, was making no commitment to put London on Europe's high-speed map – British Rail's Channel Tunnel Director Malcolm Southgate had told me earlier that year that there was 'no question' of matching the French investment in LGV Nord. The ministers meanwhile instructed their national railways to draw up detailed plans by March 1988.

The situation in France was not straightforward, however. A bitter row had broken out over the alignment, with Amiens and Lille squabbling for the privilege of hosting TGV services. It seems that the mayor of Lille, Pierre Mauroy, whose other role happened to be Prime Minister of France, threw some weight around to sway the choice towards a route through his city. Amiens was granted the sop of a parkway station near Ablaincourt-Pressoir close to the future junction of the A29 motorway with the A1 autoroute du nord. Officially called TGV Haute-Picardie, the stop quickly earned the nickname of 'Gare des Betteraves', (Sugarbeet Halt), reflecting its remote farmland location.

From Gonesse in the Paris outskirts the alignment passes west of Roissy-Charles-de-Gaulle Airport and hugs the A1 for much of the way to Lille, striding across undulating farmland whose peaceful aspect today masks the scars of First World War battlefields. A spur gives access to Arras, and a triangular junction at Fretin just south-east of Lille directs Brussels-bound trains eastward towards the Belgian frontier. Beyond Lille, where TGVs call at a cavernous through station called Lille-Europe, the alignment strikes north-west towards the Channel Tunnel portal at Fréthun, where a station serves the Calais area and provides interchange to local trains.

The declaration of public interest (DUP) for what was officially known as LGV Nord-Europe was granted on 29 September 1989, and track-laying over the 333km alignment commenced two years later using lavish parameters such as 6,000m radius curves to allow for speed increases beyond 300km/h. The construction timescale was squeezed to allow opening in time for the planned inauguration of the Channel Tunnel in 1993, but in the event contractor Transmanche-Link did not hand over the Tunnel to Eurotunnel until 10 December 1993. Long before that, on 18 May 1993, Mitterrand opened the first part of LGV Nord-Europe.

This was the French president's third LGV inauguration. 'How could I resist your invitation? I, the son and grandson of a railwayman?' he quipped at the start of his speech in Lille. He had travelled in the cab of a TGV from Paris that morning and was clearly making the most of the occasion. On arrival at Lille he stepped on to a blue carpet spread along the platform, and he did not lose the opportunity to admonish Britain for failing to make progress with a high-speed link from the tunnel to London. Services to London 'will leave the tunnel à toute petite allure to visit the beautiful countryside of Kent', he chided.

Four specials had made the Paris–Lille trip that morning. The first conveyed many of the 2,000 guests, who observed what travel at 300km/h was like when compared with cars on the parallel *autoroute* – the cars appeared motionless as we swept past. Jean-Marie Metzler, Director of SNCF's Passenger business, opined that the 130km of twinned infrastructure was 'our best publicity'. Next to zip along the pristine tracks was a security sweeper train, which was followed by the President's TGV, duly decorated with a tricolour band across the nose. A reserve train brought up the rear.

President's train. One of four TGV Réseau sets used for the inauguration of LGV Nord-Europe by President François Mitterrand on 18 May 1993. (Author)

Commercial trips from Paris to Lille via Arras commenced on 23 May 1993. The final section from the junction for the Arras spur into Lille was delayed by the mayor of the small town of Seclin who had banned contractors from access to local land, but from 26 September Paris–Lille timings over the completed 225km route were slashed to just 1 hour. The remaining section from Lille to Fréthun had to wait until the Channel Tunnel opened in 1994.

LGV Nord had barely been open six months when an early morning TGV from Valenciennes was streaking towards Paris at nearly 300km/h near the site of the Ablaincourt-Pressoir station when the unthinkable happened. Shortly after 7 a.m. on 21 December 1993, the rear four cars of the speeding train left the rails. The train took more than 2km to come to a stand, but the derailed vehicles remained upright and intact, which builder GEC-Alsthom attributed to the articulated design, showing 'excellent stability and safety in extreme circumstances'. Amazingly, only one of the 200 passengers on board was reported to be slightly injured, while another was taken to hospital with stress symptoms.

An observer present at the time remarked that the track behind the derailed TGV looked as if it had been struck by bombs. His comment was not far wide of the mark, because the derailment was caused by the track and formation collapsing into an underground bunker left over from the First World War – the ground had given way after a torrential downpour. The void had not been detected when the line was built, and the event prompted SNCF to check the rest of the line, a process which revealed numerous similar holes. They were hurriedly filled with concrete.

Just over a year before, on 14 December 1992, a TGV from Annecy was cruising at around 270km/h towards Paris when the bogie between the third and fourth cars derailed as the train was passing through Mâcon-Loché station on LGV Sud-Est. It turned out that a malfunctioning electronic component had caused two anti-skid systems to fail, locking the wheels when the train's brakes were applied. On this occasion too the train remained upright; there were no injuries on board, but about twenty-five passengers on the platform were hurt by flying ballast, requiring six of them to be taken to hospital.

The first segment of LGV Interconnexion opened on 28 May 1994, although the station at Roissy Airport was unfinished and the final 25km – which effectively formed an extension of the Sud-Est line through the Paris suburbs – was not commissioned until 1996. It was enough, however, for SNCF to make a serious bid for the inter-regional market with Lille–Lyon TGVs timed to link the two cities in around 3 hours.

THE NORTHERN FLEETS

Several types of stock were needed for LGV Nord-Europe: domestic trains for services from Paris to Lille and towns in Nord-Pas-de-Calais, plus inter-regional services; a separate fleet equipped to run through the Channel Tunnel and over British tracks; and another batch to ply between the French and Belgian capitals as well as from Paris to Amsterdam and Cologne.

Taking the TGV Atlantique stock as the design starting point, in early 1990 SNCF placed more orders with Alsthom, which on 22 March 1989 had formed a joint venture with Britain's GEC. The contracts covered ten more Atlantique sets and a fleet of ninety *Réseau* (Network) trains with eight trailers to operate Nord-Europe and inter-regional services; this meant that they had to be powerful enough to handle the grades on LGV Sud-Est. The first fifty were dual-voltage sets for domestic diagrams, and twenty-four were fitted to accept Belgium's 3kV DC power supply; the other six also had a 3kV DC ability, but were equipped to run into Italy.

The last ten trains were kitted out to accept the Dutch 1.5kV DC power supply so that they could run to Amsterdam. A quirk of the Dutch network is the large number of lift and swing bridges over navigable canals and rivers, forcing gaps in the overhead wires. The ten trains therefore had stops on the pantographs to avoid them springing up when passing through gaps. Known as the PBA (Paris–Brussels–Amsterdam) fleet, they appeared in red and silver, in contrast to the silver and blue retained for the other *Réseau* sets.

Given that all these trains were destined for journeys of up to 5 hours, the second-class seat pitch was eased and more luggage space provided. Full pressure sealing was also applied, as LGV Atlantique passengers had complained of pressure pulses in the line's tunnels.

Building trains to run in three countries was complicated enough, but adding German territory brought further complexity. Based on a performance specification finalised in April 1990, tenders for trains that could run from Paris to either Amsterdam or Cologne were issued in January 1991 to two groups, one led by GEC Alsthom and the other by Siemens.

On 25 June 1992 a joint venture formed of French, Belgian, Dutch and German railways awarded a letter of intent for twenty-seven so-called PBKA (Paris–Brussels–Köln–Amsterdam) trains to the French group, which had undercut its German rival. Contracts worth ECU548 million were exchanged on 28 January 1993 in Brussels, but in 1995, with the prospects for high-speed operation east of the Belgian capital receding into the future, the order was chopped back to just seventeen sets.

Like other TGVs, the PBKA's maximum speed was 300km/h (later 320km/h). The eight trailers with a total of 377 seats were a simple matter, as they were identical to other Réseau and PBA vehicles.

Multi-system. Two PBKA sets resplendent in their red and silver Thalys livery hurry along LGV Est at Chauconin-Neufmontiers near Meaux with a special service conveying Euro MPs from Brussels to Strasbourg. Note the wi-fi dome on the third vehicle. (Christophe Masse)

The power cars, however, were entirely different. The trains had to operate on different voltages and frequencies: 1.5kV DC and 25kV 50Hz in France, 3kV DC and 25kV 50Hz in Belgium, 1.5kV DC and 25kV 50Hz in the Netherlands, and 15kV 16.7Hz in Germany. Accommodating the equipment for this in the confined space and keeping to the 17-tonne axle load was a tough challenge, not least because of the hefty transformer needed to convert the German supply to DC for the traction inverters which fed the synchronous traction motors.

Apart from configuring the two pantographs on each power car to cope with the various overhead power supplies, perhaps the hardest job was ensuring that information from the seven signalling and automatic train protection systems in the four countries could be reliably decoded and processed. Devising ways of clearly displaying the kaleidoscope of different indications was no mean feat, but just as tricky was accommodating the numerous antennae on the bogies and under the car body. The PBKA sets were the epitome of the inter-operable train, but this flexibility came at a price. In terms of cost per seat, the trains rank as some of the most expensive ever built.

The first PBA set was rolled out by GEC Alsthom in late 1995 and demonstrated for the press on 9 January 1996. One of its seventeen PBKA cousins emerged shortly afterwards, and preparations began for launching the service. But achieving the ambitious aims of the PBKA project required progress with the Dutch and Belgian high-speed lines (Chapter 13).

In France, the prospects for expanding high-speed services were looking very promising indeed. After eight years, traffic on the Paris–Lyon route was dramatically up, and approval for LGV Rhône-Alpes, a 115km extension past Lyon towards Valence in the Rhône Valley, had been granted in October 1989.

The world record sprint in May 1990 sparked renewed interest in TGV technology, and the government saw rosy prospects for promoting France as a world leader in railway expertise and equipment. There were sound political reasons, therefore, for Minister of Transport Michel Delebarre to sign a protocol on 31 May with GEC Alsthom and SNCF covering a Fr535 million four-year research programme to develop a 'Super-TGV' able to run at 350km/h.

MASTER PLAN

There was more to come. At a press conference on 12 June 1990 Delebarre unveiled a twenty-year master plan proposing construction of no fewer than fourteen LGVs with a combined length of 3,560km. Supported by upgrading of existing lines, the star-shaped network stretched to the German, Spanish and Italian frontiers and included cross-country routes from Bordeaux to Toulouse and Dijon to Belfort. Among the more unlikely schemes, clearly of political rather than commercial interest, were a second route from Paris to Calais via Amiens and a line from Paris to Rouen, whose rate of return was a paltry 0.1 per cent. Other lines had better prospects, and SNCF was tasked with deciding how to handle such an ambitious programme. An amended version approved by government on 1 April 1992 envisaged sixteen projects and a staggering 4,700km of new line.

With eight years of high-speed experience behind it, a second LGV nearing completion and further projects authorised, SNCF was aware in 1989 that demand for high-speed rail travel was bound to rise. It had already put in hand plans to cut headways from 5 minutes to a theoretical 3 minutes with an updated version of the LGV Sud-Est TVM300 train control equipment called TVM430 – the first application was on LGV Nord. This would allow more trains to be run, but longer trains were

out of the question because of fixed platform lengths. This left the option of higher-capacity trains.

Double-deck cars had operated in Japan's Series 100 train sets since 1986, and SNCF ran double-deckers on various suburban routes. The question facing the design team was whether the fundamental TGV concept of articulation could be kept for a double-decker without busting the 17-tonne axle load limit. Saving weight was the critical issue.

Studies were commissioned, practical tests put in hand and mock-ups built. The design team turned over every stone in the search for weight-saving, quickly deciding that aluminium bodyshells would be essential for the trailers. Another big saving was in the seat design; a TGV Atlantique seat tipped the scales at 26kg, but the seat chosen for the double-decker weighed just 14kg.

The feasibility of a double-deck TGV was established, and a test train incorporating three double-deck cars, a rolling laboratory car and two TGV Atlantique power cars was assembled. This ensemble was subjected to tests on LGVs Sud-Est and Atlantique that included runs peaking at 320km/h, and in 1991

Fastest in France. Passengers on Duplex TGVs operating on LGV Est can monitor the train's speed on the information screens in each car. (Author)

SNCF placed an order with GEC Alsthom for thirty train sets plus an option for fifteen more; a pre-series train was required by mid-1994.

Among the more ingenious features of what became known as TGV Duplex was to arrange the inter-car gangways on the upper deck above a redesigned articulation. This freed space at the end of the car immediately over the bogie for equipment such as air-conditioning, so that the entire length between the bogies was available for seating. A bar car separated the two classes; the upper deck was occupied by a bar and buffet, and passengers quaffing their beer or wine stood over a mass of equipment downstairs: batteries, chargers, auxiliary converters and air-conditioning plant.

The complete ten-car train offered 545 seats, but SNCF later decided that more luggage space was needed, requiring the removal of up to thirty-five seats. Thus, 509 or 512 seats are provided in a 200m train. This compares with 817 in JR East's eight-car E4 MAX, which is approximately the same length. The difference is accounted for by the Japanese train having distributed traction rather than separate power cars, plus 3+2 and 3+3 seating for short-distance trips, whereas the French train is laid out for long-distance travel.

Starting in November 1994, a string of pre-production Duplex trailers was tested with a pair of *Réseau* power cars, before being united with its own traction units in June 1995. Immediately

recognisable by a rounded front end offering superior aerodynamics, the power cars packed the same 4.4MW punch as their *Réseau* predecessors but incorporated numerous technical advances and other changes such as a centrally positioned driver's seat.

The first Duplex sets were commissioned in time for the 1996 Christmas holiday traffic on LGV Sud-Est and quickly proved a hit with passengers who relished the generous seat spacing and the panoramic views from the upper deck. The Duplex was to prove immensely successful, and SNCF, which structures its fleet to cope with enormous peak loads at the start of summer and winter holidays, placed more orders. These will see

Double-deck. Perhaps the ultimate development of SNCF's TGV Duplex fleet, this multi-system 'EuroDuplex' set is bound for Frankfurt-am-Main on 24 March 2012. On the side of the leading power car is a white banner announcing the launch of Marseille–Frankfurt services over LGV Rhin-Rhône the previous day. (Christophe Masse)

High-Speed Cargo

Several studies have proposed a network of high-speed trains to corner some of the lucrative market for carrying time-sensitive parcels around Western Europe. Promoters point to the only operation of its kind: the specially built postal TGVs running between Paris, Mâcon and Cavaillon near Avignon. This began in 1984 using two train sets shuttling between depots at Paris-Charolais and Lyon-Montrochet; *La Poste* had an extra half set built as a reserve. Turned out in *La Poste*'s yellow house colour, these windowless curiosities can carry 120 tonnes, far more than the aircraft they replaced.

A decade later *La Poste* reorganised and moved its Lyon terminal to Cavaillon, and a third TGV was added to the fleet, which by 2008 was handling between 200,000 and 300,000 letters every weekday. However, the operation looks set to end in 2015 as *La Poste* announced in June 2014 that it planned to replace the TGVs by swap bodies that can be easily transferred to lorries.

Attempts to develop a commercial parcels service on routes such as Paris to Brussels, London or Cologne have so far come to nothing, but the EuroCarex consortium formed of SNCF, Eurotunnel, Air France, *La Poste*, FedEx and various airport operators organised a demonstration trip with a postal TGV from Lyon–Saint-Exupéry and Paris Charles-de-Gaulle Airport to London St Pancras on 21 March 2012. There is talk of a regular service between French cities and a terminal at Barking near London in 2017, but the capital cost of trains is a serious obstacle. Interestingly, in 2014 SNCF began scrapping some of its original TGV fleet.

Post haste. Sunlight catches the nose of a Postal TGV at London St Pancras on 21 March 2012 after a special run from Lyon Saint-Exupéry and Paris Charles de Gaulle Airport to demonstrate the feasibility of a high-speed rail service for commercial packages. *La Poste* will cease using its three and a half yellow-painted TGVs in 2015, replacing them with swap bodies that can be carried on freight wagons or lorries. (Chris Jackson)

deliveries stretch into 2015, taking the total fleet to 252 sets in several versions.

The single-deck TGV POS for international services via LGV Est switched to asynchronous motors, which were also fitted to later Duplex builds; forty of the last fifty-five double-deckers were intended for international routes and are, or will be, fitted with the European Train Control System. This is an automatic train protection system based on cab signalling and continuous transmission of data between track and train intended to remedy the lack of standard signalling across Europe (p70).

LURE OF THE SOUTH

Prominent among the master plan projects was a commercially attractive 295km extension beyond Valence down the Rhône Valley, splitting west of Avignon to serve Marseille and Montpellier. Not surprisingly, this Fr21.5 billion scheme, which required some spectacular engineering through a geologically tortured landscape, was controversial, not least because it passed uncomfortably close to some treasured vineyards. Even Mitterrand was moved to put in his presidential oar with a public statement on Bastille Day in 1990 that he was concerned about the famous Côtes du Rhône vines.

After lengthy consultation and negotiations with angry local residents and winegrowers, some of whom felt sufficiently moved to perpetrate acts of sabotage and vandalism, the line received its DUP in June 1994. Just over a year later, on 3 July 1995, timings from the capital to destinations in the Midi were cut again when SNCF commissioned the LGV Rhône-Alpes extension from Lyon to Valence. In September that year a start was made on LGV Méditerranée, again using generous parameters such as a 4.8m spacing between track centres to allow for speeds above 300km/h. The objective was to achieve a 3-hour Paris–Marseille timing, which SNCF's Managing Director of Passenger Services Guillaume Pepy believed would allow the railway to reverse its position in the air versus rail travel market to give it a share of 66 per cent.

According to Project Director Gilles Cartier, construction was 'very complex', requiring 500 bridges and structures and 17km of viaduct, including a pair of graceful curved twin-track structures over the River Rhône where the line bifurcates near Avignon for Marseille and Montpellier. SNCF also undertook to limit noise to lower levels than on earlier LGVs.

French President Jacques Chirac, accompanied by SNCF President Louis Gallois and Transport Minister Jean-Claude Gayssot, presided at the inauguration on 7 June 2001, but before that SNCF had marked the line's completion with another publicity stunt. On 26 May 2001 TGV set 531 staged a special run over the 1,067.2km from Calais to Marseille, completing the trip in 3 hours 29 minutes. Over a measured distance of 1,000km the special achieved a mean speed of 317km/h, a world record for sustained long-distance running. Meanwhile, a short section was authorised for 320km/h as SNCF wished to gain experience of regular operations at the proposed maximum speed for future lines.

In the first year, traffic on the Paris–Marseille route – a journey now timed at just 180 minutes – soared to 18 million trips, way above SNCF's expectation of a 30 per cent uplift. Rail's market share versus air between Île-de-France and the Provence-Alpes-Côte d'Azur regions was 60 per cent, well on the way to Pepy's two-thirds target. Traffic between Lyon and Marseille actually tripled, encouraging SNCF to predict breaking-even on the route in 2004.

EASTERN PROMISE

Next in line for construction was a route from Paris to Strasbourg, a scheme mooted back in 1983. Countless studies had been made and numerous 'green lights' accorded by government, but progressing this Fr26.8 billion LGV proved difficult because of the low rate of return of 4.5 per cent. The answer was to split the project into two, but when Prime Minister Alain Juppé announced on 15 May 1996 that he had signed the DUP, he gave no date for work to start. In December he promised that construction would begin in 1998, but although land for the entire 406km alignment could be purchased, authority to build was given only for the 270km from Vaires-sur-Marne in the Paris suburbs to Baudrecourt, between Metz and Nancy.

As it turned out, the funding package was not settled until November 2000, and civil works did not commence until June 2002. The first section, where the V150 claimed its honours, opened for commercial traffic at 320km/h on 10 June 2007 after inauguration by Transport Minister Dominique Perben on 15 March; the event included the lighting of torches to create 'a line of light' over the 300km from Vaires to Lorraine. Perben vowed that work on the final section to Vendenheim, just outside Strasbourg, would start in 2008, but the €2 billion funding package was not agreed until 2009, with tenders invited in September that year; the job will not be finished until 2016. The line will then offer some very attractive timings with

Tilting TGV. Seen here on SNCF's roller-rig testbed at Vitry, a TGV Sud-Est set dubbed P01 was fitted experimentally with two types of tilting equipment in the late 1990s. The trials were inconclusive and the tilt gear was dismantled. (SNCF-CAV J.J. D'Angelo)

Strasbourg just 1 hour 50 minutes from Paris, and the prospect of a Paris–Stuttgart time of 3 hours 20 minutes. Meanwhile, the success of the line was underlined in April 2013 by Air France's decision to replace its Paris–Strasbourg flights with chartered space on four daily TGV services to and from Roissy-Charles-de-Gaulle.

In 1996, ambitions of forging ahead with more lines in the master plan were dealt a serious blow when SNCF announced its worst financial performance of the decade, not helped in December 1995 by a disastrous strike that crippled services for much of that month. The government's biggest headache was the interest due on SNCF's long-term debts of nearly Fr178 billion, much of which related to investment in LGVs. In October 1996 Transport Secretary Anne-Marie Idrac – who later became SNCF President – described the plan as 'unrealistic'.

In the following year the government transferred ownership of the network to a new organisation called Réseau Ferré de France (RFF), which began life with the allocation of a goodly chunk of SNCF's long-term debt – RFF was conveniently out of the public eye. Cutbacks were now the order of the day, and rather than build more LGVs, government needed to find other ways to accelerate the nation's passenger services. Criticism was also being voiced that too much was being spent on new lines at the expense of the conventional network. Options up for investigation included a mini-TGV with a single power car and a tilting TGV.

Italy, which we shall visit in Chapter 5, can be described as the home of the tilting train, but the concept of tilting trains to allow faster running through curves was investigated in many countries. It is not widely known that TGV001 was to have had a sister train with cars achieving 7° of body tilt, but this train was never built. Tilting trains were cheaper than new railways, and on 1 July 1996

Transport Minister Bernard Pons said in Reims that he 'had asked GEC Alsthom to study the possibility of delivering a prototype tilting TGV … in eighteen months'. This was to test the possibilities for accelerating journeys on the Paris–Limoges–Toulouse route, where rail was losing out to air, with the prospect of a new motorway abstracting yet more passengers. Tilt looked a promising way of dealing with the problem of 130 curves in just 101km, which limited line speed between Brive and Cahors to 110km/h.

Doubtless to the concern of French train builders, a Pendolino from Italy was borrowed for tests over this route in early 1997. The following year saw the debut of trials with a converted Sud-Est TGV set branded P01 whose trailer cars were fitted with a Fiat hydraulic tilt mechanism at SNCF's Bischheim workshops. The cost was Fr170 million, including a state grant of around Fr30 million.

The trials on selected sinuous segments of the French network were not conclusive, and the train was then fitted with an electromechanical tilting system, home-grown by Alstom (which had dropped the GEC and the 'h' in 1998) for a second round of tests in 1999–2000. These demonstrated the technical feasibility of a tilting TGV, but the cost of conversion or of building new trains appeared too high, and P01 resumed its former guise as a standard train. After that the government lost interest and in 2003 dropped plans to beef up the Paris–Toulouse route.

CROSS-COUNTRY

Back in 1992, preliminary studies were commissioned into a project termed LGV Rhin–Rhône. This was an inter-regional link in Eastern France with an international dimension: at its eastern end it offered access to eastern Switzerland and south Germany, and to the west it served the Rhône Valley.

Cross-country. A TGV Duplex finished in a special livery for the opening of LGV Rhin-Rhône was tested over the new line in July 2011 before it opened in September that year. (Frédéric Tindilière)

Fast trains from German and Swiss cities to the Mediterranean seemed an enticing commercial prospect. In May 1998 Transport Minister Claude Gayssot commissioned further studies, following this up in 2000 with a formal enquiry. By this time SNCF's finances were recovering, with plans for further investment again being drawn up. Conceived in three phases, the line would first join the towns of Mulhouse and Dijon. Later, a branch would run west from Dijon to join LGV Sud-Est, while a southern arm would take the tracks towards Lyon.

The scheme was granted a DUP in January 2002, but not until 6 July was agreement reached on funding. This was hardly a surprise, as the €2.3 billion cost was shared between the French government, the European Union, the Swiss government, RFF and the Regions of Franche-Comté, Alsace and Bourgogne. Even then, the route was truncated at each end to 140km between junctions east of Dijon and west of Mulhouse, whereas the original Y-shaped route stretched to 425km.

Low-Cost Riposte

Faced with a determined assault on the inter-city market by low-cost airlines, in 2004 SNCF came up with the iDTGV formula. A subsidiary called iDTGV, later merged into the main passenger business, was set up to manage and run a low-cost TGV service. Launched in December 2004 using a Duplex set between Paris and Toulon with intermediate calls at Avignon and Marseille, the iDTGV proved an instant winner, with 4,000 seats sold within 24 hours of bookings opening. The headline fare was €19.

More services were added as SNCF refined the concept, and around thirty daily iDTGV departures now link Paris with the Côte d'Azur, the Pyrenees, the Rhône-Alpes region and Brittany. Passengers desiring peace and quiet can choose the iDzen zone while those who prefer a more lively atmosphere can elect to ride in iDzap, where various forms of entertainment are on offer. The iDzinc bar offers iDzen customers a €2 'sleep kit' consisting of an inflatable cushion, ear plugs and an eye mask. In 2012 SNCF achieved an impressive load factor of 88 per cent on iDTGV services.

In 2011 talk of competing companies entering the French rail market prompted SNCF to explore the low-cost formula in more detail. The job of developing a 'hyper-accessible' service where costs were 40 per cent lower than conventional TGVs was given to Valérie Delhinger, who at the time was SNCF's Head of Sales for Île-de-France. She and her team came up with the Ouigo concept, which SNCF launched in April 2013. Using four dedicated Duplex sets rebuilt with 630 high-density one-class seats and limited luggage space, the Ouigo fleet avoids central Paris, using the station at Marne-la-Vallée as pathing is less critical and access fees are lower than a central terminus. Ouigo trains, easily identified by their bright blue livery with pink blobs round the doors, run from Marne-la-Vallée to Lyon, Valence, Avignon, Aix-en-Provence, Nîmes, Marseille and Montpellier. The four units are diagrammed for intensive use, in stark contrast to other TGVs. Each set covers nearly 1 million km a year, which the respected magazine *Chemins de Fer* suggests is about twice that achieved by most TGV sets.

Ouigo travel must be booked via the Internet and the headline 'early bird' fare is 'from €10'; needless to say, tickets are non-refundable, although they are exchangeable, with conditions. Luggage is limited to one 'cabin bag' and one suitcase per person; an unbooked bag attracts a charge of €40. A 30-minute check-in is specified, and on-board catering is limited to vending machines.

Cheap and cheerful. In April 2013 SNCF launched an ultra low-cost TGV service under the Ouigo brand. Four Duplex TGVs were refitted with high-density seating and diagrammed for intensive use between Marne-la-Vallée TGV station and destinations in Southern France. (Christophe Masse)

President Nicolas Sarkozy cut a ribbon at Besançon to inaugurate the 320km/h line on 8 September 2011, later travelling to Belfort-Montbéliard TGV station where a rolling stock display had been laid on to mark thirty years of TGV services. The first fare-paying customers rode the route on 11 December 2011, when SNCF launched a major timetable shake-up based around the new line. Two main groups of services were routed over it, one north–south and one east–west. The core of the north–south service were eight trains a day between Strasbourg and Lyon, with the trip covered in 3 hours 15 minutes compared with 4 hours 45 minutes previously; four trains ran to and from Marseille. The east–west services included Paris–Besançon–Mulhouse and the Paris–Zurich services, which previously ran via the first part of LGV Est. A return Frankfurt-am-Main–Marseille working operated by a Duplex set joined the other services on 23 March 2012.

PRIVATE FUNDING

Towards the end of 2007 the government staged something called the *Grenelle de l'environnement*, an environmental summit embracing a cross-section of French organisations that addressed all conceivable related topics, including high-speed railways. A torrent of legislation followed, with laws proposing that construction of a further 2,000km of LGV should start by 2020, with another 2,500km to follow. The package unveiled on 30 April 2008 by Jean-Louis Borloo, who rejoiced in the title of Minister of State for Ecology, Energy, Sustainable Development & Land Use Planning, included the second section of LGV Est, the eastern, southern and western branches of LGV Rhin-Rhône, Tours–Bordeaux, Montpellier–Perpignan, a Nîmes–Montpellier bypass, Bretagne–Pays de la Loire (extending LGV Atlantique from Connerré near Le Mans towards Rennes), Provence–Côte d'Azur

(Marseille–Nice), Bordeaux–Toulouse, Bordeaux–Hendaye, and a southern Paris bypass.

Earlier in 2007 RFF was given permission to finance major projects using public-private partnerships (PPPs). This was largely because the government could not possibly fund all the major projects that it had planned from the public purse, and partly because RFF could not manage a whole raft of new projects simultaneously. Accordingly, two schemes were selected as PPP pilots, and expressions of interest were called for the 302km Tours–Bordeaux route, officially called LGV Sud Europe Atlantique, and for the Nîmes–Montpellier bypass.

The 182km Bretagne–Pays de la Loire scheme, amounting to 214km including connecting links, had been granted a DUP on 26 October 2007, and this too was proposed as a PPP. Completion would put the towns of Brest and Quimper within about 3 hours of Paris.

The economic crisis that hit Western Europe in 2008 could have ended many of these projects, but in practice it had the unexpected effect of prompting some countries to launch huge investment programmes to stimulate their economies. France was among them. In July 2012 the government published a national transport infrastructure plan for the next twenty to thirty years, with around half of the €170 billion projected spend allocated to rail. A Paris–Calais via Amiens scheme was revived, together with a second Paris–Lyon route via Clermont Ferrand to relieve LGV Paris–Sud-Est.

A financial protocol for the €3.4 billion Bretagne–Pays de la Loire scheme – endorsing contributions from the state, RFF, and the regions of Bretagne and Pays de la Loire – was agreed on 29 July 2009, and an agreement for a twenty-five-year PPP concession was signed between RFF and the Eiffage Rail Express consortium on

28 July 2011. A groundbreaking ceremony was held at Étrelles on 27 July 2012, the aim being to open the line in 2017.

A fifty-year PPP concession for the €6.2 billion Tours–Bordeaux project was inked by RFF President Hubert du Mesnil and CEO of Vinci Constructions Xavier Huillard on 16 June 2011. Completion promises a Paris–Bordeaux timing of just 2 hours, sufficiently quick to make a flight, including travel to and from the airports, a waste of time. Up to 3 million extra passengers a year are expected.

Initial bids for a concession for the Nîmes–Montpellier bypass, needed to relieve the heavily used conventional line, were submitted in 2010. Connecting end-on with LGV Méditerranée at Manduel, it was granted a DUP in May 2005. Just over seven years later, Oc'via was chosen as the private partner to finance, design, build and maintain the €2.3 billion line until 2037. In contrast to earlier LGVs, it is designed for conventional passenger and freight trains with 25-tonne axle loads as well as TGVs. Opening is planned in 2017.

Soon after President François Hollande's government took office in 2012, it dawned on ministers that their predecessors under Sarkozy had made rather a lot of commitments without ensuring that finance was in place to carry them all through. Austerity once more became the order of the day, and a review of the previous government's twenty-five-year €245 billion national infrastructure plan was ordered by Transport Minister Frédéric Cuvillier. In fact, the whole RFF-SNCF edifice was becoming rather wobbly, with RFF jacking up track access fees and SNCF complaining that running TGVs was less profitable. The solution postulated by the government was to merge RFF back into a reconstituted SNCF; this was consummated in 2015.

In October 2013 Cuvillier said that his government 'would prioritise the everyday transport needs of the French people without turning its

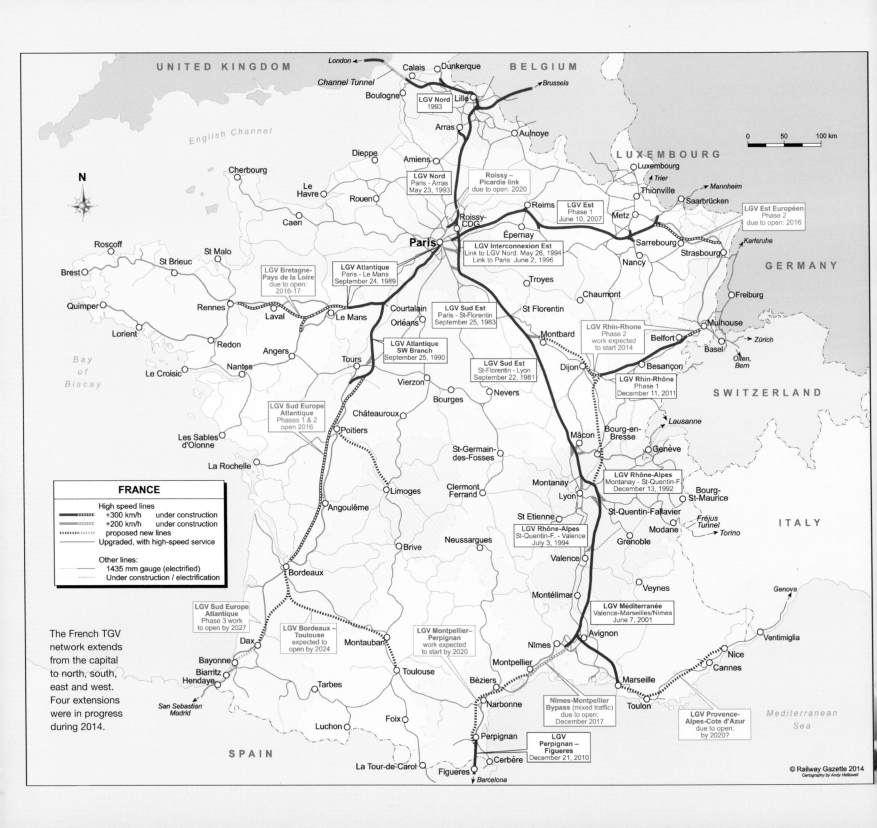

The French TGV network extends from the capital to north, south, east and west. Four extensions were in progress during 2014.

FRANCE

High speed lines
+300 km/h   under construction
+200 km/h   under construction
proposed new lines
Upgraded, with high-speed service

Other lines:
1435 mm gauge (electrified)
Under construction / electrification

LGV Nord
1993

LGV Nord
Paris - Arras
May 23, 1993

Roissy –
Picardie link
due to open: 2020

LGV Est
Phase 1
June 10, 2007

LGV Est Européen
Phase 2
due to open: 2016

LGV Interconnexion Est
Link to LGV Nord: May 26, 1994
Link to Paris: June 2, 1996

LGV Bretagne-
Pays de la Loire
due to open:
2016-17

LGV Atlantique
Paris - Le Mans
September 24, 1989

LGV Sud Est
Paris - St-Florentin
September 25, 1983

LGV Rhin-Rhone
Phase 2
work expected
to start 2014

LGV Atlantique
SW Branch
September 25, 1990

LGV Sud Est
St-Florentin - Lyon
September 22, 1981

LGV Rhin-Rhône
Phase 1
December 11, 2011

LGV Sud Europe
Atlantique
Phases 1 & 2
open 2016

LGV Rhône-Alpes
Montanay - St-Quentin-F.
December 13, 1992

LGV Rhône-Alpes
St-Quentin-F. - Valence
July 3, 1994

LGV Sud Europe
Atlantique
Phase 3 work
to open by 2027

LGV Bordeaux –
Toulouse
expected to
open by 2024

LGV Montpellier–
Perpignan
work expected
to start by 2020

LGV Méditerranée
Valence-Marseilles/Nîmes
June 7, 2001

Nîmes-Montpellier
Bypass (mixed traffic)
due to open:
December 2017

LGV Provence-
Alpes-Cote d'Azur
due to open:
by 2020?

LGV
Perpignan –
Figueres
December 21, 2010

© Railway Gazette 2014
Cartography by Andy Hellewell

back on high-speed rail'. This seemed to indicate that planning for some LGVs would continue, and Cuvillier confirmed this by announcing the alignments of links from Bordeaux to Toulouse and Dax. Completion of the Toulouse route is expected in 2024, when the Paris–Toulouse timing will be cut to 3 hours 10 minutes. However, the timescale for other schemes stretches far into the future, with completion of some not envisaged until 2050.

BEYOND THE TGV

The Duplex proved to be ultra-successful domestically, but SNCF's supplier Alstom was anxious to continue developing high-speed technology for both the home and export markets. With a new management team at the helm, SNCF dropped the plan for a 'Super-TGV' power car

in 2000. Many of the PSE sets were rebuilt to run at 300km/h, but neither the mini-TGV nor the tilting TGV progressed beyond the drawing board.

In October 2001 Alstom rolled out an experimental high-speed train with power equipment distributed along the train, known as the *Automotrice à Grande Vitesse* or AGV. The intention, claimed François Lacôte, by now Director & Senior Consultant for Alstom, was to carry more passengers on a single-decker, reduce power consumption and lower the maintenance and investment costs per seat. Describing the Duplex as 'the rail equivalent of the high-capacity wide-body jet with over 500 seats', he saw the AGV as a train suitable for 'intermediate or regional' applications; it also offered 'the prospect of raising maximum speeds to 350km/h without major changes to the train design'.

It was relatively simple to assemble a prototype, so Alstom built two AGV cars and married them with four trailers and a Réseau power car to form a test train, dubbed *Elisa*. This lash-up spent much of its life dashing up and down LGV Nord-Europe between Lille and Calais-Fréthun. Its job done, *Elisa* was dismantled, but Alstom was sufficiently pleased with its experiment to invite the press for a ride on *Elisa*'s last trip in May 2002.

In 2003–04, largely because of problems with its power station turbines, Alstom's financial performance took a distinct turn for the worse, so much so that it became a matter of pressing concern for government. Finance Minister Nicolas Sarkozy could not afford to let the manufacturer of the world-leading TGV go bankrupt, and he managed to persuade the European Commission to accept a government rescue.

Given this state of affairs, it was all the more remarkable that Alstom decided in 2005 to build, at its own expense, a seven-car AGV demonstrator. Keeping the TGV's articulation, the demonstrator had a modular design, with two independent sets of power equipment, each packaged over three cars. The principal innovation was the use of permanent magnet traction motors attached to the bogie frame, avoiding the tripod transmission used on TGVs. In terms of cost-effectiveness, the target was to achieve a cost per seat for a single-decker equal to that of the Duplex.

On 6 March 2007 Alstom submitted a bid to supply twenty-five eleven-car AGVs to nascent Italian operator Nuovo Trasporto Ferroviario. Of an order for AGVs from SNCF, however, there was no sign, although the national operator continued to place contracts for more Duplex sets. By this time the AGV demonstrator, dubbed *Pégase*, was taking shape in Alstom's La Rochelle factory, and invitations were sent out to an unveiling ceremony on 5 February 2008.

Elisa finale. Alstom's *Elisa* AGV test train rests at Calais-Fréthun after its last run in May 2002. On the platform are Alstom Senior Vice-President François Lacôte and AGV Project Manager Georges Palais. (Richard Hope)

Mission accomplished. French President Nicolas Sarkozy did not miss the opportunity to remind guests at the launch of Alstom's prototype AGV in February 2008 at La Rochelle that he had arranged a rescue for the company during his time as Finance Minister in 2003–04. (Author)

About 500 guests seated in the Bellevue test centre at La Rochelle were treated to some son-et-lumière wizardry before the guest of honour sprang into action. It was none other than Nicolas Sarkozy, now President of France, who launched into a long speech, which seemed to laud his personal rescue of Alstom. Behind the President, the silver and black form of the AGV demonstrator was bathed in brilliant light. Speech over, 'Sarko' vanished into the cab, and the press were finally allowed to inspect the train. There was plenty to write about, as Alstom had in January clinched the NTV order, a €650 million deal that included maintaining the twenty-five trains for thirty years. This appeared to justify the €100 million invested in developing the AGV.

Nevertheless, the lack of an order from SNCF was a major concern. Yet all is apparently not lost. In September 2013 President Hollande came up with a suite of projects intended to revitalise French industry, one of which was 'the TGV of the future'. A prototype is to be built by 2017…

European Train Control System

ETCS Level 1 provides automatic train protection and speed control using intermittent communication between train and track via track-mounted balises, which transmit information from the lineside signalling to the train. An on-board computer calculates the train's maximum permitted speed and the braking curve. Track circuits or axle counters detect the location of the train.

ETCS Level 2 provides the same functions as Level 1, but with continuous communication between train and track via GSM-R radio. 'Movement authorities' are transmitted to the train directly from a 'radio block centre' attached to the interlocking rather than being generated from the lineside signalling, as happens in Level 1. Lineside signalling is not required, but is sometimes provided as a back-up or if non-ETCS equipped trains use the same route. Balises are used by the train to determine its location, and an on-board computer continuously monitors the train's actual speed in relation to the maximum permissible.

5

Frecciarossa Versus Italo

Showers of rain pelted down beyond the platform canopy and dark clouds towered over Rome's Tiburtina station. It was late morning on 20 April 2012, and Platform 15 was crowded with journalists and photographers. Officials were anxious to usher everyone aboard, as Train 9915 was due to leave at 11.57 a.m. and there would be a hefty price to pay if departure was delayed – this was the launch special for Europe's first privately owned operator of high-speed trains, Nuovo Trasporti Viaggiatori.

Bound for Centrale station in Naples, the train's passengers included none other than Ferrari Chairman Luca Cordero di Montezemolo. A self-confessed 'addict of speed', di Montezemolo was one of NTV's founders and the company's president. He and his fellow investors had launched against state-owned rail operator Trenitalia, part of *Ferrovie dello Stato* (FS), to compete for a slice of the inter-city business on Italy's spanking new high-speed network. In fact, 20 per cent of the company was owned by state-owned French national operator SNCF, but NTV was essentially a private business, which saw its role as shaking up the incumbent operator's historic monopoly to give Italy's rail customers a choice.

Whistles shrill and stragglers are bundled aboard the immaculate crimson-liveried AGV train set. Radio journalists poke their microphones through the open doors to catch the sounds of departure, only withdrawing them at the last moment as the doors slide shut. Almost imperceptibly, and precisely on time, Train 9915 draws away from the platform and out from the grandiose structure of the rebuilt Tiburtina station, inaugurated by Italian President Giorgio Napolitano on 28 November 2011, a date that marked 150 years of the Italian Republic. Wild poppies beside the tracks echo the train's colour as it threads the tracks through suburban Rome. Graffiti-smothered walls slide past as we gather speed, heading for the 205km high-speed line that opened in December 2005 between the Italian capital and Naples (Napoli). The rain, which NTV Chief Executive Giuseppe Sciarrone had said earlier was a good omen, is easing off.

Inside the train, media interviews are in full swing as journalists and TV crews block the aisles in their efforts to capture the ambience of this historic trip. An electronic jingle precedes a PA announcement welcoming us on board, and the information screens tell us that we have reached 220km/h. Short tunnels and green-coloured sound barriers interrupt the view through the deep windows, and clouds mask the summits of the Albani hills to our left as we streak south.

The AGV is rock-steady on superbly aligned track, and the speedometer moves up in 10km/h increments, finally holding at 300km/h under the control of Europe's first high-speed commercial application of ETCS. Branded *italo* with a leaping

Rivals in Rome. A Trenitalia Frecciarossa ETR500 passes NTV's *italo* launch special at Rome Tiburtina on 20 April 2012. The two operators compete head-to-head for business and leisure traffic on Italy's high-speed network. (Author)

hare for a logo, NTV's high-speed service is 'a revolution', Sciarrone assures me, adding that 'we are treading prudently' in the initial phase. The term applies not just to the private sector's venture into the high-speed rail business but also to the company's choice of technology.

Our eleven-car AGV train set – it is number 07 – is one of twenty-five assembled by Alstom at La Rochelle in France and Savigliano in the Piedmont region of Italy. Even at maximum speed, there is little sound from the electronic equipment and permanent magnet traction motors below us. The motors are mounted in long-wheelbase articulation bogies whose frames are made of weight-saving high-tensile

steel; ten of the twenty-four axles are powered, with each motor delivering up to 750kW.

The train offers 460 leather seats in three 'habitats' or classes styled by Italdesign–Giugiaro: Club, Prima and Smart. A 'cinema' car at one end features high-definition ceiling-mounted screens, and a suite of communications technology means that passengers can stay connected while on the move. There is no restaurant car, but Club and Prima passengers may order pre-cooked meals provided by the Eataly company; these are served at-seat with the food rather curiously packed in glass jars. Coffee and other vending machines are available to passengers in Smart.

The AGV's traction, braking and on-board equipment had been thoroughly tested on the seven-car *Pégase* demonstrator unveiled at La Rochelle in February 2008. The train, which doubled as a full-scale prototype, was sent to the Velim test facility in the Czech Republic where a 13km ring allowed it to clock up high mileages without disrupting commercial services. Electrical isolation of the loop also meant that checks could be made on the train's electromagnetic compatibility. In the middle of the tests, *Pégase* made a short excursion to Berlin for display at the InnoTrans exhibition in September 2008 – long queues to visit the cab were evident throughout the show.

Pégase then returned to its birthplace to be thrashed up and down LGV Est at maximum speed before heading to Italy for testing and approval checks by safety and regulatory bodies. In March 2010 it clocked 300km/h on the Rome–Naples line, where our series-built *italo* is now flashing past orchards and fertile fields on its 68-minute timing to Naples. White wraiths of cloud clutch at distant hills, and there are blue patches in the sky as a brake application signals the approach to our destination. We plunge into a tunnel where sharp curves trigger a judder or two and provoke a squeal of protest from the wheel flanges. Moments later we glide to a halt at Platform 24 in Centrale station where the clocks indicate that we are 2 minutes ahead of schedule.

Photographers tumble out to form a scrum at the head of the train, betraying the presence of di Montezemolo who walks to the rear, preceded by a circus of backwards-walking film crews and microphone-hugging journos. The president poses in front of the angular nose of *italo* 07 for the cameras, finally calling a halt before striding back along the platform where a cocktail lunch is being served.

Addict of speed. A media scrum surrounds Ferrari Chairman Luca di Montezemolo, then President of NTV, on the return trip from Naples to Rome on 20 April 2012. The speed display shows 300km/h. (Author)

Sciarrone confirms that NTV will launch two round trips between Naples and Milan on 28 April, stepping up to five and then nine by the end of May. Destinations to be added later include Venice, Turin and Salerno. Three weekday non-stop return trips between Rome Tiburtina and Milan are due to start in September, he asserts, with a timing of 3 hours 10 minutes.

Another AGV pulls in to the adjacent Platform 23 as preparations are made for the run back to Rome as train 9944. The appointed departure is at 2 p.m., and smartly clad NTV staff shoo us back on board. Di Montezemolo passes along the train, batting the media's questions with expert soundbites. Hinting at a future increase to the train's design speed of 360km/h, he asserts that 'everybody is discovering and appreciating high speed; this is the future, not only in Italy, but also in Europe'.

State-Owned Rival

Back at Tiburtina, one of Trenitalia's *Frecciarossa* (Red Arrow) high-speed services rolls past. NTV has made its pitch against these trains, and Trenitalia is taking the threat seriously. On 13 December 2011 NTV took the wraps of its first fully fitted *italo* set at Alstom's specially built depot and workshop at Nola near Naples, but just three weeks earlier Trenitalia had unveiled the first refurbished *Frecciarossa*. These ETR500 train sets, dating from the late 1980s and early 1990s, were styled by Pininfarina. Each set consists of two chunky power cars and a rake of conventional coaches including a restaurant car. Originally fitted with two classes of accommodation, they were refurbished with four classes including eight seats in a plush Executive zone, with meeting rooms and wi-fi throughout; other classes are Business, Premium and Standard.

Pink faces. In September 2010, Trenitalia decorated two of its ETR500 fleet in pink and rebranded them as Frecciarosa to promote the health, rights, safety and culture of women. (David Campione)

NTV had set out to secure a 20 per cent market share of the Italian high-speed rail business by 2015. It was certainly not plain sailing, as right from the start the company encountered obstacles that delayed its plans. Rival operator Trenitalia is part of the *Ferrovie dello Stato* holding group, whose Chief Executive was tough-talking Mauro Moretti. The group also owns the infrastructure management company, *Rete Ferroviaria Italiana*, and it was with RFI that NTV had to negotiate track access, train paths and use of stations, and nobody would pretend that this was a smooth process.

Trenitalia's historic monopoly was under attack, and it was clear that relationships were strained. NTV accused RFI of amending the rules about use of the network so as to 'cause serious and irreparable damage' by delaying or even preventing NTV's launch of services. The paths that NTV finally negotiated were far from ideal, with Rome–Milan services sometimes timed to run immediately behind Trenitalia's *Frecciarossa* trains. Similarly, pathing constraints meant that NTV cold not use Milan Centrale station; it was obliged to route its trains into Porta Garibaldi instead.

NTV, however, was a young and dynamic company. Considerable sums were at stake, so there was huge motivation to get the trains up and running to earn a return. Its arrival on the Italian railway scene had clearly struck a chord: by May 2010 as many as 50,000 people had applied for the 929 jobs at NTV, half of them hoping to qualify as one of the 106 *italo* train drivers.

Trenitalia had been spurred into action too. Now certain that NTV was not a businessman's paper dream, and aware that refurbishing its elderly ETR500 fleet would only serve as an interim measure, it went out to tender for fifty non-articulated high-speed trains. The operating arm of FS had considerable experience with high-speed rolling stock; a prototype ETR500X power car and trailer had been available for tests in 1988, and these were followed by two pre-production ETR500Y train sets. FS was sufficiently pleased to place an order in 1992 for a fleet of thirty trains from the Breda-led Trevi consortium; a second series of thirty was ordered at the end of 1994. One train was unfortunately written off in 2005 when it derailed with the rear power car nearly falling off a washed-out bridge, leaving Trenitalia with fifty-nine sets.

Alstom responded to the call for tenders with a non-tilting version of its Pendolino, but the contract was won in August 2010 by a joint bid from Bombardier and local supplier AnsaldoBreda, pricing the trains at €30.8 million each. 'A good race ended with high scores by both competitors', said Moretti.

A full-size mock-up of Trenitalia's future flagship was unveiled in Rimini to Italian Prime Minister Mario Monti on 19 August 2012, and Moretti was in his element when the first ETR1000 *Frecciarossa* train emerged from the AnsaldoBreda factory at Pistoia in Tuscany on a rainy 26 March 2013. Clutching their umbrellas, crowds of guests and media watched the blazing headlights of the Bertone-styled front end appear through a cloud of smoke framed by a giant screen on which images of the train were projected. Trenitalia claimed that its latest acquisition was 'the fastest series-built train in Europe', declaring that it had been designed for 400km/h. This would translate into a Rome–Milan journey time of just 2 hours 15 minutes. Finished in red and white, the first set was named *Pietro Mennea* after the Italian sprinter and European 200m record holder who had died a few days earlier.

Red hot. NTV's *italo* services carried over 6 million passengers in 2013, but a fierce price war with state-owned Trenitalia means that revenue is below forecasts. The *italo* fleet is maintained under contract by train builder Alstom at a purpose-built depot at Nola near Naples. (David Campione)

Like the AGV, the ETR1000 has distributed power. Water-cooled IGBT inverters feed sixteen asynchronous traction motors on four of the eight cars, generating a peak output of 9.8MW geared to the possibility of commercial schedules at 360km/h. Fairings between the aluminium-bodied cars ensure a smooth aerodynamic profile along the whole train. The interior features 455 seats arranged in four classes, and one car features a swish cafe-bar.

The pre-production set was soon dispatched to the Bombardier plant at Vado Ligure for commissioning and certification. There it starred in a second presentation on 3 July, breaking a red, white and green ribbon strung across the test track in front of 300 guests. Moretti lauded the new arrival as 'the most beautiful train in the world', unknowingly echoing former FS Chief Rolling Stock Engineer Giancarlo Piro who had used precisely those words to describe the ETR500 during a demonstration trip on

20 September 1991. Assuming all goes as planned, ETR1000 formations are set to dazzle Trenitalia customers in 2015.

An ETR1000 set attained 300km/h for the first time on 29 April 2014 on test between Rome and Naples. RFI was by this time upgrading the overhead line equipment on a 57km section of the Turin–Milan AV line for ultra high-speed trials, suggesting that Trenitalia was quite serious about its plans for 360km/h. A few weeks after the *italo* launch, Moretti reiterated this ambition in an interview. The ETR1000's ability to run at 360 or 400km/h would be aided, he said, by the active suspension, which would also allow the train to outpace its rivals on the Rome–Florence *direttissima*, of which more in a moment. It was early days, but what effect had NTV's launch had on Trenitalia's high-speed business? Moretti replied that Trenitalia had retained its market share, with *Frecciarossa* load factors rising from an average of 55 per cent to 60 per cent.

This was undoubtedly down to a drastic switch in fares policy: 'every month we are offering 285,000 seats between Rome and Milan priced from €9', Moretti confessed, adding that young people booked the low fares two to three months ahead so that they quickly sold out. Trenitalia had previously offered €9 fares between Rome and Milan on a daily low-cost service introduced in December 2004 in a bid to compete with the low-cost airlines. Moretti went on to highlight improvements in service: 'we are devoting more attention to the way we present ourselves to customers, so you can say the market has reacted in the right way with an increase in the total volume of traffic'. Trenitalia is of course in a dominant position, operating more services than its rival, many of them departing major cities at ideal regular intervals on the half hour or full hour.

In October 2012 some surprising news arrived: di Montezemolo had stepped down from the presidency of NTV and handed the role to Antonello Perricone. Later, di Montezemolo also left his position as Ferrari President. There was more to come. A year later Sciarrone resigned from his post as Chief Executive, his duties being taken on by Perricone. Clearly, all was not happy in the house of the private operator. Italian media quoted di Montezemolo saying in his resignation speech that the company was 'doing well'; he had pleaded that 'other commitments' had obliged him to step down.

Seeking to assess the situation two years after the launch, I asked NTV if it would meet its 20 per cent market share target in 2015. Giuseppe Bonollo, Director of Marketing & Promotions, asserted that NTV had carried 6.2 million passengers in 2013, which was 'slightly more than 20 per cent of the domestic high-speed rail market'. NTV had launched at a time when the Italian economy was in crisis, and Bonollo noted that passengers had become 'more price-sensitive'. On the other hand, NTV estimated

Red Arrow. The ETR1000 will take over Trenitalia's premium *Frecciarossa* services from the ETR500 on Italy's high-speed network. With its aerodynamic bogie skirts removed, one of the first sets undergoes trials on the test circuit at Velim in the Czech Republic. (Quintus Vosman)

that demand for high-speed rail travel in Italy had risen by 16 per cent in 2012 and 20 per cent in 2013. NTV's 2012 annual report showed an after-tax loss of €77 million, which was 'in line with the industrial plan'; the plan has since been 'revisited'.

Time will tell whether the market will support the two rivals, but in 2014 there were ominous signs when NTV put in place a recapitalisation after running up debts of €800 million. It also complained that competition regulation was ineffective, while di Montezemolo, still the biggest shareholder, said that 'the rail adventure is not an activity for the faint-hearted'.

Naissance of a Network

There is little doubt that NTV's arrival means that Italy's high-speed network is better used than it would have been had Trenitalia remained as sole operator. The network is built in the shape of a T, with Naples at the toe and Turin and Venice at the top corners of the horizontal bar.

The first section started out as Europe's first modern high-speed line – plans to construct a *direttissima* between Rome and Florence were announced in 1969, five years after opening of the Tokaido Shinkansen. The only problem was that it took the state railway until May 1992 to complete the 254km railway, and long before then France had opened its first two LGVs. Right from the beginning the *direttissima* was plagued by financial problems, arguments over the alignment and unexpected geological hazards in the tunnels. The scheme seemed to progress on a hand-to-mouth basis, with fits of construction interspersed by long pauses when the money ran out.

In contrast to most other high-speed lines, the *direttissima* – a name which had been coined for a fast link between Rome and Naples in 1927 – was designed for passenger and freight traffic, with

frequent 'interconnections' to the old route so that trains could weave on and off the new line to serve intermediate stations. Maximum speed was 250km/h and electrification was the standard Italian 3kV DC.

In 1986 Italian State Railways became a nominally independent organisation rather than a department of the transport ministry, gaining a measure of commercial freedom. Plans for expanding high-speed operations were drawn up and the seeds sown for building a national network of new *Alta Velocità* lines that would slice hours off inter-city journey times and make rail competitive against airlines and the private car.

In the 1980s Italy's state railway was seriously overstaffed and a prodigious consumer of tax-payers' money. A zealous round of cost-cutting was instigated by industrialist Mario Schimberni, whom the government had appointed as Special Administrator to sort out the railway's affairs. The AV project was put on ice, only to be resurrected by Lorenzo Necci, successor to Schimberni, who resigned in 1990 after just seventeen months in the post. Necci's contribution was to initiate a scheme that would bring private capital into the ambitious programme, which carried the impressive price tag of 30,000 billion lire.

To emphasise that the new lines would deliver a massive boost to capacity in the north–south corridor, the project was rebranded as *Alta Velocità/Alta Capacità*. A mixed capital company called Treno Alta Velocità SpA, 40 per cent owned by FS, was set up to fund them, with consultancy Italferr-TAV SpA taking the role of client engineer, approving design and construction and managing the contract on behalf of TAV.

The parameters chosen for the AV/AC network were based on a design speed of 300km/h: track centres were generally 5m apart, the steepest gradient was nominally 1.8 per cent, and minimum curve radius was set at more than 5,000m. A significant

choice was 25kV 50Hz electrification, meaning that future high-speed trains had to be dual-voltage to run on the new routes and the old network, including the *direttissima*.

South of Rome an inland rather than a coastal route to Naples was chosen to avoid the need for tunnels and damage to the coastal scenery, and construction started in 1994. Between Bologna and Florence, however, the choice of route was another story, as here the line either had to make a long detour or pierce the Apennine Mountains, renowned for their complex geology. The alignment eventually selected for this key part of the north–south corridor was just 78.2km long, but no less than 73.1km ran in tunnel, with 1.2km on bridges and viaducts and a mere 3.9km in cuttings or on embankments. Construction was well in hand by the end of 1997, when delegates to that year's World Congress on Railway Research in Florence were taken to see tunnellers at work in the double-track Vaglia tunnel. They were impressed by its cavernous 82m^2 cross-section, needed to accommodate high-speed air flows when trains passed at a combined speed of 600km/h.

The final 182km segment of the stem of the 'T' between Milan and Bologna was badly needed as the existing double-track route was struggling to cope with up to 257 trains a day. The alignment crosses the plain of Lombardy and traverses alluvial deposits of the Po, and the choice was made to follow the A1 motorway or the existing railway wherever possible; there are eight 'interconnections' to the old line. For eight years the project was bogged down in the complexities of Italy's planning process until a definitive alignment was ratified in late-1999. This included a significant deviation from the original route near Modena, and the planners had to accept that there would be smaller radius curves and hence a lower speed limit of 240km/h. Construction finally began in November 2001.

ITALY

High speed lines

▬▬▬▬	+300 km/h under construction
▬▬▬▬	+200 km/h under construction
▪▪▪▪	proposed new lines
▬▬▬	Upgraded, with high-speed service

Other lines:

──	1435 mm gauge (electrified)
┄┄	Under construction / electrification

SWITZERLAND

AUSTRIA

SLOVENIA

CROATIA

BOSNIA HERZEGOVINA

base tunnel
(under construction –
due to open 2025)

Innsbruck
München

Brennero

Fortezza

Zürich

St Moritz

Lienz
Spittal

Villach
Wien

Brig
Bern
Lausanne

Locarno

Bellinzona

San Candido

Tarvisio

Domodossola

Tirano

Calalzo-
Pieve di
Cadore

Pré-St-
Didier

Como

Treviglio-Brescia
due to open 2016

Trento

Udine

Monfalcone

Modane
Lyon

Novara - Milano
December 2009

Brescia

Verona

Castelfranco

Padova-
Mestre
2007

Trieste

Torino - Novara
February 2006

Novara

Milano

Treviglio

Mestre

Ljubljana

Oulx

Torino

Tortona

Piacenza

Milano - Bologna
December 2008

Padova

Venezia

Gulf of
Venezia

Torre
Pellice

Trofarello

Milano-Genova
construction
began 2011

Parma

Ferrara

Cuneo

Modena

Bologna

Lavezzola

Limone

Genova

Ravenna

Alassio

Bologna - Firenze
December 2009

Faenza

Nice

Ventimiglia

La Spezia

Rimini

Gulf of
Genova

Pisa

Firenze

Pratovecchio Stia

Falconara

*Ligurian
Sea*

Livorno

Sansepolcro

Ancona

Cecina

Arezzo

Fabriano

Civitanova
Marche

Campiglia

**Firenze-
Roma**
1978-92

Foligno

San Benedetto
del Tronto

Piombino

Grosseto

Terni

Giulianova

Orte

Pescara

Civitavecchia

Sulmona

S.Vito-Lanciano

*Adriatic
Sea*

Roma

Roma - Napoli
December 2005

Peschici
Calenella

Nettuno

Cassino

San Severo

Manfredonia

Terracina

Foggia

Barletta

Napoli-Gricignano
December 2009

Napoli-Salerno
June 2008

Bari

Napoli

Salerno

Sorrento

Potenza

Brindisi

Metaponto

Taranto

Lecce

CORSICA

Porto Torres

Golfo Aranci

Sassari

Ozieri-Chilivani

Macomer

N

SARDINIA

Sapri

Gallipoli

Otranto

Iglesias

Carbonia

Cagliari

Sibari

*Gulf of
Taranto*

Paola

Ciro

Crotone

*Tyrrhenian
Sea*

*Ionian
Sea*

*Mediterranean
Sea*

0   50   100 km

The Alta Velocità/Alta
Capacità network
stretches in a huge 'T'
from top to toe of Italy.

On 1 June 2000 FS was restructured, with RFI set up as a state-owned infrastructure company and Trenitalia as the national operator. This may have given added impetus to the AV/AC project and, together with legislation permitting open access companies, it paved the way for NTV's arrival.

In 2001 the civil engineers started to prepare the trackbed for the Turin–Novara section of the 125km Milan–Turin AV/AC line, which again ran parallel to a motorway to limit its environmental impact. The Turin–Novara section opened on 10 February 2006 for the 2006 Winter Olympics in Piedmont.

By 2004 most of the track had been laid on the 205km Rome–Naples line, but progress had been severely delayed by the discovery of an ancient Roman road on the approach to the capital. Its excellent condition demanded that it be moved to a special archaeological park, which meant that construction of the 10km approach to Rome could not start until 2002; this delayed handover of the line to RFI until July 2005. Trenitalia then ran a 'shadow service', partly to bed in the ETCS Level 2 train control equipment that, after four years of tests, was in use for the first time at 300km/h. RFI's Technical Director Michele Elia freely admitted during a test run on 8 March 2006 that there had been problems – the software was being updated every night after each day's tests. 'We are tuning the system every day … this work cannot stop until we have a complete level of confidence in our system', he said.

From 22 December 2005 Trenitalia started with two commercial trains a day each way, although no fares were charged. From 23 January 2006 a flat fare of €25 was payable in both classes, and on 26 March another two round trips were added. The number of workings was stepped up during the year, one reason for the timid start being the availability of ETR500 train sets that had been

fitted with ETCS equipment. After the final section between Gricignano and Naples was completed in 2009, the fastest time between the two cities came down to 1 hour 10 minutes. Some services were extended over newly built 200km/h infrastructure as far as Salerno.

From 2019 high-speed services to Naples are due to call at a new station to be built at Afragola, about 3km north of the centre. Designed by Zaha Hadid and dominated by a spectacular curved bridge snaking across the tracks, it will form a major interchange. The design was originally unveiled in 2003, but work was put on hold in 2012 because of financial concerns. Plans to resume construction were announced in early 2014, although by mid-year there was little sign of activity. New stations are an integral part of the AV/AC package, and the awesome architecture of Afragola and the stations at Rome Tiburtina and Turin Porta Susa illustrate that the second age of rail has certainly arrived in Italy.

A national record of 355km/h was notched up by an ETR500 test train on 1 March 2008 before services were first routed over the Milano–Bologna AV line on 14 December that year, when the headline Rome–Milan non-stop timing was pruned to 3 hours 30 minutes. This was the occasion Trenitalia chose to rebrand its premium services as *Frecciarossa*, with a second tier of slightly slower trains branded *Frecciargento* (Silver Arrow). After just one month, over 1 million tickets had been sold on Italy's high-speed services, and Emilio Maestrini, Trenitalia's Technical Director, reported that both the level of traffic and the price of air tickets on the Rome–Milan route had fallen.

Earlier, on 27 November, an ETR500 test train reached 339km/h on the Florence–Bologna line, presaging its opening in December 2009. Because so much of the line is in tunnel, trains are monitored from a RFI control centre in Bologna,

with cameras available to check the passage of trains at tunnel entrances and exits.

In Florence, Rome–Milan trains are obliged to reverse at Santa Maria Novella station. To avoid this time-consuming manoeuvre, a new station was proposed at Belfiore on a 9km alignment bypassing the SNM terminus, but obtaining approval to build through and below the city proved problematic. Only in 2018 is a cross-city tunnel incorporating the new station expected to open. When it does, passengers will pass through another piece of architectural splendour – Florence Belfiore has been designed by Norman Foster + Partners.

Opening of the Florence–Bologna line on 13 December 2009 slashed the time between the two cities to just 37 minutes and the fastest non-stop Milan Centrale–Rome Termini trip to 2 hours 59 minutes. It was a very special occasion as it marked completion of the stem of the 'Grand T'. Apart from the Florence cross-city tunnel, high-speed infrastructure stretched all the way from Turin to Salerno via Milan, Bologna, Florence, Rome and Naples.

The occasion was formally acknowledged a week before when Milan hosted a celebration attended by now disgraced Prime Minister Silvio Berlusconi. Two special ETR500 trains carrying VIPs had converged on the city from each end of the route, with Berlusconi riding the train from Turin along with Moretti and FS holding group chief Dr Innocenza Cipolletta. Vincenzo Soprano, Trenitalia President, rode up from Salerno with RFI's Technical Director Michele Elia. Transport Minister Altero Matteoli also showed up, plus a host of other luminaries.

Still to be completed is the bar of the 'T' between Milan and Padua, the 25km section from there to Venice Mestre having opened in 2007. Upgraded or rebuilt routes are available from Bologna to Verona and Padua, and another line is in progress south from Milan to Genoa. A plan to build this 135km route was put forward by a consortium of banks, businesses and the North Milan Railway in 1990, but this was cancelled in July 1998 by Environment Minister Edo Ronchi, who cited the '*effeto bang*' of trains in the small valleys through which the line would pass as one reason for his decision. Known as the Terzo Valico route, the scheme was later resurrected, and approval for the initial section was granted in September 2003.

Yet another grand project is a line through the Alps from Turin to Lyon. This ambitious scheme, costing an estimated €8.5 billion plus a further €7 billion for access routes on the French side alone, has been talked about for decades, and trial boring for a 53km tunnel at the heart of the line has been in progress for some time. However, the scheme remains controversial, and despite numerous announcements by both the French and Italian governments that the line will be built, the cost and the limited volume of traffic on offer suggest that many years will elapse before it is finished – if ever.

Taking a tilt. The tilting ability of this ETR460 second-generation Pendolino is particularly evident as it leans into a curve. (David Campione)

TILTING TRAINS

No chapter about high-speed in Italy would be complete without mention of tilting trains. In terms of exporting trains and technology, Italian engineers developed the world's most successful tilting trains, and the term *Pendolino* has entered the English vocabulary – in Britain it describes the 200km/h tilting trains that form the mainstay of Virgin Trains' inter-city business on the busy West Coast Main Line from London to Birmingham, Manchester, Liverpool and Glasgow. Other versions can be found in Germany, Switzerland, Finland, Russia, Portugal, the Czech Republic and Slovenia. Confusingly, Alstom also markets non-tilting versions of the train as Pendolino, and these can be found in Spain, China and Poland.

The tilting concept – also adopted in Sweden, Japan and Australia and trialled in France and Switzerland – applies when there is a commercial need to accelerate services over sinuous routes; there is no need for trains to tilt on high-speed lines with large radius curves. As trains pass through curves at speed, passengers feel a force pushing them towards the outside of the curve. When the train travels through the curve faster than the speed at which the cant negates the centrifugal force, a 'cant deficiency' arises. Tilting compensates for the deficiency by moving the car body; this can be passive or active with hydraulic or electric actuation. Experience showed that fine judgement in tuning the tilt mechanism to the curve was essential, otherwise passengers would

suffer from what is known as 'tilt nausea'. Tilt trains have bodyshells that taper inwards towards the top so that a tilted vehicle does not protrude beyond the envelope specified for a moving train on the track.

Fiat Ferroviaria of Savigliano became famous for its tilting technology when it experimented with a single car using a concept developed by Professor Franco di Mayo in 1970–71. Around 50,000km of trial runs prompted Fiat to construct in 1975–76 a four-car ETR401 set that confirmed the feasibility of tilting trains on some of Italy's most sinuous main lines. There was a long pause before this translated into commercial action, but in 1987 FS unveiled a small fleet of ETR450 tilting trains that were pressed into service on the Rome–Milan corridor

Shapely in the curve. One of Trenitalia's ETR600 tilting trains on a *Frecciargento* service takes advantage of its tilting technology on the old main line between Florence and Bologna on 16 June 2009. (David Campione)

the following year. At that time only part of the *direttissima* was open, and here the ETR450 drivers could open up to 250km/h. On the rest of the route the tilt mechanism was used to help achieve a timing of 3 hours 58 minutes by taking curves faster than conventional trains; this gave an end-to-end average speed of 153km/h. Before long, FS managers eased the timing out to 4 hours 5 minutes, but the principle of high-speed running over old railways to gain valuable minutes had been established.

In 1995, a second-generation Pendolino followed, still only equipped for 3kV DC operation, and again limited to 250km/h. Styled by Giugiaro, this was the ETR460, which had wider bodies than the ETR450 and other refinements such as three-phase asynchronous motors; three similar trains were fitted to operate through the Alps to Lyon in France. Next, around 1996, came the ETR470, nine of which were designed to run from Milan to Zurich, Geneva and Basle in Switzerland. Their tilting ability was severely tested on the Gotthard main line, famed for its spiral curves. Unfortunately, partly because of maintenance problems, the ETR470 trains developed a reputation for unreliability, and current plans will see them withdrawn within a few years.

The ETR480, mechanically similar to the ETR460 but able to take power at 25kV 50Hz on the AV/AC lines, entered service in 1998; these trains underwent a renovation programme, re-emerging in 2005 as the ETR485. In the meantime, Alstom acquired Fiat Ferroviaria in 2000.

A third-generation Pendolino appeared in 2008/09. As with the ETR460/470, there were two versions: the ETR600 for domestic duties, and the tri-voltage ETR610 to run into Switzerland. The ETR610 fleet was ordered from Alstom Ferroviaria in February 2004 at a cost of SFr450 million, and delivery was much later than expected. When the first of these seven-car trains entered service on 20 July 2009 working the 5.45 a.m. from Geneva to Milan, the tilt was locked out of use. The Swiss safety regulator was concerned that the 450-tonne trains would impose excessive forces on the track when curving at speed. This issue was resolved in 2011, and a second batch of eight trains was ordered in July 2012, followed by four more in February 2015.

However, the ETR610 fleet may soon vanish from the Gotthard route. The Swiss government has been trying to switch freight transiting between Germany and Italy from lorries to trains, and this entailed construction of two long deep-level tunnels through the Alps. Both the Lötschberg base tunnel, which opened in 2007, and the Gotthard base tunnel, which will open in December 2016, are designed to be shared by passenger trains at 250km/h. While the ETR610 can, in theory at least, use the Lötschberg bore at this speed, Swiss Federal Railways decided to order twenty-nine new non-tilting trains for routes via the Gotthard base tunnel. A SFr980 million contract was signed on 9 May 2014 with Stadler Rail, a Swiss-based rolling stock builder. When they replace the ETR610 sets on the Milan–Zurich and Milan–Basle routes from December 2019, the new trains will run at no more than 249km/h; under European regulations, more onerous technical standards apply at 250km/h. Swiss Railways has an option for another ninety sets, which could see the Stadler trains running into Germany, our next destination.

6

ICE Lifts the Market

'Today is a fantastic day for us, with a new train, on a new line, with a new signalling system.' Chairman of Deutsche Bahn Hartmut Mehdorn's voice booms across the concourse of Frankfurt-am-Main Hauptbahnhof where a throng of guests has just checked in for the 11.35 a.m. departure to Cologne (Köln). It is 25 July 2002, and Mehdorn is thanking national and local government, his own staff, and DB's suppliers and contractors for helping to bring about the long-held ambition of building a high-speed railway between Frankfurt and Cologne. His speech is followed by tributes from Transport Minister Kurt Bodewig and a photocall with Doris Schröder-Köpf, wife of German Chancellor Gerhard Schröder, who had been detained in Berlin for an urgent cabinet meeting following the dismissal of his defence minister.

Guests are invited to board ICE 18812, a special sixteen-car train waiting at Platform 3. Security is tight, and the train is screened from a curious public by an identical train parked on the opposite side of the red-carpeted platform. Green-uniformed police with dogs and plain clothes security types are on patrol as the crowd crocodiles along the platform. Media folk jostle at the head of the train to capture pictures of Kurt, Doris and Hartmut posing in front of the immaculate front end, but red-coated platform staff are already indicating that it is time to board.

Coffee and refreshments are served as departure is announced. The doors slide shut with a solid clunk and, on the dot of the appointed hour, the train starts to move. Accelerating on to a flyover, we glimpse the spaghetti of tracks outside the station, and cynics among the journalists aboard wonder about the economics of rows of idle locomotives outside a depot below us. Hurrying through the suburbs, we spot green-and-white police vehicles beside the line and a chopper shadowing our progress. At 11.47 a.m. we glimpse the glass cupola that dominates the architecture of Frankfurt Airport station. Drinks are served as we bowl merrily along Germany's newest railway.

The front of another ICE suddenly noses alongside. It is packed with imbibing passengers who wave and lift their glasses as the two trains synchronise their speed. By 11.50 a.m. the pair of trains is streaking along at precisely the same

Dashing duo. Deutsche Bahn used twin pairs of ICE 3s running in parallel to inaugurate the Cologne–Frankfurt and Nuremberg–Ingolstadt high-speed lines. Laid with slab track throughout, these are Germany's only routes where 300km/h is permitted. (Deutsche Bahn AG)

speed – and we are still accelerating. At midday exactly DB announces we are travelling at 300km/h.

Our new neighbours turn out to be the lucky winners of a competition run by the tabloid *Bild-Zeitung*, which reports the next day that 750 readers rode a special train inaugurating the 177km new railway. It is a whopping publicity coup for DB – *Bild* was thought to have 4.2 million readers. We race through tunnels under the Taunus hills and tear through the station at Limburg. Sound barriers momentarily blot out the view of the parallel A3 *Autobahn*, where cars and lorries appear motionless as we flit past.

A sudden change of pace indicates we are braking for our scheduled stop at Montabaur, a town with around 9,000 inhabitants who had enough clout to insist on their own station on the new line. The two trains slide to a stand at platforms crowded with some of the 9,000. Security is being taken seriously, and long rakes of strategically parked freight wagons hide our train from motorists on the *Autobahn*. On the platform the town band strikes up, but its valiant efforts are drowned in an unequal battle with a hovering helicopter. VIPs are allowed out on to the platform to listen to speeches by local luminaries and to sign the town's 'Golden Book'. Members of the public beg to join us, but our 12.16 p.m. departure time has already passed. It is 12.21 p.m. before the trains restart under a grey sky, swiftly resuming our synchronised process towards Cologne.

On through the Westerwald hills, where the new line's continuous concrete slab track and singular 4 per cent gradients are especially evident. Their presence means that trains like ours, a pair of third-generation ICEs, are the only ones permitted to use the route. Distributed power driving half the train's sixty-four axles with 16MW available ensures that we could start from a standstill even on the steepest grade. At 12.36 p.m. we storm past

the nearly finished station at Siegburg (actually called Siegburg/Bonn), whose 42,000 population better justifies calls by Germany's fastest trains.

With a design speed of 330km/h, the ICE 3 is a technical pioneer. Stopping high-speed trains is arguably more important than starting them, and our train has eddy-current rail brakes that, in combination with conventional electrodynamic braking plus wheel- and axle-mounted discs, can halt it on the sharp downgrade. Mounted in the trailer bogies are electromagnets which can be energised and lowered to leave a 7mm air gap between the magnet and the rail. A braking force is generated by using the rail head as a reaction member in a similar way to a linear motor, with eddy currents induced in the rails by the electromagnet.

Use of the silent, wear-free eddy-current brakes in commercial service is restricted to the Cologne–Frankfurt high-speed line and the similarly equipped line from Nuremberg (Nürnberg) to Ingolstadt that opened in May 2006; versions of the ICE 3 designed for cross-border trips may also deploy the system on their way to Paris over LGV Est.

The restrictions are needed because the magnetic fields can affect wayside devices such as axle counters and other signalling equipment. In Belgium, for example, passage of an ICE 3 using eddy-current brakes was found to rip open the metal covers of plant embedded in the track. Precautions must also be taken to manage the problem of rails heating up after successive trains deploy their eddy-current brakes at the same location.

Back on board, Mehdorn, whose brief at the helm of Germany's national railway was to knock it into shape for sale to the private sector, passes through the train. As it turned out, privatisation had to be abandoned because of the economic downturn in 2008, and Mehdorn's cost-cutting agenda left a legacy from which some critics would say DB has never recovered. Reporters and

photographers jostle around the great man, but the time for interviews is nearly over as we are now slowing for the approach to Cologne.

We part company with the *Bild-Zeitung* revellers somewhere near Porz and wind our way past buddleia-sprouting sidings towards the twin spires of Cologne Cathedral that tower over the main station. Rumbling over the Rhine on the Hohenzollern Bridge, we draw to a halt at Platform 1 in Cologne Hauptbahnhof as the station clock ticks up to 1 p.m. Disembarking guests are ushered past a group of protesters waving placards about 'electrosmog' to a square in front of the cathedral where Jürgen Möller, Mayor of Cologne, delivers a welcome speech.

Moments later, a thunderous blast of drums and cymbals announces the start of a concert starring pop idol Sasha. Sixty minutes later, as the climax approaches, security teams carve a path through the crowd for the morning's missing guest. The music subsides and Gerhard Schröder, freshly arrived from Berlin, takes the stage. Hinting at future contracts for Siemens, he refers to the ICE 3 as 'an export hit' – see the next chapter. Meanwhile, red-coated ladies are already pointing the way back to the station; departure for Frankfurt is at 3.30 p.m.

The backdrop for Sasha's concert was a gigantic red figure one. Similar 'red ones' were evident on the station roof at Frankfurt and at strategic spots en route – and mingling with the crowd at Frankfurt were girls wearing human-size red figure ones. DB had chosen the figure to symbolise the 1-hour time saving achieved by the new line.

Over the traditional route between Cologne and Frankfurt DB's InterCity trains took 2 hours 16 minutes, rolling at a sedate pace along the castle-strewn Rhine Valley, while a trip over the A3 *Autobahn* could be accomplished in around 1 hour 20 minutes. The standard timing for ICE 3 shuttle services starting in August 2002 via the new line was 1 hour 16 minutes. '*Die Bahn schenkt*

Ihnen eine Stunde' ('the railway is giving you an hour') ran DB's publicity slogan, which was rather a cop-out as the original intention was to time non-stop trains between the two city centre stations at 1 hour or even 58 minutes. This proved to be impossible after local politicians put pressure on DB to halt services at one or other of the three intermediate stations.

NATIONAL PLAN DELAYED

Germany's fourth high-speed line was the first to be designed for trains to run at 300km/h. In terms of transport strategy, it should probably have been the first, for there was surely an excellent business case to build a fast link connecting the industrial Rhine-Ruhr conurbation with the financial centre of Frankfurt-am-Main. The scheme was conceived by DB in the late 1960s and put forward on 28 August 1970 in the railway's submission to the national transport infrastructure plan in what was then West Germany.

Adopted by the government in 1971, the plan envisaged that 3,250km of new or upgraded routes would enhance the national network. This kicked off in August 1973 with a ceremony marking construction of the first 12.8km section of a 327km new line between Hannover and Würzburg that ran partly down the country's eastern flank. This short fragment was completed in 1979, but the rest of the programme became mired in controversy.

In 1976 Transport Minister Kurt Gscheidle sanctioned construction of a 99km Mannheim–Stuttgart route, and the government confirmed in 1977 that the rest of Hannover–Würzburg would follow in stages; a decision on Cologne–Frankfurt was deferred. Only in 1985 was it included in the national transport infrastructure plan. The government agreed DB's preferred route on 19 July 1989, although uncertainty remained over how, or if, the town of Coblence (Koblenz) in the *Land*

of Rheinland-Pfalz would be served. The alignment finally agreed with DB in 1991 ran entirely east of the Rhine, although Coblence extracted a promise that it would continue to be served by InterCity trains. Only in 1995 did the project go out to tender, with Transport Minister Matthias Wissmann and DB chief Heinz Dürr presiding at a start-of-work event at Frankfurt Airport on 13 December. Speaking in a tent sheltering guests from an icy wind, Wissmann described the DM7.75 billion project as 'the bread-and-butter route of the twenty-first century'.

The long delay in moving from lines on maps to construction partly reflected the generous parameters chosen for the new routes. DB wanted them to carry both freight and high-speed passenger trains. But the presence of freight trains ruled out steep gradients, meaning that numerous tunnels and viaducts were necessary through hilly country. Not only that, but passing loops had to be incorporated where freight trains could lay over while passenger services zipped by. The mixed traffic formula was abandoned for the Cologne–Frankfurt line as it was cheaper to go up and over rather than through the hilly terrain, but even then thirty tunnels totalling nearly 47km had to be cut.

On the Hannover–Würzburg line especially, the presence of many long tunnels and magnificent viaducts underlines its dual purpose. The main issue causing delay, however, was the lengthy two-stage planning process, which in the case of the Gemünden–Würzburg section took five years. Finding acceptable routes through a landscape dotted with towns and villages was problematic, and opponents fought hard to halt or postpone the projects. In many cases DB was obliged to erect high lineside sound barriers.

Test trains limbered up on the Mannheim–Stuttgart line in February 1987, and a special train inaugurated the first section on 31 May. It was not until 1991, however, that passengers in Germany were able to sample long-distance

high-speed rail travel. On 2 June DB launched IC91, a sweeping timetable recast built around ICE services travelling at 250km/h on the two new lines; there was an understanding that they could accelerate to 280km/h to make up time. Nearly 1 hour was chopped from the Hannover–Frankfurt trip to give a 2 hours 22 minutes timing, and Hannover–Stuttgart journeys were pared down from 5 hours 37 minutes to 3 hours 45 minutes. The fastest point-to-point timing was between Hannover and Göttingen, with sixteen ICEs a day covering the 99.4km in 32 minutes at an average speed of 186.4km/h. This put Germany in third place after France and Japan in the league table of the world's fastest commercial services.

DB's timetable plans had been knocked for six by reunification in 1990, which required various cities in the former East Germany to be joined to the IC network. The timetable launch was further compromised by DB having only twenty-five out of sixty ICE train sets available. One set was delivered just two days before it was pressed into service, so it came as no surprise to learn that the first few weeks of ICE operations were plagued by teething troubles with doors, toilets and kitchen equipment. More serious were issues with fault diagnosis software flagging up minor snags as major problems. DB's staff grappled successfully with all this, and the ICE began to earn the reputation it deserved.

The ICEs were descended from the IC-Experimental, a research train completed in 1985 that was intended to help make up for lost time in developing high-speed technology. As we saw in Chapter 1, the IC-Experimental put Germany back in the race with a noteworthy speed record in November 1985. By this time, however, TGVs had been astounding passengers for four years, and German politicians were aware that their country's own prowess in the field of high-speed rail travel was lagging.

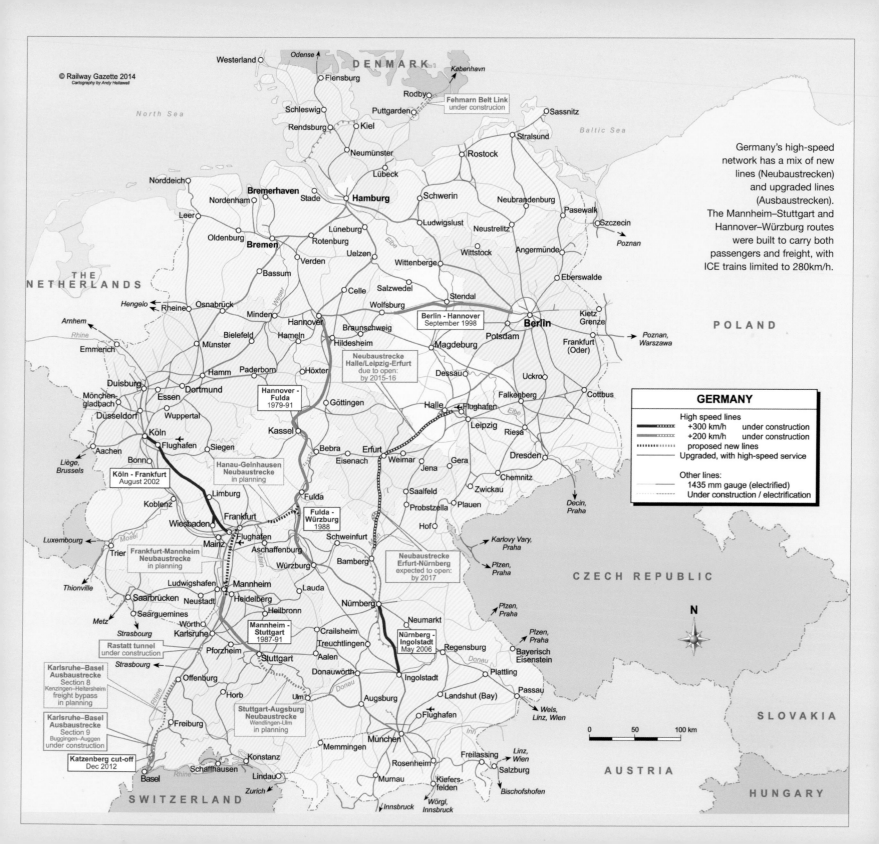

© Railway Gazette 2014
Cartography by Andy Hellawell

DENMARK

Odense ↑

København

North Sea

Baltic Sea

Fehrman Belt Link
under construcion

THE NETHERLANDS

POLAND

Poznan, Warszawa →

Germany's high-speed network has a mix of new lines (Neubaustrecken) and upgraded lines (Ausbaustrecken). The Mannheim–Stuttgart and Hannover–Würzburg routes were built to carry both passengers and freight, with ICE trains limited to 280km/h.

Berlin - Hannover
September 1998

Berlin

Neubaustrecke Halle/Leipzig-Erfurt
due to open:
by 2015-16

Hannover - Fulda
1979-91

Köln - Frankfurt
August 2002

Hanau-Gelnhausen Neubaustrecke
in planning

Fulda - Würzburg
1988

Neubaustrecke Erfurt-Nürnberg
expected to open:
by 2017

Frankfurt-Mannheim Neubaustrecke
in planning

CZECH REPUBLIC

Mannheim - Stuttgart
1987-91

Nürnberg - Ingolstadt
May 2006

Rastatt tunnel
under construction

Karlsruhe–Basel Ausbaustrecke
Section 8
Kenzingen–Heitersheim
freight bypass
in planning

Karlsruhe–Basel Ausbaustrecke
Section 9
Buggingen–Auggen
under construction

Katzenberg cut-off
Dec 2012

Stuttgart-Augsburg Neubaustrecke
Wendlingen-Ulm
in planning

N

SLOVAKIA

0   50   100 km

AUSTRIA

HUNGARY

SWITZERLAND

GERMANY

High speed lines
+300 km/h   under construction
+200 km/h   under construction
proposed new lines
Upgraded, with high-speed service

Other lines:
1435 mm gauge (electrified)
Under construction / electrification

SPACE AND COMFORT

When the first generation InterCity Express emerged on a press run from Fulda to Würzburg on 28 February 1991, it immediately commanded attention. Between the two hunky power cars with their three-phase drives and a mass of power electronics to condition DB's 15kV 16.7Hz power supply were thirteen stylish trailers with a ribbon of mirror-glass windows setting off an off-white paint scheme with a waist-level red and pink stripe. The power cars had steel bodies and the trailers were formed of long welded aluminium extruded profiles.

The accommodation in first and second class was plush and spacious. Passengers had a choice of saloons or compartments, with wardrobes and luggage lockers to stow belongings. Wide inter-car gangways were easy to walk through, even with luggage, and automatic glass doors slid aside at the entrance to saloons or corridors. A four-seat conference compartment and a small office with a fax machine were available in one car, and between first and second class was a waiter-service diner with an extravagantly high roof lit by skylights with wooden blinds; naturally, draught beer was on tap.

The ICE 1 fleet was built by a Siemens-led consortium embracing much of the national rolling stock industry. Even at this stage there looked to be good prospects for further orders as DB's engineers were planning second-generation versions for different markets, including cross-border services to France, Austria and Switzerland.

During the press trip, engineers expressed concern about a drumming vibration experienced in parts of the train when running at speed. The bogie suspension consisted of steel coils rather than air springs, and this seemed to be relevant. Damage to the rail surface by freight trains came under suspicion, but fine tuning of the suspension and adjustments to the track were expected to sort the problem. As it happened, the drumming had major significance.

Passengers were duly impressed by the addition to DB's rolling stock fleet, and the word ICE (pronounced ee-tsay-ay) quickly entered the German vocabulary. There was some resentment at having to pay higher prices for ICE travel but, as in other countries, DB found that its clientele valued faster journeys and was willing to pay for them.

In 1992 DB invited bids for up to sixty more trains classified as ICE 2. To provide more flexibility than the long ICE 1 sets, these were eight-car trains with a single power car and a driving trailer at the other end. The DM2.2 billion contract announced on 17 August 1993 went to a grouping of Siemens, AEG and Deutsche Waggonbau. Again, lightweight aluminium trailers cars were chosen, but this time with air-sprung bogies. Other changes from the ICE 1 included lighter seats, partitions instead of compartments, and better information displays.

In 1994 the ICE fleet carried nearly 22 million passengers. The trains' popularity, future expansion plans and the need to replace elderly stock on IC routes led DB to binge on new train procurement. On 22 August it disclosed that it was placing contracts worth DM3 billion, with options worth another DM2.5 billion. Heading the list of orders were fifty third-generation ICE sets officially known as ICE 2/2 as they formed an option to the previous year's ICE 2 contract. The main part of the deal covered thirty-seven units for domestic

Bright and white. The long formation of an ICE 1 emerges from a bridge at Hamburg Veddel on 17 May 2010. (Christoph Müller)

routes, plus forays into Austria and Switzerland, whose rail networks share the same power supply. Four sets were to be equipped with 1.5kV DC and 25kV 50Hz traction equipment; these would be used primarily for services to Amsterdam. Another nine would be fitted additionally to take 3kV DC power so that they could reach Brussels.

Next on the shopping list was a fleet of thirty-two seven-car and eleven five-car 230km/h tilting ICE trains to be built by the IC-NeiTech consortium of Siemens, DWA, Duewag and Fiat Ferroviaria; their tilting gear is based on that equipping Italy's ETR460 and its derivatives.

Although the ICE 2/2 was an option to the earlier order, the trains bore little resemblance to the ICE 1 and ICE 2. The essential difference was distributed power. It also emerged that only forty-four ICE 2 sets had been built under the 1993 order for sixty trains, plus the equivalent of three more supplied as individual cars. This left thirteen trains which morphed into the multi-current versions of the ICE 2/2 order. All this appeared to be a stratagem to get round European requirements to put new orders out to international tender, and by 1997 Heinz Kurz, chief engineer responsible for the technical design

of DB's fixed formation long-distance trains, was referring to the third-generation fleet as ICE 3.

Many of the ICE 3's components, including the eddy-current brakes, were tested on a five-car lash-up known as ICE-S. Formed of a pair of ICE 2 power cars, two intermediate vehicles with different versions of ICE 3 traction equipment and a laboratory car, its 13.6MW power rating was enough to accelerate it up to 393km/h on one occasion.

The first complete ICE 3 was demonstrated on the Siemens test loop at Wegberg-Wildenrath, once the site of a Cold War airfield used by Britain's Royal Air Force. On 9 July 1999 a trip round the 160km/h loop afforded the chance to examine the stylish interior in five fully fitted cars. Spacious seating in both classes, wood trim and panelling matched with chrome and glass partitions gave an impression of luxury. A twenty-four-seat dining area and bar-bistro occupied one centre car, but the greatest attraction was undoubtedly at the sharp end: behind the cab was a lounge with a glass screen affording a view over the driver's shoulder to the track ahead. Should the driver need to block the view, the touch of a button suffices to obscure a photo-electric layer in the glass.

On that occasion Kurz assured me that the four-system version, which had six pantographs to cope with power supplies in different countries, was intended to run to Paris from 2001 or 2002; discussions with SNCF had begun in 1995. The price of a 415-seat domestic set, I was told, was DM36 million; an extra DM5 million would buy the four-system version. Later, the trains were refitted with more seats, perhaps reflecting DB's drive to become a more entrepreneurial company after its 1994 restructuring from a federal agency (Deutsche Bundesbahn) into a joint stock company (Deutsche Bahn) – which incidentally required changes to the German constitution.

Journey's end. The driving trailer of an ICE 2 push-pull formation brings up the rear of a train from Berlin at Cologne Hauptbahnhof on 25 September 2014. The train had split at Hamm, with the other portion, formed of an identical ICE 2, serving Dortmund and Düsseldorf.

TILTING WITH ELEGANCE

On 3 April 1998 around 1,500 people assembled at the DWA rolling stock plant in Görlitz to witness the roll-out of DB's first series-built tilting high-speed train, the ICE-T. The factory had just been absorbed into the Canadian-owned Bombardier empire, and its claim to fame was construction in 1933 of the legendary *Fliegender Hamburger* diesel railcar set; the event saw the ICE-T posed next to its illustrious forebear.

Like the ICE 3, the ICE-T had distributed power and styling by industrial designer Alexander Neumeister; the ICE 3's elegant furnishings and see-through cab were also perpetuated. The 230km/h top speed was mainly for use when pathed between its ICE sisters on high-speed lines, but its main task was to shorten timings on regional inter-city routes such as Dresden

Built to tilt. Two of Deutsche Bahn's elegant ICE-T Class 411 sets head up the Frankenwaldrampe on the way from Leipzig to Munich. The tilting system was switched out of use in October 2008. (Deutsche Bahn AG/Jochen Schmidt)

to Saarbrücken and Stuttgart to Zurich. Later, the trains were deployed between Hamburg and Berlin, where the track was fettled up for their 230km/h design speed.

For routes without wires DB ordered a score of four-car tilting diesel ICEs with underfloor engines. Designated ICE-TD or Class 405, they had a maximum speed of 200km/h and were fitted with a novel electrically operated tilt mechanism. Entering service in 2001 after lengthy commissioning delays, their history is a sorry tale of technical hitches that saw them pulled out of service on several occasions. One set holds the German speed record for a diesel train, attaining 222km/h between Hannover and Göttingen, but another was written off in 2001 after an accident in Hof depot. They were finally put out to grass while a foreign buyer was sought, but no one wanted such trouble-prone creatures.

In 2006 some sets were restored to working order and pressed back into service, in two cases as charter trains for visiting football teams during that year's World Cup. In the following year a few ICE-TDs finally found a home on the Hamburg–Copenhagen route, where, leased to Danish state operator DSB, they ran tilt-less and won over clientele with their comfortable accommodation.

On 16 February 2001 DB announced that it was planning to top up its ICE train orders with thirteen more ICE 3s and another twenty-eight ICE-T sets. Five of the thirteen ICEs were intended to work into France. Around the same time DB confirmed that it was testing new lightweight bogies under an ICE 2 and on an E2 train set in Japan as part of a joint research programme with JR East, suggesting that a next-generation ICE was making progress. In 1997 DB had considered adopting a 3.3m wide body for a theoretical ICE 4 to fit five seats across the car width, but the idea came to nothing.

BEYOND THE BORDERS

Taking advantage of the European Commission's attempts to foster competition on Europe's rail networks, DB set out to capture some of the traffic between Brussels, Cologne and Frankfurt with ICE 3 sets making three round trips a day. These were introduced from 2002, competing for traffic with Thalys services, which since 1996/97 had been jointly run by the national railways of Belgium and France. In fact, DB had a small interest in Thalys, but in 2013 it announced that it would relinquish its 10 per cent stake.

Initially, the ICE 3s were not permitted on Belgium's high-speed lines, and maximum speed on the traditional route wired at 3kV DC was limited to 160km/h, adding around 15 minutes to the journey. In 2003, trials with ICE 3 sets began on the high-speed line, but a run at 270km/h in December that year had to be cut short because chunks of ballast were flung up by air turbulence below the train, damaging pipes and other underfloor equipment. The upshot was a series of modifications, with spoilers and shields fitted to protect sensitive kit below the floor. The Belgian track was also modified to allow the ICE 3s to deploy their eddy-current brakes.

A similar tale applied to DB's ambitions to send ICE 3s to Paris. Trials took place in 2001–05 for extended periods over various routes, including the Lille–Calais section of LGV Nord. Dealing with flying ballast was a particular concern; it was less of a problem on DB's high-speed lines as three of them were laid with long sections of slab track, while in France the TGV fleet was less vulnerable as it had been designed from the outset for ballasted track.

To introduce high-speed services between German cities and Paris via LGV Est, DB decided to modify six ICE 3 sets and fit them with the French TVM430 and KVB train protection systems at a cost of around €8 million per train. In March 2007

International ICE. One of DB's ICE 3MF fleet heads out from Paris bound for Frankfurt-am-Main.
There are four sets of pantographs spread along the roof, reflecting the train's ability to run in several countries. (Christophe Masse)

this sub-fleet was certified to run in France, including on LGV Est at the maximum line speed of 320km/h – faster than anywhere in Germany. The ICE 3 for many years sported a 330km/h speed limit on the car bodysides, but this was never reached in commercial service in Germany.

On 25 May 2007 SNCF and DB staged a simultaneous arrival in Paris Est of an ICE 3 from Frankfurt and a TGV from Stuttgart to mark the signature of an accord with SNCF to set up the *Alleo* joint venture to manage high-speed services between the two countries. The trains ran around half an hour late, allegedly because the TGV had made an unscheduled stop in Strasbourg to top up the water tanks and because of the presence of numerous photographers at other stops en route.

Stepping down from the ICE, DB chief Hartmut Mehdorn was greeted by SNCF President Anne-Marie Idrac, who declared that the move was all about 'increasing our market share against road and air'. Commercial services between Paris, Frankfurt and Stuttgart using a mix of TGVs and the modified ICE 3s (classified ICE 3MF) were launched on 10 June 2007, with more added the following December. Around twelve years had elapsed since DB first approached SNCF about its planned high-speed service to Paris. Unfortunately, the ICE 3MF fleet developed a reputation for unreliability, and for a time the Frankfurt services were operated by TGV-POS train sets after one of the modified ICEs was written off following a collision with a road vehicle near Saarbrücken.

UNITING THE NATION

As part of Germany's reunification programme, in the 1990s the government authorised seventeen major transport schemes intended to unite the country's two halves. The core of Unity Project 4 was a DM5.1 billion high-speed railway over the 263km between Hannover and Berlin. Backdrop for the start-of-work ceremony on 11 November 1992 was the River Elbe at Hämerten, where a new bridge was to be erected. Part of the line consists of tracks upgraded for 250km/h, but a new line runs for 153km between Staaken, just west of Berlin, and Oebisfelde.

DB chose to adopt ballast-less track for 180km along the route. As there was no obviously superior design, several types were installed.

Another innovation were forty-five sets of points with clothoidal turnouts whose long point blades were driven by six motors; the design meant that trains could take the diverging track at 160km/h. As with all other German lines where trains exceed 160km/h, the route has the standard inductive train control known as LZB (*Linienzugbeeinflussung*).

New lines often spell controversy, and in the case of Hannover–Berlin the culprit was a colony of great bustards. These gigantic birds had lived happily next to the old railway, but wildlife organisations insisted on special protection measures where the new line passed near the nesting site. A tunnel was rejected as too costly, and a compromise led to high bunds being built on each side of the tracks so that the bustards would not fly into the overhead wires. Similar structures were erected at other locations where migrant birds were likely to be present. Quite remarkably, long sections of this and other German high-speed lines are unfenced.

German Chancellor Helmut Kohl presided at a party on 15 September 1998 to mark completion of Berlin's high-speed link to the west, and public services rolled over the route with that year's timetable change on 27 September. The day just happened to coincide with the national election that unseated Kohl.

Unity Project 8 is a new or upgraded railway all the way from Nuremberg to Berlin that is intended to shorten the trip between the capital and Munich to less than 4 hours. In 2014 the best timing between the two main stations was slightly over 6 hours. Included in this DM8.5 billion scheme is 83km of upgrading from Nuremberg to Ebensfeld, a 107km section of new line from there to Erfurt, another new segment between Erfurt and Leipzig (113km), and 8km of upgrading between Schkopau and Halle.

Federal Transport Minister Matthias Wissmann and his counterpart from the *Land* of Bavaria Otto Wiesheu cut the first sod on 16 April 1996, but the event, also attended by DB Chairman Heinz Dürr, was interrupted by booing, shouting and whistling from protesters who wanted no new construction through the Thüringer Wald – despite an autobahn also being built there. In time, many of the objections were dealt with, but progress was slow. It became even slower in 1999 when the government scythed through the project's budget, effectively bringing it to a halt.

Work continued on tunnels and viaducts that had already started, and for years many of these stood as isolated 'investment ruins' dotted across the landscape, as *Railway Gazette*'s correspondent Ralf Roman Rossberg described them. In 2002 Chancellor Schröder felt obliged to restart the project during his election campaign, and DB resumed work so that rights for the line did not lapse. But only in 2007 did the government agree to release €400 million a year to keep the project going. Funds were also sought from the European Union, but the scale of work – there are twenty-two tunnels totalling 41km and twenty-nine bridges and viaducts with a combined length of 12km between Erfurt and Ebensfeld alone – and the slow rate of progress mean that completion is not expected until 2017.

South of Nuremberg, DB was more fortunate. An 89km new line built for 300km/h was completed in May 2006 in time for the soccer World Cup the following month. Once more, DB deployed the publicity tactic of a parallel run with two pairs of ICE 3s for the inauguration on 13 May. The 171km trip from Nuremberg to Munich via the new line to Ingolstadt and upgraded tracks from there to the Bavarian capital took around 67 minutes by ICE in 2014. DB was appointed official carrier during the World Cup, and it won many accolades for the efforts it made to handle fans and visitors travelling to the sixty-four matches at German stadia.

ANOTHER RECORD

On 2 September 2006 the line played host to over 1,000 photographers and onlookers who had come to see an attempt made on the world speed record for locomotives. The machine chosen to capture the crown worn by a pair of French locomotives since 1955 was Siemens-built 'Taurus' No 1216-050. The event kicked off at Kinding with a ceremony at which the town's mayor, Rita Böhm, named the locomotive *Kinding-Altmühltal*. The locomotive, sporting a special grey livery adorned with sponsors' names and logos, was then dispatched for the first of two record attempts. On the second trip the locomotive eclipsed the 1955 figure by accelerating up to 357km/h during a dash to Allersberg, 34km away.

In contrast to the 1955 event when French engineers were peering into the unknown, on this occasion everyone involved was confident that a new record was well within the capabilities of both train and track. Owned by Austrian Federal Railways, the Taurus had not been significantly modified. To record the exploit for posterity, it hauled a single measurement car on which thirty-two engineers and observers were travelling. Another six were crammed into the locomotive's cab, including driver Axel Dworaczek who had been instrumental in setting up the record attempt. The maximum was reached near Hilpoltstein at 4.02 p.m. and held for around 4 minutes.

Immediately afterwards, staff quickly added large yellow figure 5s and 7s to the 3s already in position on the locomotive nose and bodyside before it returned to Kinding for the waiting film crews and photographers. Huge interest was generated by the presence there of French locomotives CC7107 and BB9004, which had been awoken from their slumbers in the Cité du Train museum at Mulhouse and hauled to Germany for the occasion.

The entire event took place without disrupting DB's normal services. This was not too difficult as the only trains on the line were two-hourly ICE services. Not until the following December did DB introduce a full service, which included two-hourly regional trains timed at 200km/h that called at Kinding and Allersberg.

Several of Germany's other new line projects are on hold, but work is advancing on a 60km line between Wendlingen, south-east of Stuttgart, and Ulm, about half of which will be in tunnel. When the 250km/h alignment opens in 2021, Stuttgart–Ulm services will no longer have to ascend the famous Geislinger Steige, where in the days of steam – and even after that – heavy trains required assistance from banking engines. At its western end the line feeds into a new route, partly in tunnel, that will serve the future underground main-line station in Stuttgart. The Stuttgart–Ulm trip will come down from 54 to 28 minutes.

Of all the new railway schemes in Germany, the related Stuttgart 21 project to replace the dead-end terminus with an underground through station is the most controversial. Partly because of the cost, and partly because a wing of the historic terminus was demolished, Stuttgart 21 drew unprecedented protests in 2011–12. These made international headlines, and DB was forced to review the whole concept. The cost had risen to €5.6 billion, far beyond the original estimate, and there were suggestions in 2013 that DB was continuing only because cancellation would have been more expensive.

DISASTER

No history of Germany's ICE trains would be complete without some account of the awful events of 3 June 1998. On that morning an ICE 1 set forming service ICE 884 *Wilhelm Conrad Röntgen* left Munich at 5.47 a.m. bound for Hamburg, which it was due to reach at 11.52 a.m. It never arrived.

The train left Hannover at 10.30 a.m. with around 300 passengers. Soon after passing through the station at Celle some passengers were alarmed by loud banging and rattling from beneath the train. It took a few moments to alert the conductor, who apparently spent precious minutes hurrying along the train to ascertain what had happened as it forged on at close to the line's maximum speed of 200km/h. Before the conductor could take action, disaster struck.

The noise below turned out to be caused by a fragment of a wheel tyre breaking off from the third axle of the leading trailer car. For around 5km the train ran on unaffected, but it then encountered a set of points about 300m before a road bridge over the tracks near Eschede station. The damaged wheel struck the pointwork, forcing an 8m check rail upwards through the floor of one of the coaches, which at once began to derail. The second bogie of the third car was diverted by the points on to another track so that the car was running diagonally along two parallel tracks. By great misfortune part of this car struck one of the bridge piers, causing the bridge to collapse on to the train. The first four trailer cars had already passed the bridge, with the leading three remaining more or less upright and

Euro Sprinter. On 2 September 2006 Siemens-built 'Taurus' locomotive 1216-050 claimed the world speed record for locomotives from SNCF's BB9004 with a dash from Kinding to Allersberg on the Nuremberg–Ingolstadt high-speed line. It is seen here during the record-breaking run before the '5' and '7' were affixed to the front and bodysides. (Siemens)

the fourth overturning to one side of the tracks. The rear of the fifth trailer was sliced off by the falling bridge, and the sixth was crushed beneath it. The rest of the train smashed into the bridge that now lay across the tracks and jackknifed against it.

It was a scene of utter horror and devastation; ninety-eight passengers, one member of staff and two track workers were killed, and many more passengers were seriously injured. Over 1,000 people took part in the rescue operation, and the line through Eschede did not reopen until 9 June. This was Germany's worst rail accident since 1945, and some of the consequences were still evident in 2014.

To deal with the drumming felt in some ICE 1 cars from the start of commercial operations, DB had decided to replace the solid monobloc wheels with a design that incorporated a resilient insert and an outer tyre. Initially fitted on the ICE 1's restaurant cars, it was installed on the fleet's other trailer cars from 1992. Similar wheels had been fitted to trams in Hannover, but that was clearly a low-speed application. DB's choice of the resilient wheel design for high-speed running was not an issue for six years, and DB stated in 2000 that wheels of this type had accumulated about 10 billion km in service before the accident.

DB was responding to an official report prepared by the Fraunhofer Institute for the Public Prosecutor, which said that the wheel tyre had broken because of a crack initiated from its inner surface. This, the report said, was caused by fatigue and stresses that were excessive for the wheel in its worn condition. The authors found that, although the diameter of the wheel had not worn down to the lower limit set by DB, it had worn to the point where it should have been replaced. The limit set by DB, the report said, was out of line with the technical knowledge available at the time.

In the aftermath of the accident there was much discussion about DB's wheel-checking procedures and the phenomenon of out-of-round wheels. The wheel in question was found to exceed the out-of-roundness tolerance by 1.1mm, significantly more than specified. The problem is normally kept in check by wheel profiling – an out-of-round wheel can cause enormous dynamic loads which generate excessive stresses within the wheel.

While the focus of investigations was on the wheel, photographs of the accident showed that some of the vehicles exhibited what appeared to be an 'unzipping effect' along the longitudinal weld seams of the aluminium-bodied trailer cars. This was caused by reduced strength in the zone affected by the heat of the welding process. A similar effect had been observed in accidents in Italy in 1997, in Britain in 1999 and in Norway in 2000. This led to a research programme into aluminium welding that drew financial support from the European Commission. The work concluded in 2005 and Dennis Schut of the European Commission's Directorate-General for Research asserted at a conference in York on 7 September 2005 that 'weld unzipping has been mastered'.

On the day after the accident DB withdrew all ICE 1 trains from service for emergency wheel checks and introduced a temporary 160km/h speed limit for the remaining ICE and IC services. Despite hiring in stock from other railways, this reduced the timetable to chaos. The ICE 1 fleet went back into service at normal speed after completion of the checks, but the safety regulator, the *Eisenbahn-Bundesamt* (EBA), ordered DB to withdraw the trains again on 13 June. DB then decided to refit the entire fleet with monobloc wheels.

To put Eschede in context, over 7,500 people were killed on the German road network in 2000. It is important to note that the accident did not occur on a purpose-built high-speed railway, but on a route built in the 1840s and upgraded in the 1970s for trains to run at 200km/h. The safety record of purpose-built high-speed lines, with no level crossings and the latest technology in terms of track and structures, is, with one exception that we shall discuss in Chapter 9, superb.

Over time, DB reinstated its premium ICE services and began to restore its damaged reputation. However, on 9 July 2008 an axle broke on an ICE 3, triggering a derailment as the train was leaving Cologne Hauptbahnhof. This happened at low speed and no one was hurt. But the shadow of Eschede loomed heavily, and the EBA at once instructed DB to inspect the wheels of its ICE 3 fleet at intervals of 60,000km rather than the 300,000km that had applied until then. This played further havoc with the timetable.

Another shock came on 8 October that year when a 2mm crack was discovered in the axle of an ICE-T. The EBA decreed that ICE-T axles should be inspected every 45,000km rather than every 240,000km, at the same time tightening the axle inspection interval for ICE 3 sets to every 30,000km. On 23 October DB decided that the tilting mechanism on the ICE-T fleet should be locked out of use, which led to long delays as the trains could not keep to schedule. After consulting the trains' manufacturers, who would not agree to DB's demands, all seventy-one ICE-T trains were pulled out of service for 'additional technical checks'. This precipitated more chaos, despite valiant efforts to draft in alternative stock. The fleet resumed its duties after the checks, but the frequent wheel and axle inspections made the situation far from satisfactory.

The answer seemed to be replacement of the axles for both the ICE 3 and ICE-T fleets, but DB's negotiations with its suppliers were long drawn-out. Not only that, but the EBA proved reluctant to grant approval for a new axle design, and even by 2014 little progress had been made.

LONDON IN SIGHT

On 17 December 2008 DB signed a contract with Siemens for a further fifteen eight-car multi-voltage ICE 3 train sets for its international passenger business, which it was anxious to expand. It nursed hopes of running to the Mediterranean over France's LGV Rhin-Rhône and to London through the Channel Tunnel. However, the ICE 3s did not meet the Channel Tunnel safety rules. These specified that trains should be 400m long so that passengers could be evacuated to one of the cross-passages, which are located at 375m intervals, without having to walk outside the train. DB arranged for emergency evacuation tests in October 2010 using a pair of ICE 3s to demonstrate that passengers could leave the train safely in an emergency.

On 19 October, having finished the evacuation tests two days earlier, one of the ICE 3s travelled through the Tunnel and on to London St Pancras. DB Chairman Dr Rüdiger Grube, who had replaced Mehdorn in 2009, and German Transport Minister Dr Peter Ramsauer were received in the London terminal by UK Minister of State for Transport Theresa Villiers, and Grube said that he would like to start running ICE 3s to London in 2013, if not 2012.

London visitor. Deutsche Bahn has long held an ambition to run ICEs from Frankfurt-am-Main and Cologne to London. A demonstration trip brought this ICE 3 to St Pancras station on 19 October 2010, but no date has been set for the start of services. (Chris Jackson)

Late arriving. Deutsche Bahn's Class 407 was built for international services, but obtaining certification to run outside Germany took far longer than predicted. A test train crosses the River Loire at Orléans under 1.5kV DC catenary. Roof-mounted equipment is surrounded by curved casings to improve air flows. (Christophe Masse)

Grube had not reckoned with two factors. First was the delay in completing the fifteen additional ICE 3 sets, known as Class 407, which could be used in slightly modified form for services to Britain. This delay was the result of difficulties in obtaining certification for the trains to run in Germany, let alone in other countries. With the spectre of Eschede ever present, the EBA had become exceptionally reluctant to sign off any new trains for commercial use, and the process of obtaining approval for new stock was so long-winded that dozens, even hundreds, of new trains were at one time parked unused in sidings across Germany. Only on 20 December 2013 did the EBA accord DB permission to run the Class 407 in pairs (which DB considered commercially essential), and the first train formed of the new stock began carrying passengers on 26 December – but only within Germany.

Second was the attitude of the British customs and immigration authorities to intra-European rail travel. The UK had not signed the Schengen Agreement for free movement between countries, and the British government insisted on airport-style passport and security checks for Channel Tunnel rail passengers. Eurostar trains between London, Paris and Brussels must use special secure terminals and depots, which if replicated in Germany for the proposed thrice-daily Frankfurt–Cologne–London services, would entail considerable expense – even if the British agree to the plan. Proposals in the 1990s for overnight trains between British and German cities through the Tunnel had foundered for the same reason – and the rolling stock for this service was eventually sold to Canada. DB initially postponed the introduction of an ICE London service to 2015, but in 2014 there was no sign of DB agreeing commercially satisfactory arrangements with the British authorities.

The X generation. Deutsche Bahn's first complete ICx train emerged from its birthplace at Hennigsdorf near Berlin in December 2014 en route to the Siemens test centre at Wegberg-Wildenrath. Note the weight-saving inside-frame bogie, whose origins can be traced back to a British Rail design from the 1980s. (Bodo Schulz)

NEXT GENERATION

For domestic services DB has long planned to replace its locomotive-hauled IC trains, and after years of indecision DB finally signed a framework contract with Siemens on 9 May 2011 for up to 300 so-called ICx train sets, to be called off over a thirty-year period. The €6 billion contract envisaged 130 train sets to start with, with ninety more to follow. In the first build were two variants, one of seven cars with a top speed of 230km/h to replace the loco-hauled trains and the other consisting of ten-car sets able to run at 249km/h as replacements for ICE 1 and ICE 2, which have already undergone a major refurbishment to bring them into line with the ICE 3.

In March 2013 DB issued a variation order that will see the ICx train length increased up to twelve cars accommodating 830 passengers. Apart from various technical changes including a switch to the higher European specification for 250km/h, better standards of accommodation were specified, hopefully ensuring that the ICx will be a worthy successor to the other ICEs. Comfortable and attractive interiors are considered essential, as DB is facing new competitors following the deregulation of long-distance buses in 2013. The first complete ICx train emerged for tests in early 2015.

7

A Question of Gauge

There was a time when managers from Spanish National Railways (*Renfe, Red Nacional de Ferrocarriles Españoles*, now called Renfe Operadora) were guaranteed a laugh at business conferences. They would show a video of passengers clapping and joking on a high-speed train arriving at its destination. 'They are very happy', the presenter would say, 'because the train is late!' He or she would then proudly explain that trains were so rarely delayed on the high-speed railway from Madrid to Córdoba and Seville that Renfe offered a full refund if the train was more than 5 minutes late.

The 471.8km Madrid–Seville high-speed line signalled a revolution in Spanish transport. It was opened on 14 April 1992 by Deputy Prime Minister Narcís Serra, and on 21 April the first commercial service left Madrid Puerta de Atocha at 7 a.m. bound for Seville Santa Justa. Until then, trains in Spain had been viewed as slow, antiquated and unreliable. Worse, the railway was struggling to recover from a programme of line closures and cutbacks in 1985.

Almost overnight, the situation changed. The advent of high-speed services sporting the AVE (*Alta Velocidad Española*) brand swiftly restored pride in the national railway, and today the term AVE, pronounced ah-bay, is part of the Spanish language.

The AVE line to Seville was born out of a need to cut journey times to Andalusia. Any train travelling from Madrid to Córdoba had to negotiate a single-track bottleneck dominated by a long climb over the steeply graded Despeñaperros pass, where sharp curves restricted speeds to no more than 100 or sometimes just 70km/h.

In October 1986 an enlightened government unveiled the Railway Transport Plan, which promised to lavish over 2,000 billion pesetas on the network. Signed off in 1987, the plan allocated money for track doubling, upgrading and three new lines. All this would make the railway more productive and help it to play a part in stimulating the economy.

One of the three new lines was the 'Brazatortas cut-off', a 105km replacement for the long drag via Despeñaperros. Officially known as *Nuevo Acceso Ferroviario a Andalucia* (NAFA), it ran from Brazatortas, west of Puertollano, through Villanueva and Adamuz to Alcolea, about 8km east of Córdoba. Contractors moved on site on 5 October 1987.

Government planners had meanwhile become aware that something called the TGV was attracting new customers to rail in neighbouring France. This prompted a rethink of NAFA, leading to a decision to build a high-speed railway all the way from Madrid to Seville. In prospect was the opportunity to cut the Madrid–Córdoba trip of around 5 hours to less than 2 hours, and the go-ahead for this ambitious scheme was announced on 9 December 1987.

A critical question was the track gauge. For historical reasons the rails on Spain's national network were 1,668mm apart. High-speed trains had until then been developed only for 1,435mm gauge, and special designs for the Spanish broad gauge would incur extra development costs. So the government ruled that its new railway should match that in the rest of Europe. The line was also to be electrified at the world standard of

25kV 50Hz rather than the 3kV DC of Spain's broad-gauge network.

As Spain's railway supply industry was not geared up to build high-speed trains, rolling stock would be bought off-the-shelf from other European suppliers, and in March 1989 Renfe signed a contract with GEC Alstom for twenty-four AVE trains that were in many respects clones of the TGV Atlantique. A consortium of German and Spanish companies secured the electrification and signalling contracts, which included Germany's LZB continuous inductive train control with cab signalling.

SOUTH TO THE SIERRA

Starting from a rebuilt station at Atocha, where the old terminus was transformed into a commercial emporium based around a tropical theme, the standard-gauge line runs parallel to the broad-gauge tracks to Getafe. From there it takes over the alignment of the old line to Ciudad Real, which was closed in 1988 to permit construction of the new route. A short section parallel to the single-track Ciudad Real–Puertollano broad-gauge line comes next, and west of Puertollano the new route follows that of the Ciudad Real–Almorchón line as far as Brazatortas. From there the Brazatortas cut-off strikes through the Sierra Morena to reach Córdoba, whence it continues along the Guadalquivir Valley to Seville.

The engineering requirements for the cut-off were pretty demanding, and nearly all the line's eighteen tunnels and thirty-two viaducts are concentrated here. Gradients and curves had to be less generous, and the 300km/h line speed specified for other parts of the route was reduced to 250km/h, with the limit over the 28km from Adamuz to Villanueva set even lower at 215km/h.

There was huge pressure to complete the line by 1992 as in that year the city of Seville was hosting the Universal Expo. This warranted a special branch off the high-speed line with its own temporary expo station. King Juan Carlos I laid the first standard-gauge sleeper for the new line in 1989, and contractors worked furiously to finish the job. The cost came in at 348 billion pesetas.

Cut and dry. Building Spain's first high-speed line through the arid Sierra between Brazatortas and Córdoba was a challenge for the civil engineers. Nearly all the line's tunnels are located on this section, where one of Renfe's Talgo S-102/S-112 fleet is passing. (Renfe, Patier)

GAUGE-CHANGING TRAINS

Given the choice of 1,435mm gauge, decisions were needed on how to serve towns in Andalusia located off the new route. The answer lay in gauge-convertible Talgo technology (p104). A fleet of 200km/h Talgo 200 train sets was ordered to serve the Mediterranean resort of Málaga, plus Huelva and Cádiz – the trains would pass through gauge-changing devices at Córdoba or Majarabique near Seville. Motive power for the 1,435mm gauge trunk haul consisted of ten Class 252 locomotives from Krauss-Maffei in Germany.

On 10 October 1991 Renfe President Mercè Sala visited the GEC Alsthom factory at Belfort in Eastern France where the first AVE train set awaited her inspection. CEO Pierre Bilger was her guide as she climbed into the cab and toured the train's three classes of accommodation: *turista*, *preferente* and *club*. Chess boards were incorporated into the tables in one of the *turista* cars, and the *club* vehicle had semi-compartments resembling those on TGV Atlantique, plus an eight-seat business lounge. Ceiling-hung video screens were fitted throughout, foreshadowing the *italo* cinema cars by more than twenty years.

In reality, Renfe needed only sixteen sets for its start-up service, and the contract was renegotiated down from twenty-four trains. Four complete sets plus eight power cars were assembled in France, while the rest were put together in Spain by GEC Alsthom's subsidiaries and partner companies.

Renfe initially ran six Madrid–Seville AVEs a day each way with speed peaking at 270km/h. The AVE trip to Córdoba took 2 hours, and Seville was reached in less than 3 hours compared with over 7 hours by conventional train. Before the line opened, Renfe ferried around 357,000 passengers a year between the two cities. After twelve months, the figure had doubled, and Renfe claimed to have 50 per cent of the Madrid–Seville rail-air market. Average load factor was close to 85 per cent, and Sala asserted that by September 1994 the line had a positive cash flow and was 'close to covering its construction costs'.

A new market was also opening up. After the first six months, Renfe added some high-speed runs over the 210km between Madrid, Ciudad Real and Puertollano. Using the same S-100 sets that ran to Seville, these *Lanzadera* (shuttle) services quickly won their own clientèle.

During 1993, the S-100 fleet was joined by the gauge-changing Talgo trains. With the high-speed commuter operation, these nudged traffic up to around 3 million passengers a year. By 1994 Renfe felt confident enough to launch its 5-minute delay refund policy, securing a blaze of publicity.

Six years after France and two years ahead of Japan, from 10 September 1995 Spain became the second member of the 300 club when Renfe lifted the speed limit on part of the line to 300km/h. This put Seville just 2 hours 15 minutes away from Madrid. More travellers switched to rail so that total AVE traffic that year topped 3.8 million passengers. And out of 16,659 trains operated, Renfe reported that only ten were late enough to trigger refunds.

First generation. Renfe's S-100 and S-101 AVE trains were derived from the French TGV-Atlantique design. Set 02 is seen waiting to leave the rebuilt station at Madrid Puerta de Atocha. (Renfe, Patier)

BARCELONA NEXT

Within days of the line to Seville opening, Antonio Monfort, Director-General of Planning at the Ministry of Public Works & Transport, declared that work on a high-speed standard-gauge line from Madrid to Barcelona would commence during 1993. This was a trifle optimistic, but the government's enthusiasm for high-speed rail was clear. Compared with the route to Seville, Madrid–Barcelona was a prime business market where frequent shuttle flights dominated travel between the two cities.

Given the route's commercial importance, the rail journey was astonishingly slow: the fastest trips in 1980, just one year before France's first LGV opened, were by two return Talgo workings that trundled over the 687km in about 9 hours. A major obstacle was the sinuous single-track between Calatayud and Ricla, west of Zaragoza; single track between Zaragoza and Lleida formed another bottleneck. Various upgrades in the first half of the 1980s brought the time down to around 7 hours, and 6 hours 35 minutes was achieved in 1986.

In early 1993 the Ministry of Public Works, Transport & Environment issued another transport plan strongly favouring investment in rail; Madrid–Barcelona was top priority. With a matching standard-gauge link to the French frontier, it was seen as a way of cementing Spain's participation in the European Community. Preliminary work to replace the two single-track bottlenecks was put in hand, the idea being to lay dual-gauge track so that broad-gauge trains could take advantage of the new sections as soon as they were finished. The plan also suggested high-speed lines north from Madrid through the Sierra de Guadarrama to Valladolid and east to Albacete and Valencia. Upgrading was planned along the Mediterranean corridor from Barcelona to Valencia and from Valladolid to Vitoria and León.

At the core of the plan were target journey times for inter-city pairs, that for Madrid–Barcelona being just 2 hours 30 minutes. This meant that trains would have to sprint over the 621km of new line at an average of 248km/h, slightly faster than the 245.6km/h speed attained in 1993 by the world's fastest point-to-point service between Massy and St Pierre-des-Corps on France's LGV Atlantique. The 150-minute timing determined the design parameters, which included an unprecedented line speed of 350km/h, generous curve radii and grades no steeper than 2 per cent. Signalling would consist of Level 2 ETCS.

Whether 150 minutes would suffice to capture a worthwhile share of the business market was still not certain. Aviation had been deregulated in 1994, and competition between airlines was as fierce as ever. As AVE Managing Director Dr Juan Luis Martín Cuesta later said, Renfe would be fighting 'against one of the busiest air shuttles in the world'.

The first construction tender was awarded in October, kicking off a project that was to radically alter rail's role in the Spanish travel market. However, the mayor of Fuentes de Ebro refused to approve compulsory purchase orders for part of the alignment, and delays looked inevitable.

Changes were meanwhile afoot at a higher level, with Parliament approving the creation in 1997 of a publicly owned rail infrastructure authority known as *Gestor de Infraestructuras Ferroviarias* (GIF), reporting to the Ministry of Development. This embryonic body had a budget of 60 billion pesetas in its first year, mainly for new line construction. This became its primary role, drawing on capital sourced from the privatisation of state-owned organisations and the European Union's Cohesion Fund.

Completing the line to Barcelona was GIF's first priority, but the government was anxious to keep rail competitive on other routes before new lines could be built. The Madrid–Valencia corridor was a case in point, and Renfe ordered a fleet of ten broad-gauge three-car IC2000 tilting trains from GEC Alsthom and Fiat. Launched under the *Alaris*

brand on 16 February 1999, they were timed at 3 hours 30 minutes over the 490km, including a stop at Albacete. The market responded favourably, and in September Renfe stepped up the *Alaris* service to ten round trips.

Good progress was meanwhile being made with the Mediterranean corridor upgrade, and 16 June 1997 saw five daily return *Euromed* services launched between Barcelona and Valencia, with two continuing to and from Alicante (Alacant). The duty was allocated to six broad-gauge versions of the S-100 ordered from GEC Alsthom, along with two more standard-gauge trains to handle rising traffic to Seville.

In February 1999 Renfe received 300 billion pesetas to procure new rolling stock, including trains for the Madrid–Barcelona line. Later that year came news that Prime Minister José Malía Aznar would be allocating another large slice of state funds for high-speed rail in an updated infrastructure plan, with the EU's Cohesion Fund contributing a goodly share of the 4,700 billion pesetas to be spent in 2000–07. The plan was published on 24 January 2000, with Aznar drawing criticism for unveiling it after Parliament had been dissolved forty-eight days ahead of a general election on 12 March.

Prodigious sums were earmarked for a star-shaped network radiating from Madrid. Jáen, Málaga, Granada, Cádiz and Huelva were all to enjoy links to the Madrid–Seville line, while the regions of Rioja and Navarra would be joined to the Madrid–Barcelona line. AVE services would reach cities along the northern coast thanks to the now firmly planned line to Valladolid, while Valencia, Alicante, Murcia and Almería would also be plugged into the AVE network. Even a high-speed route to Lisbon in Portugal was included, and Minister for Development Francisco Álvarez Cascos promised that by 2007 no regional capital would be more than 4 hours from Madrid.

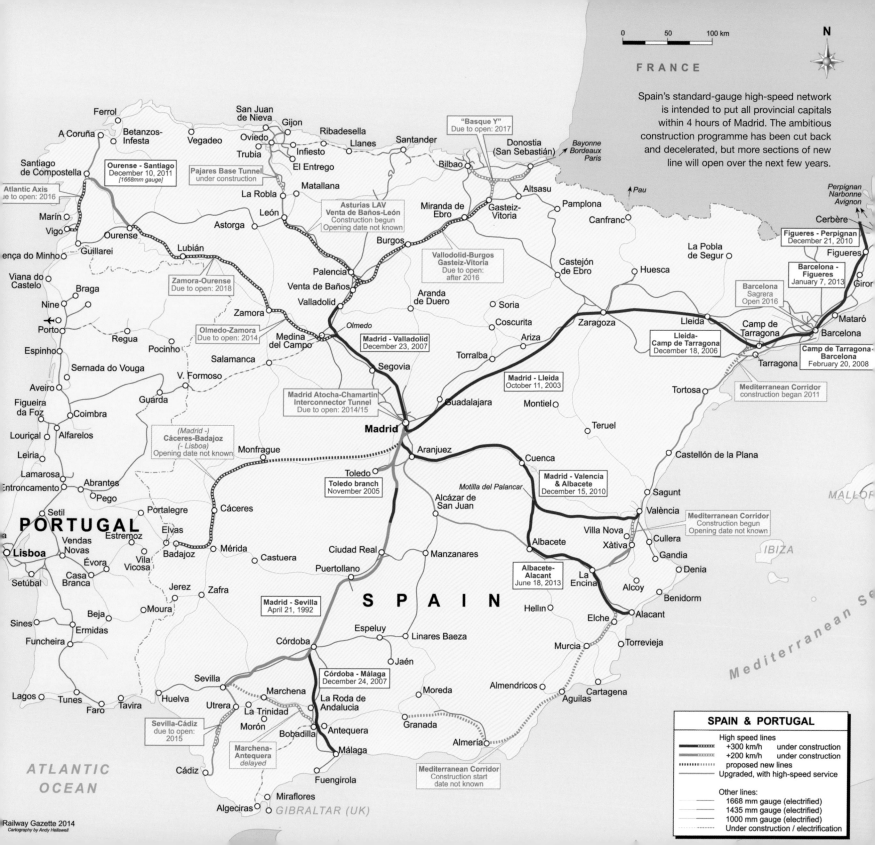

The government's serious intent was confirmed in the first quarter of 2000 when GIF awarded three contracts for the 180km Madrid–Valladolid line. These covered twin-bore 25km tunnels through the Guadarrama mountains. Another key element in the emerging network was a bypass east of Madrid to connect the Barcelona and Seville high-speed lines. This paved the way for AVEs to run directly from Barcelona to Málaga.

ROLLING-STOCK BONANZA

Renfe envisaged three types of stock for the future network: super-fast trains for premium services at up to 350km/h; 'intermediate' regional trains running at 250 to 270km/h; and 200 to 250km/h gauge-changing trains to reach cities off the standard-gauge network.

On 28 March 2000 the Renfe board signed off tenders for up to forty trains for the Madrid–Barcelona AVE service, and three bids were submitted by the closing date of 29 September. Alstom had joined forces with local builder CAF to propose both single-deck and double-deck derivatives of the TGV and an early version of its AGV. Siemens was offering a derivative of the German ICE 3, marketed as the Velaro E (for España).

Talgo had opted not to bid for the initial AVE fleet, but, conscious of the lucrative market that was opening up, it put research in hand to acquire the know-how to participate in later tenders. An unpowered eight-car development train with passive tilt was commissioned and, hauled by an S-100 set, this was clocked at 333km/h between Ciudad Real and Mora in autumn 1997. With an eye to the Madrid–Barcelona contract, in November 1999 CEO Francisco de Lorenzo announced that Talgo would spend 6 billion pesetas on a 350km/h prototype. The company's bid went in as a joint offer with Adtranz.

Duck bill. The distinctive nose shape of Renfe's S-102 and S-112 lightweight high-speed Talgo train sets earned them the nickname 'pato', meaning 'duck'. (Renfe, Patier)

The prototype's two 4MW power cars arrived from Germany in early 2000, and their distinctive shape quickly earned them the nickname *pato*, meaning 'duck'. The press were invited to view the *pato* in late April, and de Lorenzo ventured that it would reach 380km/h during tests between Zaragoza and Lleida the following year.

The big announcement came on 24 March 2001: Renfe had picked two winners. Siemens was to supply sixteen eight-car Velaro E sets – the company's first export version of the German ICE 3. Talgo and Adtranz (which later that year was absorbed by Canadian-owned Bombardier) were contracted to

build sixteen AVE S-102 train sets closely modelled on the prototype *pato*. Both deals were arranged so that some work went to Renfe's workshops.

Alstom and CAF were then chosen to supply twenty non-tilting Pendolino sets for more *Alaris* services, plus twelve gauge-changing trains, again with some local assembly. These used CAF's Brava gauge-changing bogie, which has wheels that can be pre-set to move sideways over a non-rotating axle body. Locking pins prevent the wheels from moving laterally while the train is running, and these are only released when the weight of the train is lifted off the wheel sets passing through a gauge-changer.

Velaro E. The AVE S-103 was the first export version of the Siemens Velaro design derived from the German ICE 3. (Renfe, Patier)

MORE LINES AUTHORISED

The national commitment to the high-speed line programme remained firm, and in mid-2001 the first tenders for the Córdoba–Málaga line were awarded. On 12 July Development Minister Francisco Álvarez Cascos met his French counterpart in Toulouse to agree details for the 45.5km link through the Pyrenees. At Figueres this would join end-on with the planned extension of the Madrid–Barcelona line, while in France it would connect at Perpignan with the conventional network pending completion of a high-speed link from LGV Méditerranée. Unusually, it was set up as a public-private partnership with a concessionaire appointed to build and operate the line for fifty years. The job included an 8km twin-bore tunnel through the mountains.

Flamingo flypast. The unique Talgo design feature of individual wheels with stub axles instead of bogies on the trailer cars is clearly shown in this shot of a Renfe S-130 gauge-changing high-speed train. (Renfe, Patier)

Railway events featured strongly in Prime Minister Aznar's July 2001 diary of engagements, including start-of-work ceremonies for the Madrid–Valladolid and Córdoba–Málaga AVE lines. The government also agreed to build a short branch off the Madrid–Seville line from La Sagra to the historic city of Toledo.

All this activity made Spain a magnet for the rail industry, and no fewer than 1,700 people gathered in Madrid in October 2002 for a congress on high-speed railways. King Juan Carlos I opened the event, noting that the high-speed lines were 'a symbol of development in our country'.

King Juan Carlos I inaugurated the first section of the Madrid–Barcelona line as far as the stunning new station at Zaragoza-Delicias on 10 October 2003, accompanied by Renfe President Miguel Corsini. Commercial services between Madrid and Lleida began the next day, nearly a year later than planned. There were four AVE trains each way, plus seven *Altaria* services operated by gauge-changing Talgo sets, six of

Royal opening. King Juan Carlos I is greeted by Renfe staff before boarding the inaugural train to open the Madrid–Zaragoza section of the Madrid–Barcelona high-speed line on 10 October 2003. (Renfe, Patier)

which continued over the broad gauge beyond Lleida to Barcelona. Pending satisfactory operation of the ETCS, trains relied on the standard Spanish ASFA train protection system, but this limited speed to 200km/h. While this was enough to cut the Madrid–Barcelona timing to 4 hours 30 minutes, it was 2 hours short of the target.

A report presented to the Spanish Parliament in 2005 revealed that completion of the Madrid–Lleida line had been delayed by technical shortcomings. Apart from persistent trouble in tuning the ETCS so that it was reliable enough for commercial operation at 300km/h, civil engineering standards were found wanting. The report stated that there had been a failure to plan and analyse the geological and geotechnical risks, and that 'design and construction in particularly complex areas' was inadequate. Major structures had been built with 'excessive' haste, with cracks found in tunnel linings and on viaducts. No less than 166km had been affected by subsidence and cavities below the track, meaning that some embankments were unstable, the report said.

Meanwhile, the bonanza for train builders rolled on. In late 2003 Renfe ordered forty-four gauge-changing power cars from Talgo and Bombardier to be marshalled with twenty-two existing Talgo sets. Further bids for high-speed rolling stock were then called – in 2001–03 Renfe put no fewer than ten orders for high-speed trains out to tender.

On 25 February 2004 Renfe signed contracts for 101 high-speed trains plus ten gauge-changing sleeping car sets. Just a few days later, on 3 March, the board agreed to procure thirty more high-speed trains from Talgo-Bombardier and ten more from Siemens in what the railway described as its 'largest-ever' rolling stock order. Taken together, these deals were worth around €4 billion, and several included maintenance contracts for up to fourteen years.

Attention span. A Class 130 gauge-convertible Talgo train crosses the 578m long Contreras viaduct between Motilla del Palancar and Valencia on the Madrid–Valencia AVE line. The 261m span of the main arch is the largest concrete viaduct structure on Europe's rail network. (Renfe, Patier)

Inevitably, not everything ran smoothly, and the complications of building trains at various factories in Germany and Spain were blamed for holding up delivery of the Velaro E trains, which Renfe classed as AVE S-103. Six cars for the first train reached Spanish metals in June 2005, when they were mated with two cars assembled in Spain. Changes from the German version included power uprated to 8.8MW, more powerful air-conditioning and different brakes as Renfe had eschewed eddy-current technology. On 16 July 2006 one of the fleet set a Spanish speed record of 404km/h, just 3km/h below the figure attained by the German ICE prototype in May 1988.

OPENINGS GALORE

In 2005 the Spanish rail sector was reorganised again, with GIF merged into a new national infrastructure manager, ADIF (*Administrador de Infraestructuras Ferroviarias*), and the national operator becoming Renfe Operadora. This coincided with rapid progress in new line construction, and several high-speed lines were opened in the ensuing five years. Prime Minister José Luis Rodríguez Zapatero opened the Toledo link on 15 September 2005. From then on the city could be reached in a 35-minute hop from Atocha by S-104 *Avant* non-tilting Pendolinos. In the same year S-104 trains also replaced the S-100 sets on *Lanzadera* duties to Puertollano and Ciudad Real.

Following in his predecessor's footsteps, Zapatero was present to open the Madrid–Valladolid line on 23 December 2007. Eight out of thirteen trains a day continued beyond Valladolid over broad-gauge tracks to Bilbao, Santander, Oviedo and Gijón.

Problems with tunnelling on the final part of the Madrid–Barcelona line held up completion, and construction dragged on until late 2007. Not until 20 February 2008 was Renfe able to launch a full service over this prime inter-city rail route. From that day S-103 and S-102 AVE train sets replaced gauge-changing S-120 units on the long haul from Madrid. One or two trains were timed at the original target figure of 2 hours 30 minutes, but this was later relaxed to give a standard time of 2 hours 38 minutes.

The much-delayed commissioning of ETCS Level 2 at the end of 2011 allowed the maximum speed to be raised to 310km/h, restoring the fastest time to 2 hours 30 minutes. Although passengers are entitled to some compensation if trains are late, Renfe has never replicated the generous 5-minute offer applying to the Madrid–Seville AVEs.

In 2000 Iberia and its rival airlines were shifting 3.6 million passengers a year on sixty-four daily flights in each direction between the two cities. The arrival of the AVE captured a huge slice of business for rail: more than 28,000 tickets were sold on the first day that bookings opened. Yet market share has not met expectations: in 2014 Renfe had just under 60 per cent of the air-rail market. That is not to say the line has not been a success – after starting with

A Spanish Invention

Talgo stands for *Tren Articulado Ligero Goicoechea y Oriol.* During the 1940s Alejandro Goicoechea, financially supported by José Luis de Oriol, conceived the idea of joining a set of independently rotating wheels using a triangular frame whose apex rested on a bar supporting the adjacent set of wheels. This formed an articulated structure on which short, low-slung bodies could be mounted.

The first of these unusual trains was assembled in the USA and tested in Spain in the 1950s by Patentes Talgo. The trains were very light, allowing them to run at relatively high speeds on indifferent infrastructure, which led to them operating premium services on Spanish metals.

The trains had wheels on stub axles, a feature that was used to good advantage in the development during the 1960s of a gauge-convertible version able to run into France via a gauge-changer at the frontier; other cross-border trains had to be jacked up to have their bogies swapped. Initially, only the coaches could pass through gauge-changers, but more recently Talgo has developed diesel and electric gauge-changing power cars. Many Talgo trains have passive tilt using high-level secondary airbag suspension between the cars.

A range of Talgo designs is in use for both day and night trains in Spain and elsewhere. They have operated in Germany, France, Italy and Switzerland and continue to run in the USA, Kazakhstan and Argentina. In 2014 Talgo delivered the first of seven trains to Russia; three of these are for gauge-changing services between Moscow and Berlin.

fifteen trains a day each way, six years later there were twenty-eight. As an aside, passengers generally undergo a security check before boarding AVE services, while departing and arriving passengers are normally segregated at the termini.

Completion of the Barcelona link was followed by the AVE line from Madrid to Valencia, which opened on 18 December 2010. The inaugural train conveyed King Juan Carlos I and Queen Sofía, along with Zapatero and his Development Minister José Blanco. The new line took the total length of Spain's high-speed network to 2,665km, more than any other European country. AVE trains now served twenty-one cities, and Renfe claimed that 40 per cent of the population lived within 50km of an AVE station. The longest AVE trip was from Barcelona to Málaga, a distance of 1,121km.

In 2013 it was the turn of Alicante to have direct AVE services to the capital with the opening of a branch off the Valencia line on 6 June. One year after the start, the Madrid–Alicante service, with

All-purpose train. Renfe's S-730 is a gauge-changing electro-diesel. Four out of the thirteen vehicles are used for traction, with the diesel units marshalled behind the electric power cars at each end. A train of this type derailed disastrously at speed on a sharp curve at Santiago de Compostela in July 2013. (Renfe, Patier)

stops in Cuenca, Albacete and Villena, had carried 1.7 million passengers, with load factors averaging 80 per cent. In 2014 there were eleven AVEs a day each way.

The bones of the final network were by now mainly in place, but on some routes major obstacles had to be overcome. On the route to Oviedo and Gijón, for example, a long base tunnel was needed to replace the climb over the famous Pajares pass. The Basque country will be reached by a new Valladolid–Burgos line, with reconstruction from there to Vitoria, where a new Y-shaped line will serve Bilbao and San Sebastián.

The 2008 recession knocked Spain's economy badly, and despite another ambitious transport infrastructure plan published in 2012, cuts were unavoidable. Work on many segments of new line had to be postponed, leaving some significant gaps. For some time to come, therefore, gauge-changing trains will have an important role to play.

In such circumstances versatility becomes a valuable attribute, and Talgo stole a march on its competitors by developing the ultra-flexible high-speed train: an electro-diesel version of its gauge-convertible S-130. This it did by adding diesel power cars behind the electric traction unit at each end.

BORDER CROSSING

Completion of the Perpignan–Figueres link into France proved to be a protracted process. It was finally opened for passenger and freight trains in December 2010, but the connecting Barcelona–Figueres high-speed line was not completed until January 2013. Even then, Barcelona-bound passengers from France had to change at Figueres.

No convincing reason was given for the delay to the start of through Barcelona–Paris trains, but they were finally launched on 15 December 2013. From the timetable change two days later, two Duplex TGVs a day ran from Paris to Barcelona

Cross-border AVE. A modified AVE S-100 set from Barcelona has arrived at Lyon Part-Dieu station on 22 December 2013, marking the start of regular high-speed services between the two cities via the Perpignan–Figueres route through the Pyrenees. (Didier Delattre)

and back, and a third summer-only round trip was added in March 2014. The fastest TGV covered the 1,073km in 6 hours 25 minutes. The advent of these services spelled the end for the Talgo hotel trains *Francisco de Goya* and *Joán Miró* that linked the French capital with Madrid and Barcelona overnight. Also from December 2013, Renfe scheduled modified versions of its AVE S-100 trains to link Madrid with Marseille and Barcelona with Lyon and Toulouse.

COMPETITORS ON THE HORIZON

The government expects Renfe to run its AVE network at a profit and has granted the operator some freedom to set fares. Renfe President Teófilo Serrano told me in 2009 that both the Madrid–Seville and Madrid–Barcelona corridors were 'in the black' and that AVE services covered all their costs, including track access fees paid to ADIF. 'When the whole AVE network is complete, it will generate a huge amount of money,' he asserted.

Although Renfe had previously adopted yield management techniques with lower prices for train-specific advance bookings, in February 2013 it refined the AVE fares structure, introducing hefty discounts for early booking. A young person's railcard, mobile-phone ticketing and a Renfe ticketing app were also launched. After a year Renfe reported AVE traffic to be up by over 23 per cent to 14.9 million trips, with average load factors rising from 65 to 73 per cent. In Spanish terms, the passenger total is high, but nine times as many people travel every year on the Tokaido Shinkansen.

Looking ahead, Renfe may soon face competition from rival operators. Development Minister Ana Pastor announced on 13 June 2014 that the cabinet had agreed to bids being invited to run long-distance trains in competition with the incumbent. This will apply initially on the route from Madrid to Valencia, Alicante and Murcia and the term will be seven years.

Any new operator will be able to lease some of Renfe's AVE trains pending procurement of its own fleet, but both Talgo and CAF have developed next-generation high-speed prototypes that could prove attractive. Talgo demonstrated its 'Avril' train with bodies wide enough for 2+3 seating in Berlin in 2012, and CAF unveiled its four-car 'Oaris' in late 2011. This was delivered to Renfe in place of the last Class 120 set. After early trials during which it clocked 350km/h, Oaris returned to the

Test train. The experimental Oaris design emerged from the CAF factory in 2011 and was still on trial during 2014. (CAF)

builder, but it was out and about again in early 2014. In September that year Pastor announced that another thirty high-speed trains, plus ten gauge-changing sets, would be added to the Spanish fleet over the next few years.

Spain has been criticised for building high-speed lines where they are barely justified, and this may be true for some as yet unfinished routes. On the other hand, Spaniards do not complain about their rail services, which now match the best in the world.

Spain's railway industry has come a long way in a short time, and the country is rather proud of its achievements, which have led to a huge export deal (Chapter 10). Nor is the story over yet: in 2011 plans for a high-speed test centre at Bobadilla were announced. These include what the government claims to be the world's longest test circuit: a 55km loop where trains could reach 450km/h.

Exhibit A. Patentes Talgo displayed its Avril prototype train at the InnoTrans exhibition in Berlin in 2012. (Author)

Catastrophe on the Pilgrim Trail

Spain's high-speed network shot into the headlines on the evening of 24 July 2013 when an *Alvia* service from Madrid to Ferrol in Galicia derailed spectacularly on a sharp curve on the approach to Santiago de Compostela. The train was formed of an S-730 gauge-changing electro-diesel Talgo. Of the 218 passengers on board, no fewer than eighty were killed in Spain's worst railway accident since the Second World War.

The immediate cause of the disaster was quickly ascertained – the train was travelling at 179km/h on a curve where the limit was 80km/h. A terrifying video taken from a lineside security camera emerged on 25 July, revealing that the train simply rolled over as it tried to take the curve, with the heavy diesel power cars with their high centre of gravity derailing first. A government report dated 20 May 2014 stated that the cause of the accident was the train's excessive speed in the curve. It also said that the driver's lack of attention occasioned by a telephone call from the train's conductor may have been a contributory cause. The train had just left the broad-gauge high-speed line from Ourense to Santiago and was on a connecting link to the old line which had opened with the new line from Ourense in December 2011. The new line had been fitted with ETCS, but the accident occurred in the transition area to the old line, where only the standard ASFA system was installed. This transition proved to be the weak point in the train protection system as there was no speed-control measure on the approach to the curve. This seems an extraordinary omission in the design of the railway, and after the crash Spain's rail accident investigation body quickly recommended installation of ASFA balises wherever there are major changes in speed limits.

8

Asian Tigers Join the Speed Club

The night of 31 March 2013 was a momentous one for South Korea's railway industry. The previous day had been spent preparing an experimental train for a test run that engineers predicted would shatter the country's previous rail speed record.

Shooting out of the dark on a section of the Seoul–Busan high-speed railway came the blazing headlights of the HEMU-430X. As it blasted past, the black nose was barely visible, but the white coaches gleamed as they powered through the night. On board, the speed recorders settled briefly on 421.4km/h. Engineers from the Korea Rail Research Institute (KRRI) and train builder Hyundai Rotem must have been ecstatic – this was a triumph for all the work they had put in over the previous six years.

Like Spain, South Korea did not have a home-grown ability to build high-speed trains when it set out to plan a high-speed line from the capital, Seoul, to the country's main port of Busan on the south-eastern tip of the Korean Peninsula, about 450km away. Around three-quarters of the population lived in this corridor, served by up to four diesel-powered *Saemaul* expresses shuttling to and fro every hour. The trip took 4 hours 10 minutes, including stops at Daejeon and Daegu, and in 1985 the corridor handled 57 million passengers. This, surely, was ideal high-speed rail country.

There had been talk of a high-speed railway for more than a decade. Despite Korea's proximity to the home of the Shinkansen, it was not until the mid-1980s that transport planners began to explore the options in detail. The economy was booming, and when Seoul was chosen to host the 1988 Olympic Games, politicians became acutely aware of the need for faster rail services to the country's second city. The need to move large numbers of people swiftly and safely was particularly apparent during Chuseok, the Korean thanksgiving festival, when many thousands of people departed the capital simultaneously.

All the talk had attracted the attention of the world's high-speed train builders, and French, German and Japanese politicians were blatantly hawking the wares of their respective industries. In late 1990 I travelled to Seoul to investigate the state of play.

Kim Kyu Sung, Director-General of Korean National Railroad's High Speed Rail Construction Planning Office, briefed me on the initial Request for Proposals that had been issued in October. Civil engineering would be in the hands of Korean contractors, but rolling stock, electrification and signalling would be sought from foreign consortia. 'Technology transfer and funding conditions,' Kim

Black and white. The front end of the HEMU-430X experimental train hints at its ability to push the frontiers of speed. The train reached 421.4km/h during a trial in March 2013. (Hyundai Rotem)

assured me, 'are critical factors influencing the decision.' The idea was for the foreign contractor to team up with local suppliers who, in line with government strictures, would be allotted the lion's share of the work. So not only did the bidders have to convince the South Korean government of their fitness for the job, they also had to make plans to hand over their expertise to Korean companies.

During my stay in Seoul the hotel management invited me to a cocktail party. The guest list read like a catalogue of European railway suppliers, with the names GEC Alsthom and Siemens cropping up frequently. The Japanese were presumably in a different hotel.

Fresh in my mind was that year's speed record on LGV Atlantique, which was not simply about boosting the egos of French engineers – it was also a sales pitch for TGV technology. Earlier, in December 1989, the French had pulled off another coup by persuading South Korean President Roh Tae Woo to take a trip on a TGV, where he was entertained with a visit to the cab.

The Germans dispatched an ICE power car and trailer to an exhibition in Seoul in 1991. They made great play of the similarity between the German and Korean terrain: the new line had to pass through the tree-clad Sobaek Mountains, which were punctuated by alluvial valleys crammed with rice paddies. The point was that German companies had great expertise in viaduct and tunnel construction – 35 per cent of the new line would run on viaduct, with no less than 190km in tunnel.

Japanese companies could offer similar know-how gained from building the Shinkansen, but it turned out that awarding a contract to suppliers from the country that had occupied Korea from 1910 to 1945 was a political step too far. In June 1993 the transport ministry announced that the Mitsubishi-led Japanese group was out of

the running, leaving the Europeans to fight it out.

It was a closely fought and long-drawn out battle. The Koreans drove a hard bargain, and bids and rebids went to and fro. By 15 July 1993 the sixth and final round was due. The sealed offers were spirited to a college outside Seoul, which was put under police guard. Inside was the evaluation team, consisting of senior staff from Korea High Speed Rail Construction Authority (KHSRCA), a clutch of American consultants and a bunch of Korean bankers. Not until 20 August did Transport Minister Lee Ke-ik reveal the outcome of their deliberations: a consortium led by GEC Alsthom had been chosen to negotiate the contract.

The Korean negotiators had exerted enough pressure to push the price down from US$3.7 billion in May 1992 to the point where GEC Alsthom Director-General Pierre Bilger conceded that 'in terms of financial sacrifices, we have gone to the utmost limit of the possibilities, and our philosophy is not to win business to lose money'. On 18 April 1994 KHSRCA signed a letter of intent with the Korea TGV Consortium for a deal worth US$2.1 billion covering forty-six trains, electrification equipment and TVM430 cab signalling. Chairman Park You-Kwang finally inked the 'Core System' deal with Bilger on 14 June, and a funding agreement was put in place shortly afterwards. The total cost of the project was about US$17 billion.

In the meantime, traffic on the old Seoul–Busan line was rising to the point where it rivalled parts of the Shinkansen. Civil engineering on the new route had begun in 1992, with Roh Tae Woo as principal guest at a sod-turning event for the 58km Chonan–Daejon section. This would serve as a test track for the first two trains, which were to be built in France. Design parameters for the 431km line included a 7,000m curve radius and a 300km/h maximum speed.

The target opening date for the Seoul–Daejeon section was 1999, with completion to Busan in early 2002. Trains derived from the TGV Réseau, but with capacity for 935 passengers and equipped for 25kV 60Hz operation, would then zip between the two cities in just over 2 hours.

SCHEDULE IN JEOPARDY

Construction did not progress smoothly. In 1996 the government was forced to reroute the line to avoid the centre of Kyongju, the ancient capital of the Silla kingdom, after protests about damage to historic buildings. Worse, the Korean civil contractors lacked experience in building to the exacting standards needed for 300km/h, and it emerged that the project was running up to four years late. Local media labelled the scheme a 'fiasco' and the KHSRCA chairman was fired.

In December 1996 France's privatisation commission refused to sanction the sale of the Thomson Multimedia group to Daewoo Electronics, triggering a furious row between France and South Korea. There were calls for the TGV deal to be renegotiated, and when that winter's heavy snow crippled many of France's TGV services, the Koreans set up a formal investigation to determine if the trains they were buying suffered from 'critical defects'. This did nothing to smooth relationships between the consortium members who were already struggling with cultural and language differences – plus the requirement to achieve a 50 per cent level of local manufacture.

Technology transfer was at the heart of the deal – the Koreans were determined to acquire the know-how to build their own high-speed trains. This had put the French in a very uncomfortable position during the contract negotiations, as they were understandably ultra-cautious about what knowledge should be released. But the Koreans were ambitious and resolute, and in August 1997 the South Korean government announced that it had signed an agreement with British consultants that would help local industry develop a Korean-designed train able to run at 350km/h.

The first *TGV-Corée* was presented to a Korean delegation on 29 May 1997 at GEC Alsthom's La Rochelle plant. The twenty-car set then embarked on a twenty-month test programme over French tracks. The second train was meanwhile prepared for shipment to Korea, where it arrived on 19 April 1998; ten more sets were to follow before production switched to Korean factories.

By this time it was clear that the civil works were hopelessly late, and the situation became increasingly tricky as Asia tottered through a grave financial crisis. Vincent Fertin, Executive Vice-President of Eukorail, GEC Alsthom's project management company in Korea, later said that the project slipped into 'contractual limbo'. There was even talk of abandonment and, after the 1998 election, new President Kim Dae-jung demanded a full reassessment.

PROJECT CURTAILED

The outcome was 're-scoping', which cut back construction to the 224km from Seoul to Daegu, with work on the remaining 118km to Busan deferred and removed from the Korea TGV Consortium's remit. Tunnel sections through Daejeon and Daegu were cut out to save money, with trains routed instead over the old tracks to the city-centre stations. The existing Daegu–Busan line would be electrified to allow TGVs to complete the last leg of the journey.

By this time there was tangible progress with the test section, and the President formally commissioned it on 16 December when a trial run attained 213km/h. The revised plan was to launch high-speed services, now known as KTX (Korea Train eXpress), over Phase I between Seoul

Korea Train eXpress. One of the forty-six original KTX trains built with TGV technology crosses a viaduct near Ulsan on 24 November 2013. As with the TGV Paris–Sud-Est train sets, some traction equipment is located in the first trailer car. (Kazumiki Miura)

and Daegu in April 2004, with Phase II to Busan completed by 2008.

While production of the forty-six-strong KTX fleet was in progress, Korean industry was, with the help of a generous government grant, working flat-out to develop its own high-speed train. The 350km/h ambition was no idle threat, and a seven-car prototype was completed on 13 March 2002 – a KRRI spokesman claimed that 87 per cent of the 'core technologies' had been developed in South Korea. Like the KTX trains, the 350X Korea High Speed Train had end power cars and motored bogies at the outer ends of an articulated trailer rake. Trains of this type, the transport ministry said, would initially

be deployed on a second high-speed line to the port of Mokpo in the south-west corner of the peninsula, with journey times cut from over 4 hours 30 minutes to 2 hours 10 minutes.

By early 2004 the re-scoped KTX project was in its final stages with the depot completed at Goyang, about 20km north of Seoul, and finishing touches being put to the spectacular station buildings. A shadow service was launched between Seoul and Daegu, and between 15–22 March this was opened to the public as the final test before commercial services began.

The big day arrived. On 30 March 2004 Acting President Goh Kun boarded a flag-bedecked KTX train conveying around 700 VIPs from

Seoul to Daejeon. The full service of ninety-two trains each way between Seoul and Busan on the Gyeongbu Line was launched on 1 April, with the first public KTX departing Busan at 5.05 a.m. The trip to the capital took just 2 hours 40 minutes.

Although KTX traffic was initially lower than forecast, traffic rose significantly, and two years later the government decided to construct the Honam high-speed line to Mokpo in two stages by 2020; an alternative access route into Seoul known as the Suseo Line is also under construction. The Honam Line parts company with the Gyeongbu route at Osong, about 120km south of Seoul, and runs for 230km via Iksan and Kwangju to the coast. The project was one of several schemes in a new National Rail Network Construction Plan, which ran to 2015. Also in the plan was Phase II of the original scheme covering the 129km from Daegu to Busan via Kyeongju; the missing links through Daejeon and Daegu were also reinstated.

SECOND GENERATION

KRRI had meanwhile made great progress with the 350X, and on 9 June 2006 Korail (the new name for Korean National Railroad) ordered ten KTX-II trains from Rotem, each with ten cars, to run mainly to Mokpo. In contrast to the first-generation KTX, these had alloy rather than steel bodies as well as different power electronics, reflecting recent progress in this field. In a separate development, South Korea's train suppliers were working on a six-car 200km/h experimental tilting train featuring carbon-fibre bodyshells supported on metal underframes, achieving a 40 per cent weight saving over aluminium.

That was not all: something even more ambitious was brewing. On 27 July the Ministry of Construction & Transport and the Ministry of Science & Technology declared their intention to develop a third-generation high-speed train to

Tilting Train Express. In 2007–08 the Korea Railroad Research Institute developed the TTX 200km/h tilting train with car bodyshells made from a carbon-fibre composite material; the shell was supported on a metal underframe. (KRRI/*Railway Gazette* collection)

carry passengers at 400km/h, tentatively described as Hanvit 400. An official told the *Korea Times* that 'the development of updated technologies is essential amid global competition', explaining that high-speed railways were a growth market.

This was evident from the KTX experience – 100 million trips had been made in three years. Taken with growing traffic on the route to Mokpo, this was reason enough for the KTX-II order to be topped up with nine more sets before the wraps were taken off the first train at the Hyundai Rotem factory in Changwon on 25 November 2008.

More than 6,600 people from 129 organisations had been involved in developing KTX-II. The cost of nearly 256 billion won would, the Korea

Transport Institute believed, be far outweighed by benefits totalling 7,500 billion won. Great emphasis was placed on giving the train a local flavour, with MBD Design styling the first-class cars so that they evoked a traditional Korean library. Korail's customers had complained about the lack of rotating seats in second-class on the original KTX trains, so KTX-II remedied this omission. The first of the new fleet, branded as KTX-Sancheon, was pressed into service on 2 March 2010, sharing duties with its first-generation cousins.

Research continued into the Hanvit 400 development train, and towards the end of 2010 Hyundai Rotem revealed that it would build a prototype with distributed power to be known

KTX-II. The KTX-Sancheon or KTX-II was the first series build of Korean high-speed trains after the TGV technology transfer deal between French and Korean companies. The design retains articulation, but the trailers have aluminium rather than steel bodyshells. (Kazumiki Miura)

KTX-Honam. South Korean operator Korail is taking delivery of twenty-two KTX-Honam train sets from local builder Hyundai Rotem. Another ten similar trains are to be built for Suseo High Speed Rail Corp, a new operator established in January 2014. (Hyundai Rotem)

as HEMU-430X. Intended for possible use on an ultra-high-speed line built parallel to the KTX route, the six-car train would have all axles powered, but with the axle load kept to 13 tonnes.

The HEMU-430X announcement came shortly before completion of the Gyeongbu Line extension to Busan, which was formally opened on 28 October 2010. Chairman of Korea Rail Network Authority (which was split from operator Korail in 2005) Cho Hyun-Yong professed to be 'overwhelmed that the greatest civil engineering project in Korean history has successfully concluded'. Timetabled services began on 1 November – no less than sixteen years had elapsed since the KTX contract was signed.

By 2014 the fastest Seoul–Busan timing over the 408.5km route by non-stop KTX service was 2 hours 16 minutes, an average speed of 180km/h. The fastest point-to-point timing was between Gwangmyeong (the KTX station serving the south of Seoul) and Daejeon, with one train attaining 212km/h.

Korea's high-speed services were sufficiently successful for the government to announce in April 2011 that the network would expand further as a contribution towards reducing carbon emissions and increasing GDP. The plans also embraced expansion of the conventional network, suggesting that South Korea is firmly among those countries where rail is replacing air as the prime mode of inter-city transport.

Further KTX-Sancheon trains have since been ordered, and future developments will hinge on the outcome of trials with the HEMU-430X. The extraordinary nose and the black-and-white paint of this engineering marvel evoked surprise among the onlookers when it was unveiled in Changwon on 17 May 2012, but KRRI President, Dr Soon-Man Hong, was more interested in the train's potential than in its appearance: 'rail technology has reached the point where a train can travel the length of Korea in one and a half hours', he declared. 'Where it is possible to commute across the country within an hour or so, this will help resolve issues of regional disparity,' he predicted.

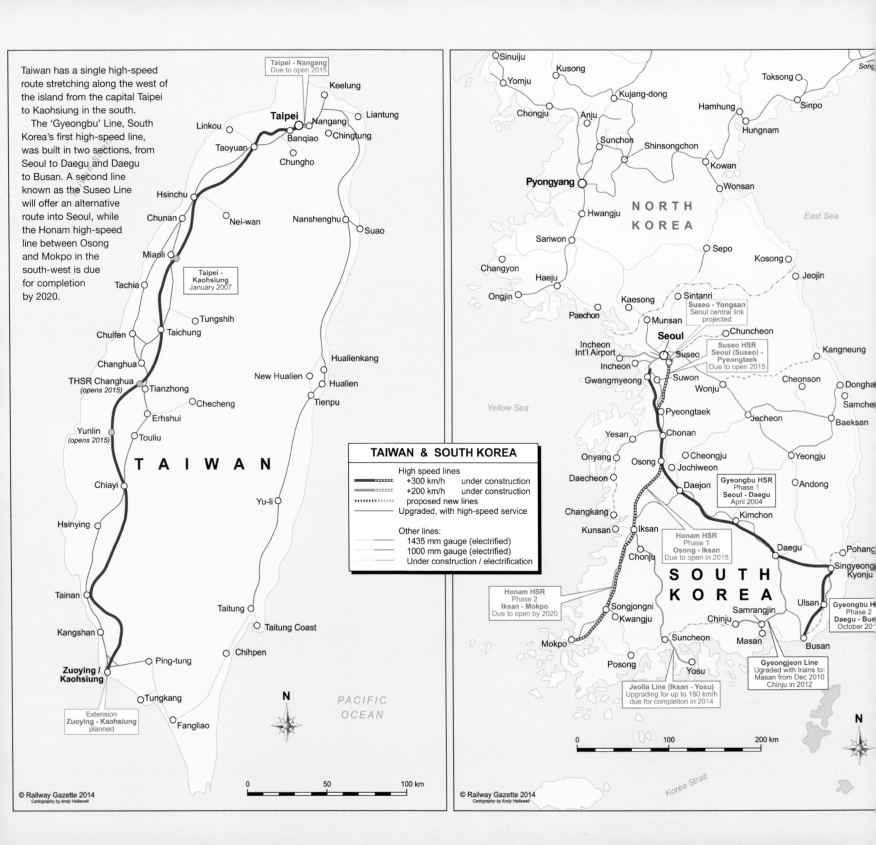

Taiwan has a single high-speed route stretching along the west of the island from the capital Taipei to Kaohsiung in the south.

The 'Gyeongbu' Line, South Korea's first high-speed line, was built in two sections, from Seoul to Daegu and Daegu to Busan. A second line known as the Suseo Line will offer an alternative route into Seoul, while the Honam high-speed line between Osong and Mokpo in the south-west is due for completion by 2020.

TAIWAN

Taipei - Nangang
Due to open 2015

Keelung
Liantung
Taipei
Linkou   Nangang
Banqiao   Chingtung
Taoyuan
Chungho
Hsinchu
Chunan   Nei-wan   Nanshenghu
Miaoli   Suao

Taipei - Kaohsiung
January 2007

Tungshih
Tachia
Chuifen   Taichung
Changhua   Hualienkang
THSR Changhua
(opens 2015)   Tianzhong   New Hualien
Checheng   Hualien
Erhshui   Tienpu
Yunlin   Touliu
(opens 2015)

T A I W A N

Chiayi

Yu-li

Hsinying

Tainan   Taitung

Kangshan   Chihpen

Zuoying /   Ping-tung
Kaohsiung
Tungkang

Extension
Zuoying - Kaohsiung
planned   Fangliao

N

PACIFIC
OCEAN

© Railway Gazette 2014
Cartography by Andy Hellawell

0   50   100 km

TAIWAN & SOUTH KOREA

High speed lines
+300 km/h   under construction
+200 km/h   under construction
proposed new lines
Upgraded, with high-speed service

Other lines:
1435 mm gauge (electrified)
1000 mm gauge (electrified)
Under construction / electrification

SOUTH KOREA

Sinuiju   Toksong
Yomju   Kujang-dong
Kusong   Hamhung   Sinpo
Chongju   Anju
Sunchon   Shinsongchon
Pyongyang   Kowan
Hwangju   Wonsan
N O R T H
K O R E A   East Sea
Sariwon
Sepo
Changyon   Kosong
Haeju   Kaesong   Jeojin
Ongjin   Paechon   Sintanri
Munsan
Suseo - Yongsan
Seoul central link
projected
Seoul
Incheon   Chuncheon
Int'l Airport   Suseo
Incheon   Suseo HSR   Kangneung
Seoul (Suseo) -
Gwangmyeong   Suwon   Pyeongtaek
Due to open 2015
Yellow Sea   Wonju   Cheonson
Pyeongtaek   Jecheon   Donghae
Samche
Yesan   Chonan   Baeksan
Onyang   Osong Cheongju
Daecheon   Jochiweon   Yeongju
Gyeongbu HSR
Phase 1
Daejon   Seoul - Daegu
April 2004   Andong
Changkang
Kimchon
Kunsan   Iksan
Honam HSR   Daegu
Phase 1
Chonju   Osong - Iksan   Pohang
Due to open in 2015
Singyeong
S O U T H   Kyonju
Honam HSR   **K O R E A**
Phase 2   Ulsan
Iksan - Mokpo
Due to open by 2020   Samrangjin   Gyeongbu H
Songjongni   Chinju   Phase 2
Kwangju   Masan   Daegu - Bus
Mokpo   Suncheon   October 20
Gyeongjeon Line
Posong   Yosu   Ugraded with trains to:
Masan from Dec 2010
Jeolla Line (Iksan - Yosu)   Chinju in 2012
Upgrading for up to 180 km/h
due for completion in 2014

© Railway Gazette 2014
Cartography by Andy Hellawell

0   100   200 km

N

Korea Strait

Taiwan Swells the Ranks

As in South Korea, Taiwan toyed with the idea of a high-speed railway for a long time before taking action; even when it did, the process was far from straightforward. Most of Taiwan's population lives in the plain that stretches along the western coast between Taipei in the north and Kaohsiung in the south. Taiwan Railway Administration's 1,067mm gauge main line between the two cities was electrified in the 1980s, but this and the parallel motorway were struggling to cope with burgeoning traffic in the mid-1990s, which is when we take up the story.

Land acquisition for the 339.3km high-speed line had already begun by 1996. In that year preliminary bids were invited for a build-operate-transfer concession whose structure reflected the Taiwanese government's insistence on at least 40 per cent private finance. The government would buy the land and allot property development rights around the stations to the concessionaire, this being a formula thought to be attractive for investors. Travel was predicted to soar spectacularly when high-speed services cut the fastest 4-hour-30-minute trip by conventional train to the target time of just 90 minutes with one intermediate stop.

Offers were received on 15 January 1997 from a European group including GEC Alsthom and Siemens and from a consortium led by the Kuomintang-owned investment bank China Development Corp, which proposed Shinkansen technology. Gauge, incidentally, was never really an issue in Taiwan – the new line would have rails 1,435mm apart.

As the plans firmed up, Taiwan's Provisional Engineering Office of High Speed Rail became the Bureau of High Speed Rail, and it was this body that was charged with evaluating the bids. Both Taiwan High Speed Rail Consortium (THSRC) and the Japanese-backed Chung Hwa High Speed Rail Consortium pre-qualified in February 1997, and more detailed bids were lodged in August. On 25 September Transport Minister Tsay Jaw-Yang informed the media that THSRC had been chosen as 'best applicant' for the thirty-year concession as it was seeking a substantially lower government contribution. After further negotiations, a symbolic start was staged near Taipei on 30 December 1997. The concession deal was initialled in February 1998, the aim being to reach financial close by 30 June.

THSRC consisted of Continental Engineering, GEC Alsthom, Siemens, Taiwan's Evergreen Marine, financiers Fubon Insurance, plus Pacific Electric Wire & Cable and electrical machinery supplier TECO. The trains would blend German and French technology, with ICE power cars and double-deck TGV trailers. Within the group, the two train builders teamed up to form their own consortium called Eurotrain with a view to winning not just the rolling stock contract, but also the other electrical and mechanical work, worth around US$4 billion in all. It seemed an improbable marriage of rivals who had tussled with each other in Korea just a few years earlier.

The marriage was consummated when Eurotrain assembled a demonstration train in Germany consisting of a pair of ICE 2 power cars and a rake of double-deck TGV trailers. This ensemble was put together to establish for a high-level Taiwanese delegation that the rolling stock was proven technology, a Taiwanese government stipulation.

Eurotrain. In 1988 rolling stock builders GEC Alsthom and Siemens teamed up to assemble a demonstration train for the contract they hoped to win in Taiwan. The ensemble of two ICE power cars and a rake of TGV Duplex trailers was shown off to a Taiwanese delegation on 4 May 1998, attaining 316km/h between Göttingen and Hannover. (*Railway Gazette* collection)

Eurotrain's guests were entertained on 4 May 1998 to a high-speed dash between Göttingen and Hannover that peaked at 316km/h, special dispensation having been obtained at the last minute to switch out the LZB train control, which would limit speed to 280km/h. On board was THSRC President Nita Ing, who at the age of 32 had been appointed President of Continental Engineering. She described the trip as 'wonderful' but warned that the 30 June date for financial close and contract signature may not be 'realistic'. Several passengers were impressed by the ride quality of the TGV cars, judged to be superior to that of Deutsche Bahn's ICE 1 trailers. The trip took place just one month before the Eschede disaster.

Negotiations over government land purchases delayed the contract until 23 July, when Nita Ing put pen to paper, her co-signatory being Minister of Transport & Communications Lin Feng Cheng. Five years were allowed for construction, and five years were added to the concession before the railway was transferred to government ownership. In the meantime THSRC had to raise enough funds to bridge the gap between the government's low-interest NT$280 billion loan and the expected cost of NT$400 billion. The project formula meant that costs had to be kept under tight rein, and separate tenders were called for civil works, for electrical and mechanical equipment, including the trains, and for track. This opened up an opportunity for the Japanese to re-enter the fray.

On 26 March 1999 ground was broken in Kaohsiung, swiftly followed by an identical event at Taipao in the home state of Premier Vincent Siew. However, major works awaited a decision on the choice of technology: despite Eurotrain's position in THSRC, the Japanese were back in contention, having lobbied furiously behind the scenes. The Kuomintang party had backed China

Development Corp in the earlier bid, and there were suggestions that the price for the party's support for the high-speed railway was a switch to Japanese technology. Meanwhile, relations between THSRC and the government were fraught, with the government only meeting its loan commitments at the last minute before an agreed milestone in June 1999.

Bids from Eurotrain and the rival Taiwan Shinkansen Alliance (TSA) for the rolling stock and train control systems went in on 15 June. Negotiations led to a second round of tenders in August, with a 'best and final offer' required by 3 December. Nothing was heard until 28 December, when THSRC, citing pricing and finance, revealed that it would grant priority negotiating rights for the NT$95 billion E&M package to TSA.

LEGAL BATTLE

Eurotrain management was furious. Having been chosen as preferred bidder for the rolling stock and other E&M kit in 1997, and having successfully demonstrated its ICE-TGV combination the following year, it seemed impossible that TSA could walk away with the deal. Apart from that, Eurotrain had imparted a great deal of expertise to THSRC for the preliminary planning of the railway. On 12 January 2000 Eurotrain announced that it was seeking an injunction with Taipei District Court against THSRC's decision, but the court dismissed the complaint on 1 February.

Eurotrain had been a partner in the THSRC consortium, but when the consortium changed its status to a company in June 1998, Eurotrain became a 'promoter'. It claimed to have an exclusive agreement to be the E&M supplier, and even with the change of status it believed it still had right of first refusal. THSRC contended that Eurotrain had not signed a formal contract and that the Europeans' willingness to bid

against the Japanese group was tacit acceptance that the earlier agreement was non-binding. Eurotrain said that it had treated this as 'a benchmarking exercise'.

Siemens dispatched its top officials to Taiwan but to no avail. Another factor had meanwhile arisen. An earthquake in September 1999 caused serious damage to Taiwan's railway installations, and Japan's well-known expertise in protecting the Shinkansen from quakes may perhaps have influenced the choice – Japanese firms had already won some of the civil works.

Eurotrain tried again to contest the decision, but a challenge through the High Court in Taipei was rejected in March. THSRC went on to sign a Memorandum of Understanding with TSA on 13 June 2000. This covered supply of thirty trains of twelve cars based on the Series 700 developed by JR Central and JR West, plus a package of power supply, signalling and communications equipment. The trains would use Series 500 bogies as the design speed was 300km/h rather than the Series 700 maximum of 285km/h; each set would seat up to 950 passengers. Negotiations dragged on until 12 December, when the Core System contract was signed by Nita Ing and Taiwan Shinkansen Corp (previously TSA) President Kazuo Sato. THSRC now had 1,760 days to finish designing the railway, build it, test it and open it for commercial service.

Visiting Taiwan in early 2001, I found the project in full swing. The civil engineering was remarkable: 61km ran in tunnel and 251km was being built on elevated structures, partly to avoid severing roads and paths between communities. Most impressive of all was a viaduct towards the southern end of the line that ran continuously for 157km. This structure was built, at least in part, to avoid parcelling out small plots of land to different owners if the railway sliced through their property.

QUARREL OVER TRACK

On 7 August THSRC called the first of five bids for the trackwork. This seemed to come as a shock to TSC, which appeared to have been working on the assumption that an entire Shinkansen package, including track, was required. But THSRC was ever mindful of costs, and competitive tendering was the order of the day. Not only that, but the alignment was based on European turnout geometry, which determined the layout of the viaducts. Despite Japan's long experience in high-speed operations, the standard arrangement for trains calling at intermediate stations was to have a set of points for the diverging track quite close to the platform, with trains approaching at relatively slow speeds. Turnouts permitting 160km/h running on the diverging track had only been used for the junction of the Joetsu and Nagano/Hokuriku Shinkansen.

What particularly horrified the Japanese was the prospect of Shinkansen trains running on European-designed track, something that had never been done before (except for some Shinkansen bogie tests on an ICE in Germany). They were very concerned that nothing should happen that could jeopardise the Shinkansen's excellent safety and reliability record.

A formal protest was lodged with THSRC, which was meanwhile struggling to raise enough money to keep the project going. The prospect of the government bailing out THSRC prompted some members of the legislative yuan (parliament) to argue that THSRC was in breach of contract, but Ing countered this with a statement that 'the lawmakers … have based their action on incorrect assumptions' and accused the government of lacking commitment.

Eurotrain in the meantime had lodged a claim for damages, which eventually went to arbitration, first in Taipei and then in Singapore and finally New York. On 15 March 2004 the International

Point taken. A Series 700T departs Taichung on a northbound service to Taipei on 24 July 2007. It is passing over a turnout supplied from Germany. (Ian Winfieldale)

Chamber of Commerce ruled that Eurotrain should be paid US$73 million as compensation for breach of contract. The final agreed amount was US$65 million, but THSRC appeared somewhat reluctant to cough up. Legend has it that pressure was successfully brought to bear by the unconventional means of impounding a Taiwanese ship in a French port.

The track contracts were let in 2002 to joint ventures of Taiwanese, Japanese, European and Australian companies. Japanese standard 60kg/m rail was used throughout, with Japanese concrete slab track chosen for the whole of the main line between stations. In contrast, German Rheda slab track was selected for all the station areas with high-speed turnouts supplied from Germany.

This prompted Japanese engineers to insist that Rheda track be used for 300m beyond the last turnout at each station.

The first Series 700T (T for Taiwan) train was rolled out in front of Nita Ing and around 200 other guests at Kawasaki's Hyogo factory in Japan on 30 January 2004. Ing described the unmissable orange and white train as a New Year's gift to the people of Taiwan and a milestone on the path to opening the high-speed line. It reached Taiwan the following May.

October 2005 remained the target opening date, but in November 2004 Ing was saying that THSRC needed 'a lot of luck' to meet the deadline.

Eight trains had been delivered by January 2005, with testing in progress on a 60km section at the south end of the route. Yet the project was far from complete, and the Japanese contractors continued to carp about the mix of technology.

On 8 September Ing announced that the THSRC board had postponed the opening until October 2006 – inspectors had concerns about the signalling and other safety-related issues. The delay would eat into the revenue-earning concession period and incur extra interest costs, obliging Ing to apologise to shareholders. Another loan from Taiwanese banks was agreed in July to keep the project rolling, but by September 2006 it

was evident that the underground section between Panchiao in the Taipei suburbs and the central station would not be ready on time.

Other issues were also coming into play. To get the service up and running, THSRC had recruited a number of experienced train drivers, many of whom were French or German, with some from Eurostar or Eurotunnel. This meant a huge technical and language learning curve before they were familiar with the Shinkansen trains. Although testing and inspection processes were well under way, the revised deadline passed, and it was not until 27 December that the Ministry of Transport granted approval for THSRC to carry the public.

Aboard a pre-launch special on 1 January, President of Taiwan Chen Shui-bian said that slicing 3 hours off the journey between Kaohsiung and Taipei 'would virtually transform Taiwan into a city state like Singapore'. The first public train left Panchiao at 7 a.m. on 5 January 2007 bound for Zuoying in the outskirts of Kaohsiung, but it was a low-profile launch for a high-profile project. Playing it cautiously, THSRC at first ran trains at hourly intervals, calling at five stops en route.

Passengers were able to travel over the section from Panchiao to Taipei Main Station by March 2007, and THSRC began to contemplate its new role of earning revenue and paying off debt. It also needed to improve connections to the Taiwan Railway Administration network and other public transport as some stations such as Taichung were located well away from the city centre. Service levels were gradually stepped up, reaching fifty-six trains a day each way by 24 October 2007 when THSRC held a 'Recognition & Appreciation Ceremony' to celebrate the end of the construction phase. Ing described the project as 'the largest build-operate-transfer project in the world'; it had swallowed NT$513 billion.

Damage Contained

On 4 March 2010 southern Taiwan was hit by an earthquake measuring 6.4 on the Richter scale. Train 110, a limited-stop service from Zuoying to Taipei, was travelling at 270km/h when the rear axle of the leading bogie derailed as the quake struck. It took about 2km to come to a stand, but in a remarkable tribute to the track and rolling-stock designers, the train remained upright. Five other trains were affected, but none of them derailed. Not a single person was hurt or killed.

The track was damaged by the derailed bogie, and the loss of a pantograph on this train and one other brought down lengths of overhead wire, but that was the extent of the damage. THSRC coped well with the interruption, quickly repairing the track and wires so that a near-normal service ran next day.

On 4 March 2010 a northbound Series 700T derailed at around 270km/h about 20km north of Tainan as a result of an earthquake. The rear axle of the leading bogie derailed towards the anti-derailment wall on the left, but a brake disc running on the gauge side of the left-hand rail prevented further lateral movement. The right-hand wheel of the derailed axle struck every alternate J-slab, causing considerable damage to the surface. No one was hurt. (Ian Winfieldale)

Track event. The transition between the Japanese J-slab track in the foreground and the German Rheda slab track beyond is plain to see. Japanese engineers insisted that the Rheda track must continue for 300m past the last turnout at each station. (Ian Winfieldale)

Although the service was up and running, there was not much else to celebrate. Interest and depreciation were eating away income from fares and property, and after restructuring its finances in 2009, THSRC agreed more loan facilities. The first operating profit was earned in 2011, and although traffic was growing steadily, with about sixty-five trains a day carrying 47.5 million passengers in 2013, it was well below forecast. At the company's AGM in June 2014 newly appointed Chairman Tony Fan was able to report a pre-tax net profit of NT$2.7 billion, but he also relayed the bad news that cumulative losses had topped NT$52 billion by the end of 2013. This, he warned, meant that THSRC could be staring at bankruptcy during 2014 if its finances were not restructured again.

More income was in prospect thanks to completion of three more intermediate stations and a northern extension to Nangang, which had all been put on hold as an economy measure during the construction phase; four more trains were also ordered. Nevertheless, a rescue package seemed essential. The transport ministry had earlier suggested reducing the company's capital and injecting a further tranche of funds, making the government the controlling shareholder. Another option was to extend THSRC's concession from thirty-five to sixty-five or even seventy-five years, giving it much longer to recoup the original investment. Not, perhaps, what the shareholders had envisaged.

Kept in the dark. A line-up of seven of THSRC's Series 700T train sets stabled at the Zuoying depot at Kaohsiung just after midnight on 4 September 2007. (Ian Winfieldale)

Bitter orange. Taiwan's government was adamant that the high-speed line be built as a private-sector enterprise, but Taiwan High Speed Rail Corp found that interest payments and depreciation were eating away its income to the point where a government rescue was mooted in 2014. (THSRC)

9

The Dragon Storms on to the Stage

If South Korea and Taiwan ranked among Asia's 'tiger' economies, then the People's Republic of China was surely the lion – or more appropriately the dragon. This vast country roared into prominence after the economic reforms of December 1978, racking up double-digit growth rates to become the world's second largest economy in 2008. Titanic changes were under way, and there is no better illustration of China's transformation than the explosive development of its rail network.

A stunning amount had already been achieved by December 2010 when China played host to an international conference on high-speed railways. Anxious to prove to the rest of the world just how far it had come, Chinese Railways (CR) staged an event designed to secure headline treatment by the world's media.

Old and new. A freight rickshaw passes the leading car of a 380km/h CRH380A distributed-power EMU on show outside the Beijing Conference Centre on 6 December 2010. (Author)

Crowded cab. Former Minister of Railways Liu Zhijun watches intently as the driver of the sixteen-car CRH380AL accelerates up to a record speed of 486.1km/h on 3 December 2010. Behind him on his right is the ministry's Chief Engineer, He Huawu.

At 11.05 a.m. on 3 December 2010, a sleek silver-nosed train pulled away from Zaozhuang station in Shandong Province bound for Bengbu in Anhui Province, 220km away. This was not an ordinary scheduled service; nor was it an ordinary railway. This was the first completed section of the world's longest high-speed line stretching for over 1,300km between Beijing and Shanghai, and the train was a sixteen-car CRH380AL EMU with distributed power that represented the most advanced product of China's rolling stock industry. Its design speed was an incredible 380km/h, and CR's engineers and the train's manufacturers were confident that higher speeds were within reach – a train of this type had already reached 416.6km/h between Shanghai and Hangzhou on 28 September 2010.

In the cab was Minister of Railways Liu Zhijun and his Chief Engineer, He Huawu. Ensconced in the cars behind, glued to screens monitoring the pantograph and a myriad of other components, was a crew of researchers and engineers. Also on board were approved media representatives that included a broadcasting team from China Central Television. According to a *China Daily* reporter, the train quickly smashed the previous record and then held steady at around 420km/h before accelerating again. By 11.20 a.m. the train was approaching the site chosen for an attempt on an even higher speed where a downhill grade was in the train's favour. It continued to accelerate until 11.28 a.m. when the train's digital display screens flashed up 486.1km/h. The train reached Bengbu in 34 minutes, averaging a scorching 388.2km/h from Zhaozhuang.

The Ministry of Railways (MoR) at once cranked its publicity machine into action, and videos of the event quickly appeared on the Internet. The record dash had been carefully timed to precede the

Chinese sword. The CIT500 research train has reportedly attained a simulated speed of 605km/h on a roller-rig in Qingdao. Unveiled in December 2011, the train with a nose said to resemble a Chinese sword is understood to be subject to a speed limit of 385km/h pending a more propitious time for ultra-high-speed trials. (Liu Jialiang)

conference starting on 7 December in Beijing, where the world's high-speed rail experts were convening. Chinese officials made great play of the exploit, claiming it as a world record for a series-built train. This raised eyebrows around the world, nowhere more so than in France – whereas the V150 was unquestionably a specially adapted train, TGV Set 325 consisted of production vehicles, admittedly modified for the record attempt.

The story does not end there, because China is intent on going further. Conference presentations confirmed that a huge research effort was being devoted to ultra-high speeds, and confirmation of this came on 9 January 2011. On that day a CRH380BL formation, a rival design to the CRH380A, notched the Chinese speed record up to 487.3km/h. Not long afterwards news arrived that an ultra-high-speed experimental train had been commissioned from CSR Qingdao Sifang, the same company that had built the CRH380AL. CRH, incidentally, stands for China Railway High Speed, with the H also meaning Hexie (harmony).

The experimental train emerged in a brief blaze of publicity at the end of December 2011. Termed CIT500, it was a six-car set with all axles motored and a power rating of 22.8MW, 3.2MW more than the V150. One end car had a long aquiline nose described as resembling a traditional Chinese sword; the other mirrored the shape of the CRH380A. This train embodied all the knowledge gained over the previous few years, and many hopes rested upon it. However, for reasons that we shall discover later, the CIT500 was effectively mothballed in Qingdao. Activity did not resume until early 2014, when the train was tested on the Qingdao roller-rig, attaining a speed equivalent to 605km/h. It was out on the tracks again by April 2014, but a ministry edict restricted speed to 385km/h.

PACE OF DEVELOPMENT

In 1993 the average speed of passenger trains in China was a lamentable 30km/h. Less than twenty years later, CR was contemplating testing a train at 600km/h. How was this possible?

In the early 1990s it was evident that the country desperately lacked the railways to meet the demand for transport. In 1993, during a technical visit to a heavy-haul coal railway at Qinhuangdao, north-east of Beijing, I observed an endless stream of long freights and passenger trains loading to fifteen or more coaches crawl past from signal to signal. The process went on for hours, suggesting that parts of the network were indeed overwhelmed. If this were true, the MoR had a serious problem, as it would be held responsible if lack of transport capacity held back economic development.

An economy growing at remarkable rates in the early 1990s needed the transport capacity to feed it, but CR was hard pushed to keep pace. Pent-up demand on the trunk routes led to congestion at busy junctions. Shen Zhijie, then Chief Engineer at the MoR, told me that in many countries the priority was to make capacity available for freight trains while in others the first requirement was to move more passengers. 'In China,' he said, 'we have to do both.'

A mighty push was under way to update the network with modern technology, and the knowledge and expertise for this could only come from outside China. The then Minister of Railways Han Zhubin took the opportunity during a formal interview to make it clear that China would welcome foreign investors – they would share in 'a golden opportunity' to develop China's railways, he said.

UPGRADES PAVE THE WAY

The first move towards higher speeds was a decision in August 1990 to fettle up the line from Guangzhou to Shenzhen, which formed part of the Kowloon–Canton Railway. Rebuilt for 160km/h, it was termed a 'quasi-high-speed' railway. Trials with new types of train developed by China's maturing rolling stock industry were generally staged on the 9km test loop at the China Academy of Railway Sciences (CARS) in Beijing, but the quasi-high-speed line soon became another proving ground.

On 27 March 1995 an express hauled by a prototype 5,000hp DF11 diesel was dispatched from Guangzhou with the aim of cutting 39 minutes off the 2-hour-40-minute trip to Kowloon. Three years later, the line had been electrified, making it an ideal route for testing some of the latest electric traction from other countries. First to arrive was a set of double-deck coaches from Japan matched with a pair of Swiss electric locomotives. Ordered in November 1995, they were followed by a modified Swedish X2000 seven-car tilting train capable of 200km/h. This ran in commercial service between Kowloon and Guangzhou for some years, eventually returning to its birthplace in 2012, its job accomplished.

SPEED-UP PROGRAMMES

CR soon began to upgrade its trunk lines to 'quasi-high-speed' standards, and in April 1997 the limit on seven key routes radiating from Beijing was raised to 140km/h, permitting the launch of fast services to Shanghai, Shenyang, Guangzhou and Wuhan. CR followed this on 1 October 1998 with twenty-seven pairs of expresses timed at 160km/h.

The domestic rolling stock industry was by now turning out locomotives and multiple-units capable of higher speeds. On 24 June 1998 a SS8 electric locomotive notched up a national speed record of 239.7km/h on the Zhengzhou–Wuhan section of the Beijing–Guangzhou line. Two years later Zhuzhou Electric Loco Works outshopped a high-speed EMU called the DDJ1 whose power car boasted a continuous rating of

1MW per axle; a version of this entered service as the *Blue Arrow* on the Guangzhou–Shenzhen route in January 2001.

On 30 March 2000 the MoR announced that passenger train speeds would be raised to 160km/h on all trunk lines, which meant that many overnight services could be retimed to offer convenient early morning arrivals in major cities. More upgrading permitted a further acceleration from November 2001, and a fifth speed-up programme was implemented on 18 April 2004, by which time 7,700km had been cleared for 160km/h. On the Shanghai–Nanjing line the maximum was raised to 200km/h, lopping over 2 hours off the 14-hour Beijing–Shanghai timing.

DEDICATED LINES

History was made in 1999 when China began to construct the first of many so-called passenger-dedicated lines (PDLs). This 405km racetrack linking Shenyang to Qinhuangdao was ready for trials in 2002. On 27 November that year the *China Star*, a Zhuzhou-built EMU with two power cars and three trailers, streaked up to a new record speed of 321.5km/h on this brand-new railway. The train now resides in the Zhengyangmen Branch of the China Railway Museum.

In the early 2000s it became clear just how serious China was about high speed. Missions to study high-speed operations in Europe and Japan were sent out to gather data. While European and

China Star. On 27 November 1999 this Zhuzhou-built EMU formed of two power cars and three trailers recorded a speed of 321.5km/h between Shenyang and Qinhuangdao. (*Railway Gazette* collection)

Japanese suppliers were keen to win contracts, they were also wary about giving away their expertise. On the other hand, the size of the potential market dwarfed anything in Europe or elsewhere, but the price was to give the Chinese the technical knowledge that they sought – the Chinese insisted on setting up joint ventures with local companies having a majority interest.

In 2000–02 China's state-owned railway equipment industry was grouped into two giant corporations, China Northern (CNR) and China South (CSR). In 2004 CNR produced the nine-car *Changbaishan* EMU, a nine-car train with distributed power and a speed of 210km/h.

It was painted in a white livery with a red stripe bearing an extraordinary resemblance to a German ICE. Although it was pressed into service between Guangzhou and Shenzhen, the design was not satisfactory, and it vanished from the radar.

OLYMPIC OPPORTUNITY

In July 2001 Bejing was nominated to host the 2008 Olympic Games. This was a triumph for the Chinese government, which saw the event as an opportunity to showcase the country's prowess, not just in sport, but in economic terms too. Enormous resources were channelled into the preparations, which included construction of a 14.3 billion yuan

high-speed railway between the capital and Tianjin, 118km to the east, where some of the Olympic venues were located. The trip would take just 30 minutes compared with 1 hour 14 minutes by conventional train.

CR's speed-up programmes were meanwhile posing a problem as the speed differential between passenger and freight trains actually reduced the number of paths available and hence cut line capacity. This was unacceptable, and further speed-ups were cancelled or postponed. Instead, the MoR decided to segregate fast passenger and slow freight trains by building more PDLs.

The scale was breathtaking. Minister of Railways Liu Zhijun announced the details in February 2004: China would construct 28,000km of new lines by 2020, of which 12,000km were to be PDLs and 16,000km were new railways to open up Western China. The PDLs would form a gigantic grid along four north–south and four east–west corridors, while three regional sub-networks of high-speed inter-city routes would also be constructed.

In January 2005 the MoR set out the initial stages of the programme. This included the Beijing–Tianjin route as well as lines from Wuhan to Guangzhou, Zhengzhou to Xi'an, and Nanjing to Hefei. On 1 July 2005, a start was made on the Beijing–Tianjin line, for which Tianjin Mayor Dai Xianglong said the city had been 'longing day and night'.

Project management was placed in the hands of French engineering consultants Systra, working with CARS. The Beijing–Tianjin line had all the attributes of high-speed railways in other countries, including full-grade separation at junctions, and it was viewed as a model for future PDL projects. Around 85 per cent ran on viaducts across flat ground, and precast concrete decks were chosen to speed construction. German slab track obtained under a technology transfer arrangement was laid on the decks. The design speed was 350km/h.

ICE clone? CNR produced the Changbaishan EMU with distributed power in 2004, but the design did not appear to be successful. (*Railway Gazette* collection)

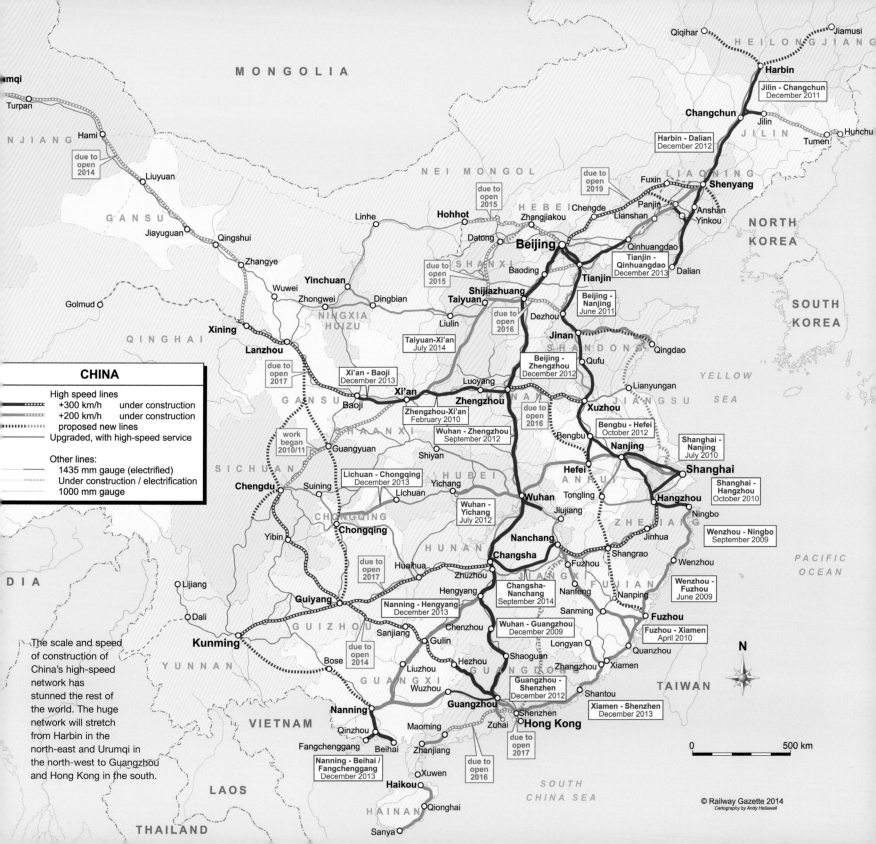

CHINA

High speed lines
+300 km/h under construction
+200 km/h under construction
proposed new lines
Upgraded, with high-speed service

Other lines:
1435 mm gauge (electrified)
Under construction / electrification
1000 mm gauge

The scale and speed
of construction of
China's high-speed
network has
stunned the rest of
the world. The huge
network will stretch
from Harbin in the
north-east and Urumqi in
the north-west to Guangzhou
and Hong Kong in the south.

Jilin - Changchun
December 2011

Harbin - Dalian
December 2012

Tianjin -
Qinhuangdao
December 2013

Beijing -
Nanjing
June 2011

Taiyuan-Xi'an
July 2014

Beijing -
Zhengzhou
December 2012

Xi'an - Baoji
December 2013

Zhengzhou-Xi'an
February 2010

Wuhan - Zhengzhou
September 2012

Bengbu - Hefei
October 2012

Shanghai -
Nanjing
July 2010

Shanghai -
Hangzhou
October 2010

Lichuan - Chongqing
December 2013

Wuhan -
Yichang
July 2012

Wenzhou - Ningbo
September 2009

Changsha-
Nanchang
September 2014

Nanning - Hengyang
December 2013

Wuhan - Guangzhou
December 2009

Wenzhou -
Fuzhou
June 2009

Fuzhou - Xiamen
April 2010

Guangzhou -
Shenzhen
December 2012

Xiamen - Shenzhen
December 2013

Nanning - Beihai /
Fangchenggang
December 2013

due to open 2014

due to open 2015

due to open 2019

due to open 2015

due to open 2016

due to open 2017

due to open 2016

work began 2010/11

due to open 2017

due to open 2014

due to open 2017

due to open 2016

0   500 km

N

© Railway Gazette 2014
Cartography by Andy Hellawell

IMPORTED TRAINS

Despite efforts by CNR and CSR to develop high-speed trains, none offered the speed, comfort and reliability that the MoR was seeking. But the imminent completion of a vast network of new railways meant that a large fleet was needed, and quickly. So the MoR called international tenders for 140 train sets, and on 9 October 2004 three deals were agreed with different consortia. A group of six Japanese companies led by Kawasaki agreed to supply an eight-car version of the E2-1000 Shinkansen trains used by JR East for ¥140 billion. Of sixty trains in the contract, three would be sent complete from Japan, with six more following in kit form. The other fifty-one would be assembled by Nache Sifang, part of CSR, in Qingdao.

Alstom, working in conjunction with China Northern subsidiary Changchun Railway Vehicles and other Chinese companies, also signed up for sixty eight-car trains. Rather than a version of the TGV, Alstom offered a non-tilting wide-bodied Pendolino derivative. Three were to be built in Italy at the former Fiat plant in Savigliano, six sent as kits and fifty-one assembled locally.

A contract for the other twenty trains was won by Bombardier, which was already well-established in China with a coach-building joint venture in Qingdao known then as Bombardier Sifang Power (now Bombardier Sifang Transportation). These were an eight-car variant of the wide-bodied Regina design originally developed for services in Sweden. All three contracts were for 200km/h trains and all included technology transfer; a separate accord between the ministry and Bombardier included a 'strategic co-operation framework agreement'.

Siemens did not share in this initial tranche of contracts, but the German company's turn came on 10 November 2005 when it agreed to supply sixty wide-bodied derivatives of its Velaro family in partnership with CNR's Tangshan Locomotive & Rolling Stock Works. The €1.3 billion deal was signed during a visit to Berlin by Chinese President Hu Jintao. Three of the 8.8MW trains were to be manufactured in Germany, with the rest put together locally. These were the first trains to be built for regular operation in China at 300km/h.

The first of the Kawasaki EMUs reached the port of Qingdao in early 2006, and they were followed in December 2007 by the first of the Alstom trains from Italy. The Sifang-built Bombardier fleet was due to make a debut on routes from Shanghai over the 2007 lunar New Year. All three types ran in 160km/h timings until 18 April, after which they were authorised to run at 200km/h. CR was by now designating its new fleet as CRH: the Bombardier trains became CRH1, the Japanese fleet CRH2, the Siemens trains CRH3, and the Alstom units CRH5.

In mid-2007 Bombardier agreed to work with its Chinese partners on more versions of the CRH1, including one variant with sleeping cars. Sifang meanwhile unveiled a CRH2 eight-car derivative of the E2-1000 in December 2007, claiming that it was suitable for 300km/h. This was just the start of a massive train-construction programme that included a sleeping-car version of the CRH2 and the two CRH380 types: the CRH380A was based on the CRH2, and the CRH380B was a derivative of the CRH3.

The MoR wanted to have five CRH3 sets and five of the uprated Japanese trains available to provide a 10-minute interval service to whisk athletes and spectators between Beijing and Tianjin during the

Chinese Shinkansen. Under an agreement reached in October 2004, a consortium of Japanese companies supplied a batch of sixty CRH2 train sets derived from the E2-1000 used by JR East. Chinese manufacturers have since built hundreds of trains derived from the original design. (Andrew Benton)

Olympic Games, and it asked Siemens to bring forward delivery of the first CRH3. In January 2008, two months early, the maiden CRH3 reached Chinese soil and was immediately put through a programme of tests at Tangshan before being sent to the CARS test loop. Soon afterwards, a garlanded locally assembled CRH3 emerged from Tangshan on 11 April 2008 – significantly, the builder was now claiming that it was designed for 350km/h.

The CRH3s were dispatched for tests on the line to Tianjin, and on the morning of 24 June Minister of Railways Liu Zhijun witnessed one of the trains rocket up to a new Chinese record speed of 394.3km/h. Siemens project manager

Ernst Reuss modestly described it as 'quite a respectable achievement'. Next day it was the turn of Chinese President Hu Jintao, who described the high-speed trains as 'a milestone in the history of China's railway development'.

These events foreshadowed the launch of the Olympic service on 1 August, which duly won accolades for its efficiency and punctuality. Mystery surrounded the maximum speed, with some reports asserting that they travelled at 330 or 350km/h. Either way, this was faster than any other scheduled service in the world.

I was able to see for myself on 25 June 2009 when I made a return trip from Beijing to Tianjin.

Arriving at Beijing South station, I found that it was a stunning advertisement for train travel in China. Vast, light and spotless, it outclassed many airport terminals. However, access to the concourse with seats for 4,000 passengers was strictly controlled by airport-style security and luggage checks, and ticket purchase required an identification or passport number. Tickets were checked at gates giving access to escalators to the twenty-four platforms; departing and arriving passengers were completely segregated.

Train C2055 from Platform 21 was a CRH3 assembled at Tangshan. We averaged 236km/h on the outbound sprint, briefly touching 328km/h,

Multiple-units. The CRH5 is a wide-bodied version of Alstom's non-tilting Pendolino for 250km/h operation. A pair of units awaits departure from Beijing's main station. (Author)

Overnight express. Both the CRH1 and the CRH2 families include sleeping-car EMUs able to run at 250km/h. Ideal for long journeys and offering excellent ride comfort on modern track, the trains include comfortable beds in four-berth compartments. (Author)

Better than an airport. Beijing South is the departure point for high-speed services to Tianjin and Shanghai.
The concourse is huge, light and airy, but access requires passengers to pass through a security check. (Author)

but on the return trip Train C2166, also a CRH3, accelerated up to 348km/h, confirming reports that this was indeed a 350km/h railway. MoR officials assured me that the CRH service had been extremely successful, with 80,000 passengers a day travelling between the two cities, four times as many as before the launch.

Hostess service. Tibet spring water was on the drinks menu on this CRH3 service between Beijing and Tianjin. (Author)

Tianjin trio. Three CRH3 sets await departure from the rebuilt station at Tianjin on 9 December 2010. The trip to Beijing over the high-speed line built for the 2008 Olympic Games takes just 30 minutes. (Author)

Land of contrasts. High-speed trains are quite the norm in many parts of China. A barber on a bridge clips away as a CRH1 EMU passes below. The CRH1 family was developed with Bombardier Transportation. (Andrew Benton)

FASTER THAN EVER

The timescale for building the Beijing–Tianjin line had been tight, but the job was straightforward although it did entail constructing a huge new station at Beijing South and rebuilding the station in Tianjin. Far more ambitious was the spectacular project for a 350km/h line from Wuhan to Guangzhou. After a ceremonial start on 23 June 2005, just fifty-four months were allowed to build and test 968km of double-track electrified railway before opening in December 2009 – this astonishing project boasted 691 bridges with a combined length of 468.5km and no fewer than 226 tunnels totalling 177.6km. Long sections were built on viaducts, partly to conserve farmland and to avoid severing paths and roads. Companies from France, Germany, South Korea and the Netherlands with experience of high-speed line construction were integrated into the project team, their role being to supervise construction and to ensure that international standards were used. The CTCS-3 signalling was a version of ETCS Level 2 supplied by Bombardier.

The route crosses the Jiangshan Plain and traverses the Changsha, Zhuzhou and Hengyang basins. Hilly country is encountered in Hubei, Hunan and Guangdong, but the most formidable obstacle is formed by the Yaoshan Range of the Nanling Mountains, which the MoR's Chief Engineer He Huawu described as 'stupendous, with deep river valleys and steep terrain'. Over

300km of the alignment runs through areas of karst, requiring special techniques to ensure stability.

On 26 December 2009 China stunned the world with the launch of trains running at 350km/h over this spectacular railway. Train G1001, the first southbound departure, streaked over the 922km between Wuhan Xi and Guangzhou Bei in just 2 hours 48 minutes at what *Railway Gazette*

World's fastest railway. A CRH380A streaks through the spectacular landscape of northern Guangdong Province on the Wuhan–Guangzhou high-speed line. When this route opened in December 2009, non-stop trains were timed at average speeds of up to 312km/h. (Andrew Benton)

On time arrival. A CRH3 EMU arrives in Guangzhou South station. (Andrew Benton)

International described as 'a blistering average' of 329.3km/h. At a stroke this train had smashed the world record for the fastest non-stop timing of a publicly scheduled train. That was a special inaugural run, but the regular timetable was hardly less impressive. Non-stop timings were 2 hours 57 minutes southbound and just a minute faster northbound, averaging 312.5 and 310.8km/h respectively. China had shot to the top of the world speed table with an undisputed lead. Never before had a railway exceeded an average timetabled start-to-stop speed of 300km/h.

By the end of 2010 the line was handling fifty-two trains a day each way, plus a further twenty-eight short workings between Guangzhou and Changsha. On busy days these trains were carrying around 115,000 passengers, with the end-to-end timing cut to 3 hours or less compared with 11 hours before the line opened. As long-distance passenger traffic switched to the new line, paths were released on the original tracks for more freight trains. In He's words, the line brought about 'a dramatic change in the spatial structure, industrial pattern and development philosophy' along the route.

BEIJING–SHANGHAI

Construction had in the meantime started on the 1,318km line from Beijing to Shanghai. All eyes in the railway business had been watching this enormous and long-anticipated scheme. The State Council gave its seal of approval in March 2008,

and on 18 April Premier Wen Jiabao shovelled some earth for the cameras at a ground-breaking party, officially kicking off the project. With the help of standardised construction methods for bridges and other structures, work progressed at a phenomenal rate from forty separate sites, so fast, in fact, that the *People's Daily Online* was able to report in November 2010 that the opening date would be brought forward from 2012 to 2011. The speed record with the CRH380AL in the following month suggested that this was credible.

Foreign consultants had made huge efforts to sell their technology to the Chinese for this project, but by the time the Beijing-Shanghai High-Speed Railway Co was created in December 2007 to manage the scheme, the Chinese had absorbed enough knowledge to effectively go it alone. Construction might have started earlier had it not been for a political faction favouring maglev technology, but this idea was dropped in 2004 and planners were able to concentrate on designing a railway with steel rails.

Designed to handle trains operating at an unprecedented 380km/h, the line serves twenty-two stations in major cities, catering for both short and long-distance travel. Of the 244 bridges and viaducts, one traverses the Yellow River at Jinan and another crosses the Yangtze River at Nanjing. This is a fantastic structure no less than 9.2km long: the two main steel truss spans, each 336m long, are designed to carry six tracks with trains travelling at up to 300km/h. At the southern end of the route is the Danyang-Kunshan Grand Bridge across the Yangtze River Delta, which at 165km is the longest in the world. There are twenty-one tunnels, and hundreds of wind-speed sensors, rainfall monitors and seismic detectors are strung along the route. The MoR claimed that the 220 billion yuan line had used twice as much concrete as the Three Gorges Dam and 120 times the amount of steel as in the famous 'Bird's Nest' stadium in Beijing.

Liu Zhijun attended a track-laying completion ceremony at Bengbu on 15 November 2010, and the line opened with simultaneous departures at 3 p.m. from Beijing and Shanghai on 30 June 2011, but by then Liu was no longer in charge at the MoR. On board the southbound special was Premier Wen Jiabao – the launch was one of several events timed to coincide with the ninetieth anniversary of the Chinese Communist Party. Regular services began the next day, with sixty-three trains each way timed at 300km/h

using a mix of CRH380A and CRH380B sets and a further twenty-seven slower services in the hands of CRH2 and CRH5 sets. The fastest timing was under 5 hours. CRH380 passengers could book seats with a view through the driver's cab, and some trains offered premium fare 'de luxe' or 'business class' seating as well as a dining car.

Domestic airlines had already cut fares by up to half in anticipation of a loss of traffic; they had been stung by the super-fast trains on other routes. A World Bank report published in 2012

noted that 'air routes from Zhengzhou to Xi'an and from Wuhan to Nanjing both survived only a few months' after the opening of high-speed railways. On the Changsha–Guangzhou route passenger demand for air travel fell from 90,000 trips a month to 30,000, with a similar but less dramatic drop over the longer route between Wuhan and Guangzhou. However, between Beijing and Shanghai the longer distance meant that the impact on air travel, at least initially, was much less.

Crossing the Yangtze. The enormous Dashengguan Bridge over the River Yangtze at Nanjing is over 9km long and carries six tracks, at least two of which are designed for trains to cross at 300km/h. (Andrew Benton)

Light fantastic. China Railway Corp's extensive CRH380A fleet is diagrammed for services on the world's longest high-speed line stretching for over 1,300km between Beijing and Shanghai. (Liu Jialiang)

Business class. Passengers on selected Beijing–Shanghai trains can elect to pay a higher fare for luxury travel. (Liu Jialiang)

DOUBTS EMERGE

While China's official news media can be relied on to give a positive version of events, there were some intriguing undercurrents. When I visited the country in June 2009 there were repeated assurances that the high-speed trains and infrastructure were built with Chinese technology, and some officials made a point of saying that it was all Chinese intellectual property. A Western observer would find this difficult to believe, given that the CRH trains appeared identical to the various European or Japanese trains supplied at the outset (p138).

A conversation with a senior manager of a Western supplier was especially interesting. He said that the train sets supplied for the Beijing–Tianjin service were designed for 300km/h. He assured me that the maximum speed notices in the driving cabs had suddenly been changed from 300 to 350km/h – a remarkable claim. He explained that increasing the speed to 350km/h would not be a problem with new wheels, but once they became worn, the smaller diameter could lead to mechanical problems. Supporting his assertions was his imminent departure for Beijing, where he said he was going to discuss the supply of replacement components.

I had also heard from a Western contractor involved in the Wuhan–Guangzhou line how the project was run – there was no room for mistakes or delay, and the opening date was absolute. Any deviation from the schedule simply had to be corrected. Nor was there any leeway to negotiate costs – if they exceeded the contractor's budget, that was just tough.

All this suggested that problems were being stored up for the future. Adhering to deadlines is fine, but if there are genuine issues to sort out then they need to be dealt with at once, not hidden away to be tackled later. Rumours were also rife that corruption was taking place on a grand scale and there were unsubstantiated reports about safety problems.

Services between Beijing and Shanghai were badly disrupted on several days during the weeks after opening, with trains stranded for hours without power. Thunderstorms had affected the power supplies, but there were worrying hints of other problems too, with suggestions from the National Audit Office that billions of yuan had been 'embezzled'.

These issues surfaced at the highest level in early 2011 when Liu Zhijin was suddenly removed from his post as Secretary of the Communist Party in the MoR. News agency Xinhua said that he was being investigated for an alleged 'severe violation of discipline' by the Central Commission for Discipline Inspection; this appeared to centre on 'commission' payments from contracts and sub-contracts. His replacement was Sheng Guangzhu, previously Head of the General Administration of Customs.

Sheng said on 2 April in a television broadcast that the ministry had conducted a six-week railway safety audit at the behest of Vice Premier Zhang Dejiang, revealing what Sheng termed 'some deep-rooted problems'. Interviewed in the *People's Daily* on 14 April, Sheng said that the 350km/h maximum speed on PDLs would be cut to 300km/h, suggesting that the 380km/h planned for Beijing–Shanghai would not be sanctioned.

When the line opened, the speed of the CRH380 trains was indeed restricted to 300km/h, with other types limited to 250km/h. This 'will allow more variation in ticket prices based on market principles', Sheng said. This comment was attributed to widespread complaints about high fares, but the speed reduction also reflected concerns about line capacity, energy consumption and wear of rails and wheels. It may also have been prompted by high operating costs at a time when CR's finances were under tight scrutiny following the spending spree during the Liu era. Sheng's statements suggested that investment in new projects would be scaled back, at least in the short term.

THE DREAM IS SHATTERED

Dramatists have often used stormy weather as an omen for a tragic event. But on the night of 23 July 2011 at Wenzhou in southern China the thunderstorm was for real. Lightning caused the signalling at Wenzhou South to fail, and controllers decided to keep the trains running on the coastal line linking Ningbo, Wenzhou and Fuzhou by reverting to manual operation over the 18km between Yongja and Wenzhou South. This meant overriding the CTCS-2 train control equipment, a Chinese derivative of ETCS Level 1. Built to handle passenger trains at up to 250km/h, the line had opened in September 2009; it was not a PDL, but one of many higher-speed mixed-traffic routes built as part of the vast expansion programme.

A short-distance inter-city train from Hangzhou to Fuzhou formed of a sixteen-car CRH1B set had been allowed to precede a late-running long-distance service from Beijing to Fuzhou.

Under control. China's Passenger Dedicated Lines are fitted with CTCS, a Chinese version of ETCS. The driver in charge of a CRH5 heading along the PDL towards Beijing from Qinhuangdao appears unperturbed by a murky windscreen. (Author)

Accident aftermath. The collision at Wenzhou on 23 July 2011 sent shock waves across China. The surprising official reaction was to bury the coaches that had fallen from the viaduct – hence the diggers at the bottom of the photo. This move backfired spectacularly on China's social media, and the vehicles were removed for examination. (Press Association)

The first train halted at Yongja at 7.51 p.m., where it was held until instructed to leave at 8.15 p.m.; the driver was told to pass the defective signals at 20km/h. In the meantime the express from Beijing, consisting of a CRH2E sleeping-car train set, was ordered to make an unscheduled stop at Yongja, where it arrived at 8.12 p.m.

The first train reached the failure site at 8.23 p.m., where it was brought to a stand. As instructed, the driver then switched to manual mode to pass through the failure area at 20km/h, but it took him several minutes to restart his train. The sixteen-car train from Beijing had meanwhile left Yongja at 8.24 p.m., reportedly on a 'clear signal'. In fact, the signal should have been showing a red aspect, but the lightning strike had damaged a critical component, meaning that a false proceed aspect was shown. The train travelled at around 140km/h, rapidly catching up with the Hangzhou–Fuzhou train ahead. As soon as the control centre realised what had happened, controllers tried to contact the Beijing train's driver by radio to warn him of the train ahead, but it was too late. The Beijing express struck the rear of the slowly moving CRH1B at about 8.30 p.m.

The collision happened on a viaduct, and the CRH2E over-rode the last car of the CRH1B before the first three cars crashed down into the fields below. The fourth car also fell, landing end-on in a near-vertical position, leaning against the viaduct. On board the two trains were 1,630 passengers; official sources said that forty people died and 192 were injured.

The government's next move was surprising and extremely controversial. It issued instructions to break up and bury the damaged coaches in a pit excavated below the viaduct, allegedly to 'protect' any innovative technology. There was a furious reaction, and the government reportedly issued instructions to Chinese media on how to cover the crash. But it was too late. A storm of activity on Chinese social media outstripped attempts to censor or control the news, and within two days the authorities were obliged to reverse their decision: the buried coaches were dug up and taken away for examination.

China had become the only country in the world where high-speed trains had collided on a newly built railway, and its ambition to lead the world in high-speed train technology was in tatters. The MoR at once instructed CR to reduce speed on the PDLs and slammed the brakes on the frenetic new line programme. Pursuing ultra-high-speed rail research in the aftermath of the accident was now unacceptable, which explains why development of the experimental CIT500 was put on a back burner.

An official report on the collision was published by the State Administration of Work Safety on 28 December 2011. On the same day a meeting of the State Council was told that fifty-four people could be held accountable, one of whom was former railways minister Liu Zhijun; both train drivers were exonerated.

The report attributed the accident to a wrong-side failure of the signalling equipment, with a signal erroneously displaying a green aspect following the failure of a fuse. It found that there were 'serious design flaws' in the system, exacerbated by 'sloppy management and the mishandling of a lightning strike'. The report also suggested that pressure to complete new lines from the MoR may have been a contributory factor. This followed allegations that lightning protection equipment had been omitted from locally supplied signalling systems in order to cut costs and save time. It is important to note that there was no failure of the equipment on the trains – the key issue was an inherent software problem revealed by the lightning strike.

FINANCIAL WOES FAIL TO HALT EXPANSION

In time, the furore generated by the crash subsided, and CR began the long haul to try and restore its lost reputation. But other issues were becoming pressing. Borrowing by the MoR to fund network expansion was approaching unmanageable levels, so much so that leading academics were suggesting that there was a risk of bankruptcy by 2015 if the MoR did not alter course. When Liu was appointed to head the MoR in 2003, capital spending was around 57 billion yuan a year, but by 2010 the figure had exploded to 770 billion. The cumulative debt in 2003 totalled nearly 400 billion yuan, but by the end of September 2012 the total had reached 2.7 trillion yuan, which someone remarked was higher than the entire GDP of Denmark. It was no surprise that the huge fiefdom controlled by the MoR with nearly 2 million employees was put under scrutiny by the State Council.

When recession gripped the world in 2008, China decided to accelerate the pace of construction to stimulate its economy. The astonishing rate of construction is illustrated by the completion of no less than 5,000km of new railway in 2010 alone, nearly all of which were PDLs or other categories of high-speed line. Despite the Wenzhou accident and other setbacks, over 2,000km of new railway was completed in 2011.

The government pruned the 2011–15 spend from 280 billion yuan to 230 billion, but in 2012 new PDLs begun earlier were being finished

Fast to Hong Kong. These sleek aerodynamic high-speed trains will serve the Guangzhou–Shenzhen–Hong Kong Express Rail Link from 2017. (MTR Corporation Ltd)

Doctor Yellow, Chinese version. China Railway Corp has several high-speed infrastructure inspection trains. Seen at Qingdao, this one is based on the CRH380A. (Liu Jialiang)

one after the other. The 536km from Wuhan to Zhengzhou opened on 28 September 2012, paving the way for direct CRH services all the way from Shenzhen to Xi'an, saving more than 12 hours compared with conventional trains. Just three months later, the 663km PDL from Beijing to Shijiazhuang and Zhengzhou opened on 26 December, so completing a high-speed route all the way from the capital to Guangzhou, a distance of 2,298km. Whereas the trip previously took around 21 hours, Beijing–Guangzhou CRH services sped between the two cities in 7 hours 59 minutes. The northern part of the route is used by Beijing–Xi'an trains as far as Zhengzhou, where

they join the Zhengzhou–Xi'an PDL opened in February 2010.

At the southern end this route continues beyond Guangzhou to Shenzhen and Kowloon. The final part of the line from the border of the Shenzhen Special Administrative Region to the terminus at West Kowloon was approved by Hong Kong's Legislative Council in January 2010, at which time opening was envisaged in 2015. The entire 26km Express Rail Link runs in tunnel, culminating in a huge underground terminus with fifteen platforms, of which nine will be for long-distance CRH trains and six for shuttle services to Shenzhen and Guangzhou. The cost of this complex project

was HK$66.8 billion at money-of-the-day prices, which was one reason why it attracted strong protests from local people when the legislation was going through the Council.

In March 2014 a torrential storm led to a section of partly finished tunnel being flooded, damaging one of the tunnel boring machines. This, combined with unexpected geological difficulties encountered at the terminus, prompted Hong Kong's MTR Corp, the organisation managing the scheme, to announce on 15 April 2014 that the line would not open until the end of 2017.

In autumn 2012 the MoR announced another tranche of spending on new projects, partly restoring the earlier cutbacks. Testing on the most northerly PDL over the 921km from Harbin to Dalian commenced on 8 October 2012, with opening following on 1 December. Temperatures in this region can fall to −38°C, and snow melting equipment was installed along the route, as on the Joetsu Shinkansen. Different summer and winter schedules apply, with a lower top speed in winter.

The increased investment level became evident in January 2013, when the capital spend was over 60 per cent higher than in January 2012. But the continued high outlay on new railways was called into question in March 2013 when the State Council suddenly abolished the MoR, with 'administrative functions' passing to the Ministry of Transport and 'commercial functions' handed to a new entity called China Railway Corp (CRC). The Ministry of Transport, at least initially, was responsible for supervising service quality and setting technical and safety standards. The move also appeared to be designed to reduce opportunities for corruption, with CRC controlled by the Ministry of Finance.

So far, the government seems convinced of the benefits springing from the huge investment in high-speed railways, and the expansion programme is set to continue. CRC has been granted the same preferential tax policies as MoR, and the government made clear that it would not have to shoulder the MoR's debt burden alone as some debts had been incurred as a result of providing public services.

How China Obtained High-Speed Technology

The Ministry of Railways first invited international tenders for high-speed trains in mid-2004. The process was structured to ensure that Chinese companies obtained the know-how to build the trains themselves. Looking back, the strategy was immensely successful.

In each case the bidding organisation had to be Chinese, but with the backing of a foreign supplier who could demonstrate expertise in building high-speed trains. At the heart of the arrangement was a technology transfer agreement that embraced the 'core technologies' needed to manufacture high-speed rolling stock. It covered traction equipment, assembly and quality control processes, systems integration and training.

Within China, a huge programme to develop high-speed technology was simultaneously put in place by the Ministry of Railways and the Ministry of Science & Technology. The programme involved the 'State Engineering Laboratory for System Integration of High Speed Trains', plus other organisations. According to Duan Liren, who was Deputy Director-General of Transport Management in Beijing, and Dennis Li, Vice-President of the International Chinese Transportation Professionals Association, it was 'the biggest research project ever undertaken by the Ministry of Science & Technology' and covered ten major fields of research. Also involved were twenty-five of China's leading universities, eleven top research institutions and fifty-one national laboratories. More than 10,000 engineers and technicians took part, together with over 500 professors and 200 other senior researchers.

All these resources were pooled to assimilate the technology and implement it on an industrial scale. In this way China could meet the demands of the huge domestic travel market that was opening up. And by working with Chinese companies who had obtained the expertise under technology transfer agreements and developed it further, it was possible to claim Chinese intellectual property rights.

Many of the world's high-speed train suppliers took part in this process: Kawasaki and other Japanese companies that built Shinkansen trains, Siemens, Bombardier and Alstom. There was reportedly anger in Japan that Kawasaki had agreed to transfer Shinkansen technology, while Alstom was careful not to release its TGV know-how, let alone that for the AGV. Another view was expressed by Heinrich von Pierer, President & CEO of Siemens from 1992 to 2005: 'the risk of not being in China is bigger than the risk of being in China'.

There is no doubt that China wants to sell its own high-speed rail products on the world market. As long ago as 2007 Chinese companies were in the frame for supplying inter-city trains to British open-access operator Grand Central. Nothing came of it, but China has become a force to be reckoned with in the passenger-train market; it has also assimilated track and signalling technology, giving it the ability to bid for almost any type of high-speed rail contract.

The CRH380D is designed for 380km/h. Built by Bombardier Sifang Transportation, it is part of Bombardier's 'Zefiro' family; seventy of these eight-car trains are being delivered to China Railway Corp. (Bombardier Transportation)

By the time the MoR was replaced, around 10,000km of high-speed line had been completed, with another 12,000km under construction or planned, ultimately ensuring that all cities whose population is 500,000 or more are connected by high-speed trains. Already, the total length far outstrips that in any other country, with the massive scheme taking high-speed trains to Urumqi in the far north-west, opening in stages during November and December 2014; at the end of 2014 China had 12,183km of high-speed railway. On the other hand, it is only fair to say that in China major projects are not subject to long enquiries and legal challenges.

While more rails are being laid, so the production of high-speed trains has continued on a truly industrial scale. By the end of 2013, CSR alone had assembled 751 eight-car CRH sets. More high-speed train designs have since emerged, including the 200km/h CRH6 family and the CRH380D, a 380km/h version of Bombardier's Zefiro family related to the ETR1000 in Italy. The first of twenty eight-car and sixty sixteen-car versions of these trains began a 600,000km test programme on the Guangzhou–Changsha section of the Beijing–Shenzhen PDL on 22 December 2013. And in September 2014 CSR revealed that it had developed a CRH train with permanent-magnet traction motors for the Shanghai–Kunming route.

The World Bank, which has been closely monitoring China's high-speed line programme, notes that CRH services typically have a 70 per cent load factor and have generated much extra travel, despite fares being three or four times higher than for conventional trains – they are generally pitched at a similar level to discounted air travel. Other commentators remark that fares

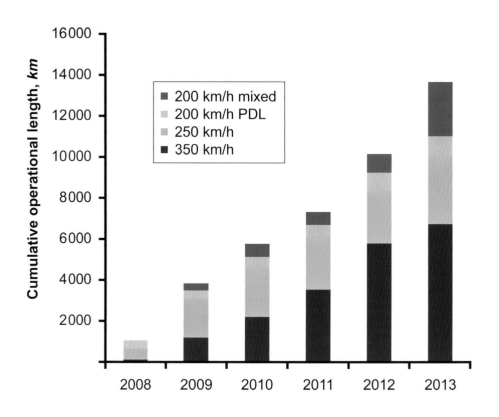

Length of high-speed line in China by year and category from 2008 to 2013. (World Bank report: High-Speed Railways in China: A Look at Construction Costs. Original source: Yearbooks of China Transportation & Communications, China Railway Yearbooks and Planning & Statistics Department of CRC)

have not risen in line with wages, meaning that many more Chinese can afford to travel than even a few years ago. The World Bank noted in a 2014 report that 672 million trips were made on CRH services in 2013, 530 million being on PDLs.

China has rocked the world with its ability to build high-speed railways at a rate that no one thought possible. Despite Wenzhou and a cutback in maximum speeds, there is little doubt that

CRC runs the fastest timetabled trains in the world. On the basis of the best information available, the fastest timings in 2013 were between Shijiazhuang and Zhengzhou Dong, with three trains booked to cover the 383km in 81 minutes at an average of 283.7km/h. These outpaced the fastest French timing at the time of 271.8km/h between Lorraine TGV and Champagne-Ardenne TGV.

10

Desert Dreams Come True

China's expertise in building railways in other countries dates back to construction of the Tanzania–Zambia Railway in the 1970s. By 2005 this knowledge had been honed considerably, and China National Machinery Export & Import Corp and China Railway Construction Corp were chosen, along with Turkish companies, to build sections of a 250km/h railway between Ankara and Istanbul. China supported the project with a loan, reportedly worth US$750 million, while another €850 million came from the European Investment Bank.

Plans for a fast rail link between the Turkish capital and Haydarpaşa on the Bosporus date back to 1972, when a 280km cut-off was proposed between Arifiye and Sincan. This would have shortened the 577km trip by 118km. Although a start was made, the cut-off was never finished, but a high-speed service was finally launched forty-two years later over the longer route via Eskişehir.

On 25 July 2014 Prime Minister Recep Tayyip Erdoğan and his wife were guests of honour on a special train from Ankara to Pendik – an interim terminus on the outskirts of Istanbul – that preceded the launch of six scheduled services a day. The train ran over a new line electrified at 25kV 50Hz for most of the route, switching to newly upgraded tracks over the last 56km from Közeköy to Gebze in the Istanbul suburbs. The train was reportedly delayed because of an overhead wire problem, but this was a very minor issue in the context of a long-awaited and much-needed project. The first part of the Ankara–Eskişehir line had opened in 2009, and the Prime Ministerial special marked completion of the Eskişehir–Istanbul section; the end-to-end distance via the new line is 533km.

At 3 hours 45 minutes, journey times are spectacularly shorter than anything up to 9 hours over the old route. A further cut to 3 hours is in prospect, but this depends on reopening the line between Gebze and Söğütlüçeşme, which was closed in mid-2013 for upgrading to carry a frequent suburban service through the Marmaray tunnel linking the Asian and European halves of Istanbul under the Bosporus. The work includes construction of a bidirectional third track, which will carry inter-city trains, allowing high-speed services to reach Haydarpaşa.

Construction of the initial section of new line between Ankara and Eskişehir began in 2003. This marked the launch of an ambitious programme to build several high-speed lines radiating from the capital – after years of neglecting the national railway, the Turkish government had

Flagship event. The initial section of Turkey's first high-speed line opened between Ankara and Eskişehir in 2009, six years after construction began. (Türker Ahi/TCDD Photography)

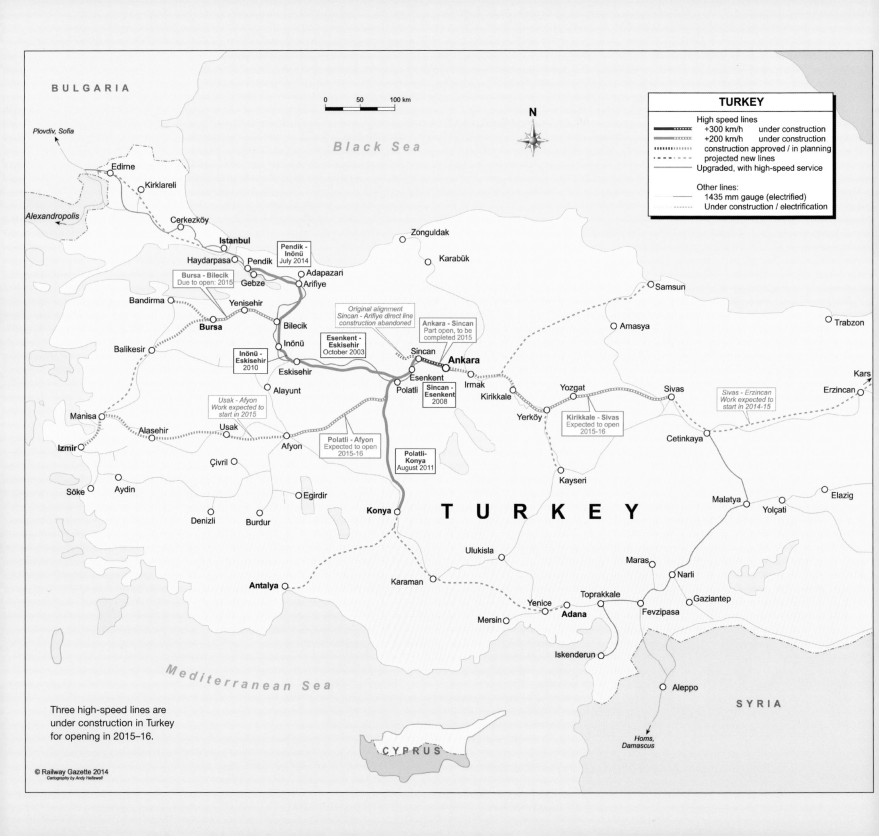

TURKEY

High speed lines
+300 km/h   under construction
+200 km/h   under construction
construction approved / in planning
projected new lines
Upgraded, with high-speed service

Other lines:
1435 mm gauge (electrified)
Under construction / electrification

BULGARIA

Plovdiv, Sofia

Black Sea

Alexandropolis

Edirne

Kirklareli

Cerkezköy

Istanbul

Haydarpasa   Pendik

Pendik -
Inönü
July 2014

Adapazari

Gebze   Arifiye

Bursa - Bilecik
Due to open: 2015

Bandirma

Yenisehir

Bursa

Bilecik

Zonguldak

Karabük

Samsun

Trabzon

Original alignment
Sincan - Arifiye direct line
construction abandoned

Ankara - Sincan
Part open, to be
completed 2015

Amasya

Balikesir

Inönü -
Eskisehir
2010

Inönü

Esenkent -
Eskisehir
October 2003

Sincan

Ankara

Eskisehir

Esenkent

Irmak

Kirikkale

Yozgat

Sivas

Kars

Erzincan

Alayunt

Polatli

Sincan -
Esenkent
2008

Yerköy

Kirikkale - Sivas
Expected to open
2015-16

Sivas - Erzincan
Work expected to
start in 2014-15

Manisa

Alasehir

Usak

Usak - Afyon
Work expected to
start in 2015

Afyon

Polatli - Afyon
Expected to open
2015-16

Polatli-
Konya
August 2011

Kayseri

Cetinkaya

Izmir

Çivril

Söke   Aydin

Egirdir

Denizli   Burdur

Konya

T U R K E Y

Malatya

Yolçati

Elazig

Ulukisla

Maras

Narli

Antalya

Karaman

Yenice

Toprakkale

Gaziantep

Mersin   **Adana**

Fevzipasa

Mediterranean Sea

Iskenderun

Aleppo

S Y R I A

*Homs,
Damascus*

Three high-speed lines are
under construction in Turkey
for opening in 2015–16.

C Y P R U S

© Railway Gazette 2014
Cartography by Andy Hellewell

finally recognised rail's potential and decided to invest in its forgotten asset. A decision was taken to limit speed to 250km/h as a compromise between journey times and energy consumption; trains were initially controlled using ETCS Level 1, but Level 2 is now being installed. In terms of journey time reductions, the results are sensational (Table I).

Even before the line to Eskişehir and Istanbul had been completed, work began on a high-speed line to Konya, providing a direct link south from the capital to a region previously only accessible by a roundabout route. Testing began in December 2010, and the line opened on 24 August 2011. On 23 March 2013 a 5km cut-off linking the Ankara–Eskişehir and Ankara–Konya high-speed lines near the junction at Polatli allowed the introduction of two daily direct Eskişehir–Konya high-speed services taking just 2 hours. Speaking at the launch of the first train, Erdoğan said the high-speed network would soon connect fourteen provinces, reaching south beyond Konya to Karaman, Mersin, Adana and Osmaniye.

Due to open in 2015 is a 75km high-speed link from Bilecik to Bursa, which is not yet served by rail. Contracts for the first stage of a 250km/h line to the important city of Izmir were signed off by the transport ministry in June 2012; the new alignment leaves the Ankara–Konya line about 25km south of Polatli at Kocahacili. At the moment the train trip over a roundabout 825km route takes around 14 hours, but the new line will cut the distance to 624km and put Izmir just 3 hours 30 minutes away from Ankara. Yet another new route is under construction to Sivas, 405km east of Ankara.

TRAINS FROM SPAIN

For its launch fleet of high-speed stock, Turkish Railways (TCDD) ordered ten six-car trains from Spanish builder CAF. Based on the Renfe S-120, the first of these 411-seat train sets arrived in

Train from Spain. Turkish Railways has a dozen six-car train sets supplied by Spanish rolling stock builder CAF. The design is based on Renfe's Class S-120. (Türker Ahi/TCDD Photography)

Turkey in 2007, and two more sets were ordered. TCDD had in the meantime begun trials with an ETRY500 test train on loan from Italy for four months to help commission the new infrastructure. The Italian visitor distinguished itself with a Turkish speed record of 303km/h on the first section of the Ankara–Istanbul route between Beylikova and Esenkent in September 2007.

The Spanish trains, driven by Renfe-trained drivers, were marketed as YHT (*Yüksek Hizli Tren*). They quickly demonstrated that rail could outclass bus or air travel in terms of speed, comfort and ease of use, so much so that the government determined in 2010 to lavish further spending on the rail network – and on a truly spectacular scale.

Plans called for no less than 14,500km of new line by 2023, when Turkey will celebrate its centenary as a republic. This will absorb an astronomic US$45 billion, but even more expansion is planned up to 2035 so that around 12,000km will eventually be suitable for 250km/h. All this is designed to restore rail's lost market share, which for many years has languished in single figures as new motorways removed TCDD's long-distance traffic.

TCDD clearly needed a much larger fleet of high-speed rolling stock. The government's network expansion plans attracted plenty of interest, and Alstom hoped to sell TCDD a version of its AGV, while Siemens offered a version of its Velaro. The German company won the day, walking off

Luxury ride. The popularity of TCDD's Yüksek Hizli Tren services is partly explained by comfortable interiors, but huge cuts in journey time will drive business as the network expands. (Türker Ahi/TCDD Photography)

in 2013 with a contract for seven trains; seven years of maintenance took the contract value to €285 million.

Remarkably, Siemens dispatched the first train a few weeks after the order was signed. Pending agreement with Deutsche Bahn, this train set had been intended as a seventeenth Class 407, partly as compensation for late delivery of the rest of the fleet. Siemens decided, however, that this train could usefully earn its keep, and on 20 September 2013 sent it by rail through Hungary, Romania and Bulgaria to Turkey.

In April 2014 TCDD called tenders for ten more trains, and the €400 million order was confirmed on 18 February 2015. Meanwhile, Turkish factories have been building rolling stock for many years, and a group of companies and universities

has completed a 'concept design' for a locally made 250km/h EMU. A high-speed technology test centre is also planned.

Table I   Selected journey times in Turkey

Route	Journey time	
	via old line	via high-speed line
Ankara–Eskişehir	3 h 55 min	1 h 30 min
Ankara–Istanbul	8 h 48 min	3 h 45 min
Ankara–Konya	10 h 30 min	1 h 39 min
Eskişehir–Konya	8 h 00 min	2 h 00 min
Ankara–Izmir	14 h 00 min	3 h 30 min (planned)

Pilgrims to Makkah

Every year, at the appointed time in the lunar calendar, hundreds of thousands of Muslims converge on the holy city of Makkah in the Kingdom of Saudi Arabia. Every Muslim is encouraged to make this Hajj pilgrimage at least once in their lifetime if they are physically able and can afford it. At other times of the year, and particularly during the fasting month of Ramadan, Muslims may perform Umrah, also a pilgrimage to the holy sites. During their visit, many pilgrims also visit Madinah, Islam's second most holy city.

Pilgrims first travelled by train to Madinah in 1908, when the 1,050mm gauge Hedjaz Railway offered a faster, cheaper and more comfortable alternative to the camel caravans that plied the harsh desert trail from Damascus, a distance of more than 1,300km; from Madinah the pilgrims could continue south to Makkah. Six years after opening, the steam-hauled trains chugging through the arid wastes were carrying 300,000 passengers a year. Much of the railway was famously destroyed by Lawrence of Arabia during the First World War, and the Saudi Arabian section has long been defunct. Today, pilgrims arrive in

Turkish delight. TCDD's second contract for high-speed trains was won by Siemens with a version of its Velaro. The first train arrived in 2013. (Siemens)

Jeddah by sea or air, and transporting the crowds to and from the holy cities presents a serious challenge for the Saudi authorities; hundreds of buses and taxis are marshalled to shuttle the visitors between the sites.

By the mid-2000s the annual total of Hajj and Umrah visitors was touching the 20 million mark, prompting the government to seek a more efficient way of moving the crowds. Rail transport was once more invoked, and the government determined that a rail link between Madinah, Jeddah and Makkah would fit the bill nicely. Making use of the latest technology, it would relieve traffic congestion between the three cities and generate economic benefits for their rapidly growing populations – Jeddah alone is home to around 3.4 million people. Planners accordingly sketched out a route from Makkah to Jeddah and then north along the Red Sea coast to the development area of King Abdullah Economic City (KAEC) near Rabigh; from there the route climbs inland through Saudi Arabia's western desert to Madinah, 620m above sea level.

Ship to the desert. The first of thirty-six Talgo trains for the Haramain project was loaded on to the ro-ro vessel *Jolly Quarzo* at Barcelona on 12 December 2014. Just ten days later, newly appointed Saudi Transport Minister Abdullah Al-Muqbel warned the Saudi-Spanish consortium supplying railway equipment that it needed to make up lost time on the scheme. (Patentes Talgo)

A done deal. The Haramain Phase 2 contract was inked on 14 January 2012 in Riyadh by Al Shoula Group CEO Abdul Aziz Bin Mishaal Bin Abdul Aziz, Saudi Minister for Development Dr Ibrahim Al-Assaf and Saudi Minister for Transport Dr Jabara Bin Eid Alsuraiseri. (*Railway Gazette* collection)

On 23 May 2006 Saudi Railways Organisation (SRO) held a 'project day' in Jeddah before inviting contractors to prequalify. Tenders for a build-operate-transfer concession were called, and on 25 June 2007 SRO announced a shortlist of six bidders. King Abdullah approved the project in February 2008, and in the following month four consortia were invited to tender for a long-term concession to build and operate the 450km double-track railway. However, the project was so colossal that the Saudi government decided to split it in two.

The first phase, worth around US$4 billion, covered civil engineering and construction of stations at Makkah, Jeddah, KAEC and Madinah. The civil works contract went in February 2009 to the Al Rajhi Alliance, which included Arup, the French group Bouygues and China Railway

Engineering Corp. The station contracts were awarded two years later to local contractors Saudi Bin Laden Group and Saudi Oger, with design in the hands of a joint venture of renowned architects Foster + Partners and BuroHappold, working with local firm Dar el Riyadh. Drawing on modern Islamic architecture, the stations will form striking gateways to each city. Taking a modular design concept built around high traditional arches, the stations will reflect some of the key individual features and colours of the four cities. They will offer all conceivable facilities including mosques, and above all shade from the sun. Special arrangements are envisaged to control boarding, with segregation of arriving and departing passengers.

Much interest centred on the second phase, which covered all the railway systems including rolling stock, plus commissioning and maintenance for twelve years. Tenders were called in 2010, attracting attention from French, German and Spanish groups, among others. France deployed some heavy political guns to press the case for TGV technology, and the French were widely tipped to walk away with the deal. However, rumours suggested that the Spanish bidder was in pole position – although SRO refused to confirm this. Only on 26 October did SRO reveal that it had concluded negotiations with the Al Shoula Consortium of two Saudi and a dozen Spanish companies to supply trains and other equipment for what had become known as the Haramain High Speed Rail project; Haramain is Arabic for 'two holy cities'.

Worth a whopping €6.7 billion, the railway systems contract covered 1,435mm gauge track, 25kV 60Hz electrification, signalling, telecoms and a fleet of thirty-six Talgo trains based on Renfe's S-112 design with its *pato* nose; an option exists for twenty-three more. As the largest export contract ever won by Spanish companies, it was a huge coup for the country's railway industry: Pablo Vásquez, President of the Spanish Consortium for the Makkah–Madinah High Speed Line, described it as 'wonderful news'.

SAND HAZARD

Some of the Turkish lines traverse inhospitable terrain, but never before has a 300km/h railway been built in such a harsh environment as western Saudi Arabia. Apart from temperatures that can reach nearly 50°C, sandstorms are a particular menace, hurling fine sand particles through the air with abrasive force that can erode electrification and other exposed equipment. Moving sand dunes are another threat as they can quickly bury the permanent way. Apart from the sand, the saline air along the Red Sea coast is likely to corrode equipment and materials.

The Spanish contractors came up with a portfolio of anti-sand measures that included special trackforms, ditches, multiple fences, trackside walls and belts of vegetation to trap the sand. Sand-collecting machines, as developed for other lines in the Arabian Peninsula, were envisaged to keep the rails clear in the most vulnerable areas.

THE PILGRIMS' AVE

Although trains in Spain are tailored to the warm climate, they are not designed to cope with the searing heat of Saudi Arabia. So the 'pilgrims' AVE' could not simply be a carbon copy of the S-112. Apart from more powerful air-conditioning and customised interiors for Saudi passengers, the trains needed to be sand-proof; this meant fitting special air filters, grilles and seals to ensure that sand and

Cool design. The Haramain stations have drawn on modern Islamic architecture to provide a wide range of facilities for pilgrims travelling to the Hajj. (SRO/BuroHappold Engineering and Foster + Partners)

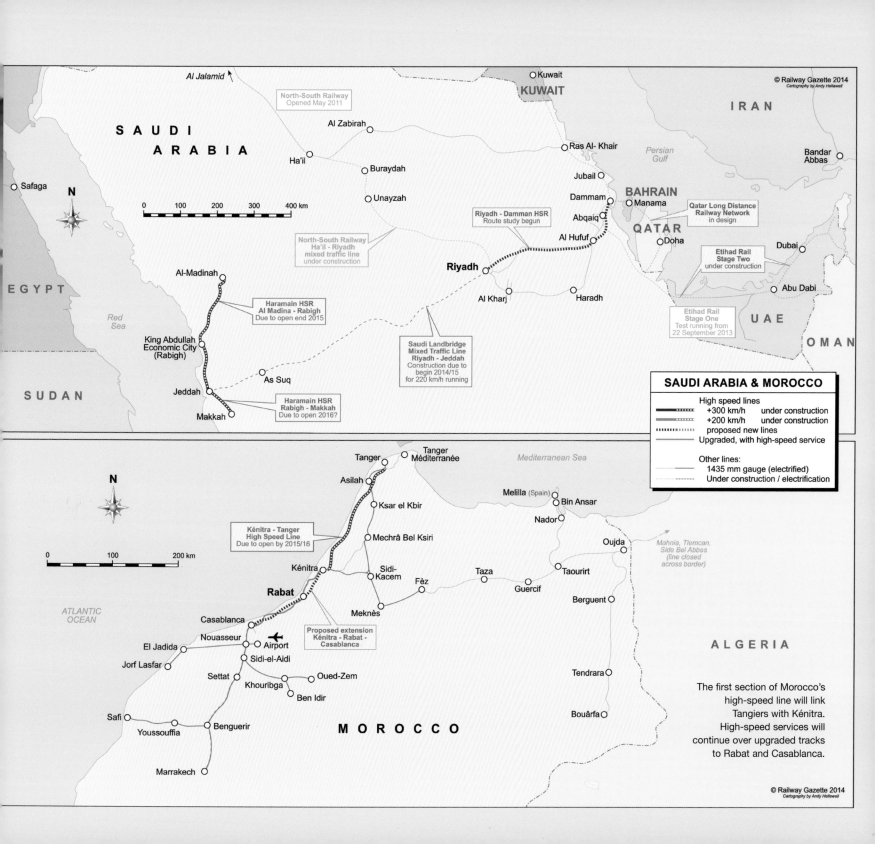

© Railway Gazette 2014
Cartography by Andy Hellawell

SAUDI ARABIA

Al Jalamid

SAUDI
ARABIA

North-South Railway
Opened May 2011

Al Zabirah

Ha'il

Safaga

Buraydah

Unayzah

EGYPT

Red
Sea

North-South Railway
Ha'il - Riyadh
mixed traffic line
under construction

Al-Madinah

King Abdullah
Economic City
(Rabigh)

Haramain HSR
Al Madina - Rabigh
Due to open end 2015

As Suq

SUDAN

Jeddah

Makkah

Haramain HSR
Rabigh - Makkah
Due to open 2016?

Kuwait

KUWAIT

IRAN

Ras Al- Khair

Persian
Gulf

Bandar
Abbas

Jubail

Dammam

BAHRAIN

Manama

Abqaiq

QATAR

Qatar Long Distance
Railway Network
in design

Al Hufuf

Doha

Etihad Rail
Stage Two
under construction

Dubai

Riyadh - Damman HSR
Route study begun

Riyadh

Abu Dabi

Al Kharj

Haradh

Etihad Rail
Stage One
Test running from
22 September 2013

UAE

OMAN

Saudi Landbridge
Mixed Traffic Line
Riyadh - Jeddah
Construction due to
begin 2014/15
for 220 km/h running

0   100   200   300   400 km

SAUDI ARABIA & MOROCCO

High speed lines
+300 km/h   under construction
+200 km/h   under construction
proposed new lines
Upgraded, with high-speed service

Other lines:
1435 mm gauge (electrified)
Under construction / electrification

MOROCCO

Tanger
Méditerranée

Mediterranean Sea

Tanger

Asilah

Melilla (Spain)

Bin Ansar

Ksar el Kbir

Nador

Kénitra - Tanger
High Speed Line
Due to open by 2015/16

Mechrâ Bel Ksiri

Oujda

Mahnia, Tlemcan,
Side Bel Abbes
(line closed
across border)

Kénitra

Sidi-
Kacem

Taza

Taourirt

ATLANTIC
OCEAN

Rabat

Fèz

Guercif

Berguent

Casablanca

Nouasseur

Airport

Meknès

Proposed extension
Kénitra - Rabat -
Casablanca

El Jadida

Sidi-el-Aidi

ALGERIA

Jorf Lasfar

Settat

Oued-Zem

Khouribga

Ben Idir

Tendrara

Safi

Benguerir

Youssouffia

Bouârfa

Marrakech

MOROCCO

0   100   200 km

The first section of Morocco's
high-speed line will link
Tangiers with Kénitra.
High-speed services will
continue over upgraded tracks
to Rabat and Casablanca.

© Railway Gazette 2014
Cartography by Andy Hellawell

dust particles could not penetrate the interior or damage sensitive components. Accommodation is spread over twelve trailers between the two power cars, a thirteenth car houses a cafe and 'dry' bar.

One of the Saudi AVEs will be rather more luxurious than its sisters. This will be kept for use by the Saudi royal family and their retinue; the formation will include a royal suite, sleeping cars with guest suites, a dining car and cars with meeting rooms. In addition to electric traction, there will be a diesel power plant to ensure that the train can still run if there is a power failure.

The first metal was laid down in December 2013, and the first complete train left Barcelona port for Jeddah on board the *MV Jolly Quarzo* on 12 December 2014. By then, considerable progress had been made with the stations and civil works, but when newly appointed Transport Minister Abdullah Al-Muqbel visited the project's worksites soon after his appointment on 8 December, he was less than satisfied with progress. On 22 December *Arab News* reported that Al-Muqbel had issued a formal warning to the consortium of contractors, demanding that they submit plans within two months to guarantee no further delays. An extraordinary general meeting was convened in Spain on Boxing Day and the consortium committed to starting commercial services 'as soon as possible'. If all goes well, the Middle East's first pilgrims to travel by high-speed train should reach Madinah 108 years after their first rail-borne predecessors. The planned service will see five departures an hour, with additional trains during the Hajj when over 160,000 passengers a day are expected to ride the desert rails.

The Haramain project may be just the start of a Saudi Arabian network of high-speed lines. On 2 September 2014 SRO announced that it had signed a contract with Spanish consultants to study a high-speed line between Riyadh and Dammam. The conventional train service takes 4 hours 20 minutes to cover 450km, but this could one day be slashed to 1 hour 30 minutes if the study is followed through.

MAGHREB CHALLENGE

An interesting comparison between high-speed rail technologies in harsh desert environments should be possible around 2017. Another high-speed desert railway is under way in North Africa where sand and dust plus a saline environment present the contractors with formidable headaches.

The Kingdom of Morocco's standard-gauge network is used heavily by both passenger and freight trains. Reflecting a buoyant and relatively liberal economy, passenger travel more than doubled between 2002 and 2013 to reach a total of 38 million trips. Rail-borne freight is expected to grow rapidly thanks to a link serving a multimodal container complex built in conjunction with the recently opened deep-water harbour at Tanger Med – by 2015 this is expected to be Africa's busiest port. Tangiers is already an important trading hub, and good links to the commercial capital of Casablanca and the political capital of Rabat are essential.

The present main line between Tangiers and Casablanca is partly single-track and far from direct, running inland to Sidi Kacem before swinging west to reach Kénitra on the coast, from where it turns south towards Rabat and Casablanca. A cut-off has been built recently to avoid Sidi Kacem, but there were concerns in the early 2000s that the railway would not keep pace with long-term demand. Apart from that, the relatively slow trip means that national operator Office National des Chemins de Fer (ONCF) has a paltry 5 per cent of the market in this corridor as the train is outpaced by cars and coaches on the A1 and A3 motorways. In 2002 the government's investigation into ways of raising capacity determined that the best option was a high-speed line. Although this had a cost premium of 30 per cent over a conventional railway, ONCF was convinced that the benefits would outweigh the extra cost.

A master plan for two high-speed routes stretching to a total of just 1,500km by 2035 was drawn up. One route follows the Atlantic Coast from Tangiers to Kénitra, Rabat and Casablanca before turning south to serve Marrakech and then regaining the coast at Essaouira, ending up in the popular holiday resort of Agadir. The second strikes inland from Rabat to Meknes, Fez and Oujda near the border with Algeria. Priority went to the coastal line because of the capacity shortage; it also offered a healthier rate of return.

ONCF publicity for the project helpfully notes that the scheme was put forward just when France was fostering a policy of promoting rolling-stock exports, providing 'a welcome convergence of the interests of the two countries'. The French government lost no time in offering its formal support, seeing it as an opportunity for Alstom to export its flagship TGV.

A feasibility study for the Casablanca–Marrakech route was completed in 2006, and this was followed by the award of planning contracts to French consultants in 2007, when ONCF Director-General Mohamed Rabie Khlie wrote that 'there can be no doubt that high speed is the future of rail in Morocco'.

In that year significant events included the V150 record and the election of Nicholas Sarkozy as President of France – his first state visit was to Morocco. In October he met King Mohammed VI in Marrakech, where the two heads of state signed a protocol 'emblematic of the partnership between the two countries' that provided for construction of a *Ligne à Grande Vitesse* from Tangiers to Casablanca. Within days

Alstom announced that it had been chosen to supply eighteen Duplex TGVs to ONCF, subject to negotiation of a contract.

The protocol included a generous French financial package supporting the scheme. Covering 51 per cent of the cost, it included a grant of €75 million and two loans together worth €845 million. Loans at favourable rates were also agreed with the Saudi Fund for Development, the Kuwait Fund for Arab Economic Development, the Abu Dhabi Fund for Development and the Arab Fund for Economic & Social Development, which together were worth €380 million. Morocco's

contribution was €500 million, with about 17 per cent of this provided by the Hassan II Fund for Economic & Social Development.

Negotiations dragged on until late 2010, when King Mohammed VI was present at the signature in Tangiers of a contract worth 'nearly €400 million' for Alstom to supply just fourteen TGV-Duplex train sets to run on the initial 200km section of the LGV between Tangiers and Kénitra at up to 320km/h – the company's only Duplex export deal. Pending construction of the second phase to Casablanca, they will continue over souped-up tracks between Kénitra and Casablanca. Here the electrification is

at 3kV DC, requiring the trains to be dual-system. The first part of the double-track route electrified at 25kV 50Hz runs through terrain demanding construction of 286 bridges and thirteen viaducts; the El Hachef is the longest at 3,500m.

Sarkozy crossed the Mediterranean again in September 2011 for a ceremony on the 29th of that month when he and King Mohammed VI laid the first sleeper in Tangiers. The main civil engineering work commenced in 2012. However, problems with station design and acquisition of land, particularly in Tangiers, have added to the project timescale, and the target opening date of December 2015 has been put back by at least a year.

The first train was completed by Alstom in 2014, but it was largely kept under wraps. The fleet will be based at a specially built workshop in Tangiers, where there will also be a staff training college.

When the LGV opens, journey time from Tangiers to Rabat will tumble from 3 hours 45 minutes to 1 hour 20 minutes, with Tangiers–Casablanca taking 2 hours 10 minutes instead of 4 hours 45 minutes. ONCF hopes that the TGVs will attract 6 million passengers a year, with around one-third switching from road or air.

If you thought that Morocco did not need a high-speed railway, you would not be alone. At one stage the project drew furious protests. ONCF pointed out that other major infrastructure schemes had attracted similar criticism and that it was essential to tackle the capacity shortage on its busy network. As Director-General Mohamed Rabie Khlie said in 2012: 'had we agreed to spend exactly the same amount of money on a conventional line or a route modernisation, nobody would have said a thing. It's simply because it's "the TGV in a developing country".'

Wadi crossing. By early October 2014 the first major viaduct on Morocco's high-speed line from Tangier to Kénitra was well on the way to completion. The 250m-long structure traverses the Wadi Sebou, which rises in the Atlas Mountains and is subject to sudden fluctuations in water level. (Systra)

Trial and Error on Russian Metals

Back in the USSR, in the late 1960s, Soviet railway engineers took good note of the Tokaido Shinkansen. Could something similar be built in the Soviet Union?

However great an impression the Japanese wonder-railway may have made among rail specialists in Moscow, the money, know-how and political will for constructing high-speed railways was absent in the communist superpower. But perhaps something could be done…

The fastest speed on the USSR's extensive broad gauge (1,520mm) network was generally 120 or 140km/h, with 160km/h permitted in a few locations. But the prime inter-city route from Moscow to Leningrad, now St Petersburg, was perfectly straight for almost the entire 650km length. This was the famous October Railway, electrified at 3kV DC and used heavily by both passengers and freight. Overnight expresses handled much of the passenger traffic, and the

only noteworthy timing was the summer-only daytime *Aurora*, which hustled between the two cities in 4 hours 59 minutes with an 8-minute halt at Bologoye. If 200km/h were achieved over some of this potential racetrack, perhaps a 4-hour timing was possible.

By early 1971 Soviet engineers had the detailed design of a 200km/h EMU on the drawing board, and construction of the ER200 flagship experimental train with distributed power was entrusted to Soviet Railways' traditional EMU supplier, Riga Carriage Works.

The ER200 electrified visitors to a rare public exhibition staged by Soviet Railways at its Shcherbinka research institute, south of Moscow, in July 1977. A four-car formation resplendent in blue-and-white paint stole the show with joyrides round a test loop. High-speed travel it wasn't, the limit being 80km/h. But the ER200 was reported to have touched 206km/h during tests in 1975.

After modifications back at Riga, a fourteen-car ER200 formation reportedly entered trial service between Moscow and Leningrad on 6 November 1977 in the timings of conventional trains. Problems with rail damage and current collection delayed the introduction of faster timings, but in March 1984 this non-standard train was authorised to run at 180km/h. Even then, it was restricted to a weekly trip in each direction.

Modifications were made to track and train, and in the following year the ER200 was accelerated to achieve a 4-hour-39-minute timing, averaging 139.8km/h between the two cities. It shared high-speed duties with the *Russian Troika*,

Soviet experiment. The ER200 first ran between Moscow and Leningrad (now St Petersburg) in 1977, with accelerated timings introduced in 1984. However, it only made the trip once a week in each direction. (V. Urvantsev)

a Czech-built ChS200 twin-unit locomotive matched with conventional coaches. Half of the twenty-strong fleet of ChS200 locos were geared for 200km/h, but the ER200 stole the limelight.

In the early 1980s serious attention was being paid to a bold proposal for a 250km/h line striking directly south from Moscow towards the Black Sea. The rationale for this 1,140km super-railway was the congestion caused by heavy goods traffic lumbering between the Moscow area and the industrial Donetz basin, making it difficult to find paths for express passenger services. Nothing much happened until a fresh proposal for a 350km/h alignment with branches stretching to Rostov and almost to Simferopol surfaced in 1987, but the 5 billion roubles price tag meant that this scheme

was stillborn. Nonetheless, the concept of switching long-distance passenger services to a new line was identical to that of France's LGV Paris–Sud-Est.

By 1986 cab signalling had been installed over parts of the October Railway, paving the way for a few spurts at 200km/h, and two years later Soviet Railways announced plans to procure ten ER200 sets – the 4-hour timing was finally in prospect.

It was not to be. The break-up of the USSR at the turn of the decade came with a heavy cost and massive loss of traffic for Soviet Railways. Plans for high-speed trains were temporarily off the agenda. The ER200, however, continued to run. My chance to ride the former Soviet flyer came in 1994, when I travelled to Moscow to interview Russia's Minister of Railways, Gennady Fadeyev. The interview

over, I found myself at Moscow's Leningradski station with a ticket for that day's ER200 run to St Petersburg – the train offered a single class of accommodation with a supplementary fare. Departure was precisely on time at 12.21 p.m. and, as the ER200 accelerated away through the bleak Moscow suburbs, hostesses distributed drinks and snacks from a trolley. My preference was to visit one of the two buffet-bars squeezed into the end cars. Here I found the clientele already quaffing Austrian beer and munching on sausages and caviar rolls.

Accompanying me was Professor Evgeny Sotnikov, Deputy Director-General of the Russian High Speed Railway Shareholding Co. (RAOVSM), an organisation set up in 1991 with an aspiration to introduce high-speed services over a new Moscow–St Petersburg line. Drawing attention to lineside fences along the route, the professor explained that these were upgraded sections for high-speed running.

During the trip Sotnikov related the remarkable events of 5 October 1993 when Russia claimed a world record speed for diesel traction. The vehicle concerned was one of two massive experimental TEP80 diesel-electric locomotives. Somewhere between Shluze and Doroshikha, near Tver, this eight-axle monster had thundered up to a speed of 271km/h. The speed has never been independently confirmed, but in December 1992 the locomotive had reached 260km/h during tests hauling a dynamometer car. The exploit sufficed to secure the leviathan a home in St Petersburg's railway museum.

During my trip the ER200 did not exceed 180km/h, and I was told that station staff and other railway workers along the route had special instructions to monitor our passage. As it happened, we were brought to a stand at Bersevka as a track worker had spotted smoke emanating from one of the cars. It turned out to be a false alarm, possibly caused by oil on a brake disc, but it underlined the precarious nature of Soviet-era high-speed

Monster traction. In 1997 two eight-axle EP200 electric locomotives were built at Kolomna to haul passenger services at 200km/h. The four-axle bogies of this huge machine were based on those fitted to the TEP80 which reportedly attained 271km/h between Shluze and Doroshikha on the Moscow–St Petersburg main line. (*Railway Gazette* collection)

train technology. Despite the unscheduled 2-minute stop to investigate, our arrival at St Petersburg's Moskovski terminus was punctual at 5.20 p.m. The once weekly trips spawned jokes that the rest of the week was spent putting the train back into working order, but pathing constraints were a more likely explanation – at almost every station a passenger or freight train had been looped to allow the ER200 to pass.

Looking back, any hope of the ER200 emulating the Shinkansen was pretty far-fetched. Apart from anything else, the October Railway was a far cry from the pristine infrastructure in Japan. My journey to Moscow had been by overnight train from Helsinki, and I was awakened several times as the elderly Soviet sleeping cars clattered alarmingly through sets of points. The ride on the ER200 was better, but this was not a dedicated high-speed railway.

Some of the ER200 cars have survived in preservation – testimony to a brave attempt by visionary engineers to advance the conservative technology of Soviet Railways.

SECOND SHOT

In the early 1990s, freed from the constraints of Soviet government, it was the turn of the nascent Russian Railways (RZD) to explore opportunities for high speed. Given the dire state of the Russian economy, this seemed somewhat surprising.

When I interviewed Fadeyev, he refused to see a contradiction in the pursuit of high-speed technology when ordinary freight and passenger services were crying out for modernisation. 'Our task is to research technology so that we can be properly integrated with the European high-speed network. If we do not pay attention now, we will construct a new Berlin Wall in railway communications. That's why we are working on the most important route from Moscow to St Petersburg.'

The arrival of the market economy unleashed a wave of activities and projects, some of them unlikely and some enjoying a measure of support from the West. One such scheme was the privately financed high-speed line between the capital and St Petersburg developed by RAOVSM. The route ran to the south of the October Railway with stations at Valdai and Melnikovo. Again, the rationale was easing congestion on the existing line.

RAOVSM Director-General Alexei Bolshakov assured me in 1994 that 'this project is not a fantasy, but a scientific scheme based on the results of serious analysis'. It had first been proposed by the Soviet government in December 1988, and Russia's new President Boris Yeltsin then signed a decree laying the foundations for the enterprise. A symbolic start-of-work ceremony was held on 30 July 1993 near St Petersburg; this included interring a time capsule in the foundations of a bridge over the Kuzminka River.

Details of the company's finances were published just under a year later: shareholders included the city administrations of Moscow and St Petersburg, the Russian government and the October Railway. Part of the government's stake took the form of state-owned military enterprises chosen to be transformed into civilian companies making useful products like rolling stock. Soviet Railways' traditional EMU supplier in Riga was now in the independent state of Latvia, and Russia needed to build up its own expertise in manufacturing modern electric trains.

SOKOL IS BORN

On 10 July 1994 RAOVSM signed a contract for a prototype 250km/h train called *Sokol* (falcon). The job was placed with the Transmash factory at Tikhvin, 200km east of St Petersburg. The company envisaged a fleet of *Sokol* trains dashing up and down thirty times a day each way,

with non-stop timings of 2 hours 25 minutes; an advanced version would travel at 350km/h. Forecasts for 1998 suggested that the conventional line would carry 7.8 million passengers a year, but traffic would more than double by 2005 if the high-speed line were built.

In parallel with construction of the prototype *Sokol*, a 30km test section of the new line was planned, starting around 13km outside St Petersburg. Next would come the 118km segment to Melnikovo near Novgorod, with successive chunks of the route following. The job would culminate in completion of the entire line by 2001.

It did not happen quite like that. In 1998, Yeltsin revoked the decree authorising construction of the line. His volte-face did not, however, halt the *Sokol* programme, and the six-car set emerged on 28 July 1999 at a roll-out ceremony attended by Russia's new Minister of Railways Vladimir Starostenko and RAOVSM Director General Vladimir Tulaev. Around sixty companies had been involved in building the train, although many had little or no experience of railway engineering. *Sokol* was in due course hauled to Shcherbinka for tests.

Alas, at a shareholders' meeting in January 2000 a decision was made to hand the project to the Ministry of Railways. RAOVSM's sources of finance were running dry, and the idea of a privately funded high-speed railway was clearly not going to fly – and sadly nor was *Sokol*.

By April 2001 the prototype had logged 10,000km of test runs, many of them over the Chudovo–Lyuban section at the northern end of the Moscow–St Petersburg line. An assessment later that year determined that *Sokol* could not be signed off to carry the public. The dual-voltage train had three-phase traction motors, but some components were unreliable, and protection against winter weather fell short of requirements. Dynamic performance at 210km/h was poor,

In the loop. In January 2001 Russia's six-car *Sokol* prototype high-speed train was tested in winter conditions at the All-Russia Railway Research Institute at Shcherbinka near Moscow where a circular track permitted continuous running. In the foreground is a preserved FD21-3125 steam locomotive dating from 1932 that forms part of the Russian Railways collection of historic rolling stock. (Igor P. Kiselev)

Cosy corner. One car of the *Sokol* prototype was laid out with luxury accommodation for VIPs. (Igor P. Kiselev)

noise levels gave cause for concern and some internal fittings did not meet the fire regulations. Numerous modifications were needed, but the question of who paid for them was not answered.

The train seemed to have no future, but Russian engineers put a brave face on it, saying that valuable experience had been learned. All six *Sokol* cars have been preserved in St Petersburg.

THIRD TIME LUCKY

The next attempt to develop a Russian high-speed train entailed a fundamental change of tack. Instead of relying on home-grown technology, Russia sought foreign expertise.

On 21 December 2004 an agreement to set up a joint venture to build sixty high-speed trains using German know-how was signed by RZD, Siemens Transportation and an organisation called New Transport Technologies. The proposed transaction was big enough to warrant the presence of Russian President Vladimir Putin and German Chancellor Gerhard Schröder.

Fadeyev, now President of Russian Railways, announced on 5 May 2005 that a contract was being prepared for a fleet of broad-gauge Velaros.

Broad-gauge record. The test team poses in front of a *Sapsan* unit on 2 May 2009 after attaining a Russian speed record of 281km/h between Okulovka and Mstinskiy Most. (Siemens)

The deal would entail technology transfer with Siemens assembling the trains in Russia – RZD had identified sixty-nine companies as potential component suppliers, including some that had been involved in *Sokol*. Less than a month later RZD confirmed that Siemens had chosen Transmashholding as its partner to assemble the ICE 3 derivatives at the Demikhovo Engineering EMU factory.

Not long after that, Fadeyev was replaced as RZD President by Vladimir Ivanovich Yakunin, a powerful and well-connected member of the Russian oligarchy. A new RZD board was

also appointed. In September 2005 RZD agreed a series of financial deals to fund a clutch of investment projects, but funding for a fleet of high-speed trains was not among them. Yakunin made clear that priorities had changed, and in December he confirmed that revised terms had been agreed with Siemens under which the German company would supply just eight trains. Signatures by RZD Vice-President Valentin Gapanovich and Siemens President Hans Schabert on 18 May 2006 confirmed the €276 million deal. The ten-car Velaro RUS trains would be built at Krefeld in Germany, with delivery commencing in 2008.

Allegro Across the Border

In 2006 Russian Railways and Finnish Railways, which share a near-identical track gauge (1,520 and 1,524mm respectively), set up a joint venture called Karelian Trains to run accelerated passenger services between St Petersburg and Helsinki. A €120 million contract for four seven-car dual-voltage Pendolino tilting trains was signed with Alstom on 28 August 2007. Similar to the S220 Pendolinos operating in Finland, the fleet was branded *Allegro* and launched on 12 December 2010.

The *Allegro* sets replaced the loco-hauled *Repin* and *Sibelius* services, which required around 5 hours 30 minutes to cover the 416km. Track upgrading, a 220km/h maximum speed and the ability to tilt cut the journey time dramatically, and by 2014 the trip took just 3 hours 36 minutes with six stops.

Four broad-gauge Pendolino tilting trains entered service between St Petersburg and Helsinki under the *Allegro* brand in December 2010. (Alstom Transport)

In September that year Yakunin disclosed during unveiling of the first three cars in Berlin that RZD's new train would be known in Russia as *Sapsan* (peregrine falcon). Half the fleet would run between Moscow and St Petersburg and the other four would link Moscow with Nizhny Novgorod, which required a dual-voltage version, as part of that route was electrified at 25kV 50Hz.

Apart from the gauge, differences from the German ICE 3 included measures to cope with temperatures down to a very chilly −50°C, bodyshells that were 330mm wider, and the ability to add four extra cars. Installed power would total 8MW, and maximum speed would be 250km/h with provision for uprating to 300km/h.

The broad-gauge Velaro RUS could not travel over German tracks from Krefeld, and so the first set went by road to the Baltic port of Sassnitz-Mukran. There it was loaded aboard the *MV Vilnius* train ferry, whose rail deck had broad gauge tracks. On 13 November 2008 the vessel set sail for Baltisk and the Russian Baltic port of Ust-Luga. The final 150km was overland to St Petersburg, future home for the *Sapsan* fleet. Maintenance of the trains was placed in the hands of the manufacturer for thirty years under a €354 million contract sealed in April 2007.

The test crews got to work with their new toy, and further sets arrived from Germany. On 2 May 2009 a *Sapsan* hit the headlines by attaining a Russian speed record of 281km/h between Okulovka and Mstinskiy Most. 'This is the first time that such a speed has been achieved on a Russian railway', claimed Gapanovich.

The record signified that good progress was being made, and on 30 July a *Sapsan* carried Yakunin and St Petersburg Governor Valentina Matviyenko on a demonstration trip from Moscow to St Petersburg to mark the opening of the *Sapsan* maintenance centre.

On 17 December 2009 Yakunin joined other passengers on the 7 p.m. departure from Moscow to St Petersburg – the first *Sapsan* to carry fare-paying passengers was a sell-out, tickets having gone on sale on 20 November. 'This is not just a train and these are not just carriages; this is a different life, different technology, a different means of transport,' proclaimed the President. The fastest of three journeys each way was timed at 3 hours 45 minutes, knocking 45 minutes off the previous best thanks to the trains' 250km/h capability.

The start of *Sapsan* services to Nizhny Novgorod was marked on 30 July 2010 with the launch of a daily train from St Petersburg. This followed upgrading of the 460km Moscow–Nizhny Novgorod route, but despite this the *Sapsan* sets could not exploit their high-speed capability and were restricted to 160km/h. The journey from St Petersburg took around 8 hours 20 minutes.

There were reports of local discontent as *Sapsan* services obliged rescheduling of commuter trains in Moscow and St Petersburg, but the accelerated timings quickly proved popular. The five millionth passenger was carried on 17 December 2011, and two days later RZD announced an order for eight more *Sapsans* with more premium accommodation and a VIP zone offering 'superior comfort'.

In mid-2014 RZD decided to concentrate all its *Sapsan* trains on the Moscow–St Petersburg route.

Winter wonderland. Just days after entering commercial service in December 2009, a morning *Sapsan* service from Moscow stirs up a snowstorm at Tosno in the St Petersburg suburbs. (Ivan Kurtov)

The Nizhny Novgorod *Sapsan* would be replaced by Talgo trains – in 2011 RZD had ordered seven 200km/h train sets with passive tilt from Patentes Talgo, three of them equipped for gauge-changing trips between Moscow and Berlin. The first of these arrived in Moscow in May 2014.

ANOTHER PROJECT

The *Sapsan* service prospered, jogging memories of earlier plans for high-speed lines, and in April 2010 RZD took the wraps off yet another proposal for a Moscow–St Petersburg route. This one was even more ambitious, with a 400km/h maximum speed, fast enough to give a 2-hour-30-minute timing over 658km of high-speed infrastructure. This, the forecasts predicted, would attract 10.5 million passengers a year by 2030.

Much excitement preceded the launch of plans for a PPP to fund and build the line. RZD had set up a high-speed rail agency called Skorostnye Magistrali and Chief Executive Denis Muratov told a London press conference on 20 October 2011 that 'the time to build the line has arrived'. The concessionaire, he said, would be expected to have the line up and running by 2017 in time for the FIFA World Cup football tournament the following year. Bidders had already registered interest, and tenders were due to be launched in December 2011, with the Russian government coughing up half the 696 billion roubles cost.

Yet, once again, a Moscow–St Petersburg project hit the buffers. Muratov was replaced by Alexander Misharin, whose job appeared to be to garner support for an alternative scheme from Moscow to Kazan. The line was to be built for 400km/h with trains covering the 770km in around 3 hours 30 minutes, carrying 10.5 million people a year by 2020. Services would continue over existing tracks to cities such as Samara, Perm, Ufa and Chelyabinsk.

A deluge of publicity was pushed out by the RZD press office, and a roadshow event on 5 March 2014 attracted around 150 companies and banks. 'This is the first major infrastructure project in the railway industry in Russia implemented through public-private partnership', said Misharin as RZD announced that ten consortia had expressed interest. Throughout the summer of 2014 RZD continued to extol the benefits of the project in terms of macroeconomics – for a construction cost of US$31 billion would spring benefits worth US$341 billion over the first decade, Misharin declared. Prime Minister Dmitry Medvedev announced on 23 December 2014 that the federal budget for 2015 would include 6 billion roubles towards the scheme, in which 'foreign investors have shown great interest, including our Chinese partners'. Bids for a contractor are due to be called during 2015.

Moscow bound. With non-stop timings of around 3 hours 50 minutes between Moscow and St Petersburg, *Sapsan* services proved popular enough for Russian Railways to place an order for eight more trains. One of the fleet awaits departure from St Petersburg. (Ivan Kurtov)

12

The American Enigma

The President waved to the crowd penned behind the security cordon and climbed into the cab of the gleaming bullet-shaped streamliner. Behind him followed the Secretary of State for Transportation and the usual security detail. Below the cab window the brilliant colours of the Stars & Stripes indicated that this was a truly special rail service. As the train's horn blared to announce departure, officials on the platform watched as the sleek coaches slid away, taking the President and his entourage on the fastest rail trip of their lives on American soil. The USA's first high-speed railway had finally been completed, and the President was on board. The superpower had finally joined the club of nations operating passenger trains at 300km/h…

On past performance, this little fantasy will remain just that. So many proposals for high-speed railways in the USA have been dreamt up and shot down that it is almost unsporting to list them. Yet, as these words are being written, there is one project that is making headway, albeit slowly. This is a proposal to link San Francisco with Los Angeles in California by a high-speed line along the San Joaquin Valley through Merced, Fresno and Bakersfield. It would ultimately be extended to Sacramento in the north and San Diego in the south. Plans call for the San Francisco–LA section to be finished by 2028, when trains would speed between the two cities in under 3 hours.

The proposal harks back to a project conceived around 1980 for a Los Angeles–San Diego line based on Shinkansen technology. That suffered a rapid demise as soon as someone realised that the traffic predictions were hopelessly optimistic. The present scheme is in the hands of the California High-Speed Rail Authority (CHSRA), which has made more progress than any other US high-speed rail promoter. In June 2013 it awarded its first civil engineering contract; this covers earthworks along a 47km section from Madera to a point just south of Fresno, which forms part of the 480km Initial Operating Section between Merced and the San Fernando Valley, due to open in 2022 at a cost of $31 billion. However, progress is halting because of a long-winded land acquisition process – *The Fresno Bee* reported in August 2014 that only seventy-one out of 550 parcels of land needed for this section had been purchased.

By September 2014 three groups had qualified to bid for CHSRA's second and third construction packages covering 96km through the Central Valley from East American Avenue in Fresno County to a location just short of the Tulare-Kern County line. Worth $1.5 to $2 billion, this contract was due to be followed by a fourth package that will take the line to the outskirts of Bakersfield. CHSRA moved rapidly to progress the scheme, staging a ceremony on 6 January 2015 to 'commemorate the start of sustained construction' at the site of the future Fresno station.

Downtown interchange. CHSRA envisages that high-speed rail services will penetrate the centre of San Francisco. This is its concept for Transbay Terminal A. (California High-Speed Rail Authority)

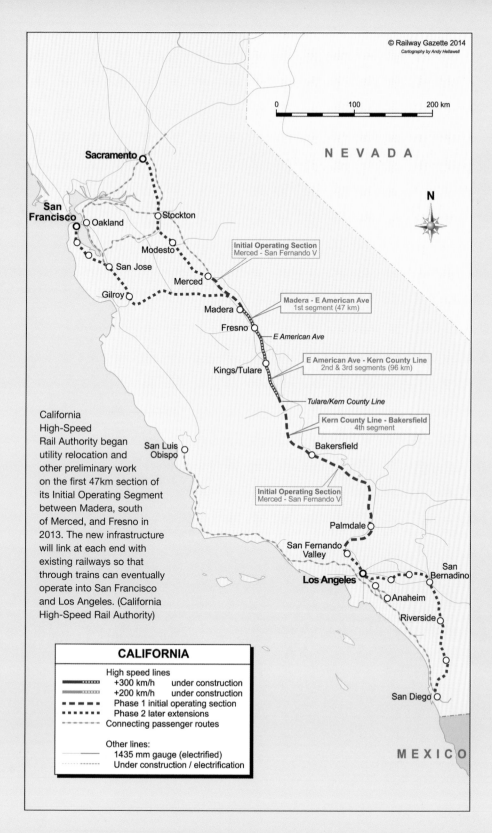

© Railway Gazette 2014
Cartography by Andy Hellawell

0   100   200 km

N E V A D A

N

Sacramento

San Francisco
Oakland
Stockton
Modesto
San Jose
Merced
Gilroy

Initial Operating Section
Merced - San Fernando V

Madera
Fresno

E American Ave

Madera - E American Ave
1st segment (47 km)

Kings/Tulare

E American Ave - Kern County Line
2nd & 3rd segments (96 km)

Tulare/Kern County Line

Kern County Line - Bakersfield
4th segment

San Luis Obispo

Bakersfield

California High-Speed Rail Authority began utility relocation and other preliminary work on the first 47km section of its Initial Operating Segment between Madera, south of Merced, and Fresno in 2013. The new infrastructure will link at each end with existing railways so that through trains can eventually operate into San Francisco and Los Angeles. (California High-Speed Rail Authority)

Initial Operating Section
Merced - San Fernando V

Palmdale
San Fernando Valley
San Bernardino
Los Angeles
Anaheim
Riverside

San Diego

CALIFORNIA

High speed lines
+300 km/h   under construction
+200 km/h   under construction
Phase 1 initial operating section
Phase 2 later extensions
Connecting passenger routes

Other lines:
1435 mm gauge (electrified)
Under construction / electrification

M E X I C O

It has been a struggle to get this far, and the future remains uncertain. Partly to avoid the high cost of building through densely populated urban areas at the start of the project, federal government insisted in 2010 that CHSRA should build the initial part of the route in a rural area. The idea is to extend this in stages at each end, in the meantime using connections to existing tracks to allow trains to operate from end to end until a high-speed alignment is available. At the north end trains would reach San Jose, from where they would continue over Caltrain tracks to San Francisco, while in the south they would share tracks with Metrolink commuter trains to reach the centre of Los Angeles and Anaheim. The decision drew criticism that CHSRA was building 'a line to nowhere', but in December 2010 CHRSA announced that the initial section would after all reach the outskirts of Bakersfield as additional federal funds had been secured.

The extra money had been destined for upgrading projects to raise train speeds in Ohio and Wisconsin, but newly elected Republican governors who had campaigned on anti-passenger-rail tickets in both states cancelled the plans. This prompted the Department of Transportation (DoT) to withdraw the promised grants worth $1.2 billion and reallocate the money – California benefitted to the tune of $616 million.

This in itself was remarkable, as federal funding for inter-city passenger trains in the USA is a rare commodity – Amtrak, the state-funded national inter-city and long-distance operator that inherited a rump of the privately run US passenger train network in 1971 has for decades eked out a miserable existence on annual grants wrung out of Congress. That any high-speed line proposal is active at all is down to the change of attitude following President Barack Obama's arrival in the White House in January 2009. It was significant, perhaps, that the President-elect travelled by Amtrak train from Wilmington to Washington DC for his inauguration.

One of Obama's first moves was to put in hand a national economic stimulus package that included a tranche of funds for rail projects. Signed by the President in Denver on 17 February 2009, the American Recovery & Reinvestment Act allocated $787 billion of stimulus funding, including $1.3 billion for Amtrak and more than $8 billion for 'high-speed' passenger services. Note that high speed in American terms is defined as 145km/h (90mph).

On 16 April 2009 Obama announced an ambitious plan to spend $13 billion on ten 'high-speed' rail corridors as part of an initiative to cut fuel consumption, traffic congestion, air pollution and airport overcrowding. This figure included the $8 billion of stimulus funds, to which was added $1 billion a year from the transport budget for five years. Included were two true high-speed projects: the one in California and another in Florida. At the same time states and regional bodies were invited to compete for the federal funds.

Dangle a pot of honey, and the bees will arrive. Secretary of Transportation Ray LaHood announced on 29 July 2009 that 278 'preliminary applications' had been received for funds amounting to $102 billion. 'The response has been tremendous and shows that the country is ready for high-speed rail', he declared. The bids were duly fed into the federal sausage machine, and on 28 January 2010 Obama announced the winners during a visit to Tampa. The Florida project was the recipient of $1.25 billion, while that in California received $2.25 billion. The rest of this federal largesse was spread thinly across thirty-one states and the US capital.

Further federal grants were announced a few days before the mid-term elections on 2 November 2010, with California allocated another $515 million and Florida a further $800 million. CHSRA was also able to draw on funds from the so-called Proposition 1A bonds intended to help finance the Initial Operating Segment. The 'Safe, Reliable, High Speed Passenger Trains Bond Act for the 21st Century' was approved by referendum in 2008, but on 25 November 2013 Judge Michael Kenny ruled in the Sacramento County Supreme Court that the measure required CHSRA to identify 'sources of all funds to be invested in the corridor' before construction began. CHSRA had envisaged that $2.6 billion towards the $6 billion budget for the first 47km section of the Initial Operating Segment would come from Proposition 1A, but still unidentified was the funding needed to complete the rest of the Segment into the Los Angeles basin.

Happily, this ruling was overturned by three judges of the State Appellate Court in Sacramento on 31 July 2014. Not only that, but California Governor Jerry Brown has pledged to use revenues from the state's emissions trading scheme to set up a long-term funding stream. In August 2014 the cost was put at $68 billion for the 837km of Phase 1 between San Francisco and Los Angeles.

Obama's vision. In 2009 the US President's ambitions for high-speed rail services embraced ten inter-city corridors plus the Northeast Corridor (NEC).

FAILURES IN FLORIDA

While the California project is still going, the Florida one had a short life. On 12 May 2010 the Federal Railroad Administration (FRA) issued a 'Record of Decision' that paved the way for Florida DoT to start design and land acquisition for a $2.6 billion line along the Interstate 4 corridor between Tampa and Orlando; it included a station at Walt Disney World. This was just the first stage of a planned network that stretched to Miami, Jacksonville, Tallahassee and Pensacola. Governor Charlie Crist rejoiced that 'we now have the green light to move forward quickly to build America's first true high-speed rail system'. Preliminary tender documents were drawn up for a PPP, which would see a contractor build, operate and maintain the railway, and some soil samples were taken along the alignment.

And that's about as far as it went. In the November 2010 election Crist stood down and was replaced by Republican Rick Scott. The new governor announced in February 2011 that he had decided to reject any federal funds for the Tampa–Orlando line on the grounds that the project could be 'far too costly for taxpayers'. They would be 'on the hook for an additional $3 billion', he predicted, if there were a cost over-run. Scott contended that the traffic forecasts for high-speed lines were 'overly optimistic' – any shortfall could leave the state paying operating subsidies. His decision stopped the project in its tracks.

This little debacle followed a proposal dating from 2000 under which Florida voters endorsed by a margin of 53 per cent a constitutional amendment requiring the state to set up a high-speed rail service linking the state's five largest urban areas. The plan had been dreamt up by retired business-man C.C. 'Doc' Dockery, who succeeded in obtaining enough signatures on a petition to force a vote. The unexpected outcome put officials, virtually all of whom had opposed the amendment, in a spin.

The amendment required a start to be made within three years, and a Florida High Speed Rail Authority was set up; this organisation then chose a consortium to build the first phase of a network. However, the state legislature, backed by Republican Governor Jeb Bush, refused to release any seed funds to kickstart the plan, and in 2004 Florida voters reversed their decision and repealed the amendment.

To take the history back a stage further, in the mid-1990s there was a TGV-based proposal called Florida Overland Xpress. But despite a hopeful start, that too was killed off by Jeb Bush almost as soon as he took office in January 1999…

Although Florida has rejected true high-speed rail for now, it may become the testbed for a new generation of privately promoted inter-city passenger services. In March 2012 the parent company of the Florida East Coast Railway launched the All Aboard Florida project to develop services running at up to 200km/h between Miami and Orlando, closely tied into property development around stations. This will use 315km of the FEC main line, which last saw passenger trains in the early 1960s, plus 65km of new alignment paralleling a main road from the coast to a multi-modal interchange at Orlando International Airport. With detailed design under way, the promoters hoped to start construction by the end of 2014 for launch in 2016. An hourly service would cover the 380km from downtown Miami to Orlando Airport in 3 hours, including intermediate stops. An initial fleet of five diesel-powered trains was ordered from Siemens in September 2014.

LONE STAR STATE GOES IT ALONE

Texas is another state with a predilection for high-speed rail. Texas Central Railway (TCR) is a private company set up with ambitions to build a 386km link between Dallas and Houston using Shinkansen technology. The concept is supported by JR Central, which envisages adoption of a complete Shinkansen package using the N700-I train design, an eight-car export version of the Tokaido Shinkansen's Series N700. Running at up to 330km/h, trains would offer end-to-end timings of 1 hour 30 minutes. TCR notes that congestion and bad weather can extend the drive between the two cities to 5 hours or more.

Dallas and Houston are each home to more than 6 million people, and the population of both cities is forecast to double over the next two decades. Dallas has an excellent and expanding light rail network that could usefully feed traffic to a high-speed line. In Houston, after a much-delayed start, a light rail network is also growing rapidly. So this would appear to be an ideal high-speed rail market, but whether TCR will succeed in jumping through the forest of hoops that surround US rail projects is another matter. The first major hurdle is the Environmental Impact Statement, the preparation of which TCR says is being led by the Federal Railroad Administration and the Texas DoT, albeit with funding from the promoters.

Another issue is that a Shinkansen scheme would have to be segregated from other railways as lightweight Japanese trains would not meet the draconian US crashworthiness standards. Persuading US safety regulators to accept this – despite the unblemished safety record of the Shinkansen – may prove difficult.

TCR is aware that an earlier project called the Texas Triangle foundered in 1994 because of fierce opposition from Southwest Airlines and landowners along the route. A franchise had been awarded to Texas TGV Corp, but the company defaulted by not raising sufficient equity to launch the $8.4 billion project, despite being granted an extra year to find the funds. At that time officials and the public were extremely sceptical. They may be less so in 2014–15 – the mayors of both cities are supportive – but TCR will need to convince a lot of politicians and investors if it is to succeed in launching N700-I services at 30-minute intervals by the target date of 2021.

TCR has to date deliberately eschewed any form of state funding, but Obama's administration has tried hard to provide capital for high-speed projects and upgrades around the country that would enable speeds to be raised for conventional passenger trains. On 8 February 2011 Vice-President Joe Biden and Ray LaHood unveiled an ambitious programme to make $53 billion available over six years, with the first $8 billion included in the next budget period. The plan was submitted to Congress, but immediately ran into trouble, attracting criticism from the Chairman of the House Transportation Committee John L. Mica.

Mica also blasted the previous year's round of grants, claiming that 'what the Administration touted as high-speed rail ended up as embarrassing snail-speed trains to nowhere'. It was Mica's contention that any available funds should be spent on the Northeast Corridor (NEC) between Washington DC, New York and Boston, which in March 2011 was officially designated as a high-speed corridor eligible for federal funds. The proposals came before the Senate Appropriations Committee on 21 September 2011, which was meeting to set the DoT's budget for 2012. It promptly voted to sanction just $110 million for inter-city rail enhancements rather than the $8 billion that the President had requested.

NORTHEAST CORRIDOR

Mica pointed out at a conference organised by the US High Speed Rail Association in New York in November 2011 that 'this is the most densely populated region of our nation, and its highways and airports are increasingly congested'. It is

Metroliner memory. Originally ordered to a demanding specification from the Budd Company by the Pennsylvania Railroad in the 1960s, the 257km/h (160mph) *Metroliner* EMUs became part of Amtrak's Northeast Corridor fleet but never made it in regular service at their design speed. Eastbound Metroliner 885 passes Metuchen, New Jersey, led by a car rebuilt with a prominent equipment pod on the roof. (Amtrak Corporate Archives)

also the location of the only US rail service that qualifies for what the rest of the world defines as high speed, and that is Amtrak's *Acela Express*.

Trains had been running at up to 160km/h since electrification was completed between New York and Washington DC in the mid-1930s, but the first real attempts to turn the NEC into a high-speed artery date back to the 1960s, when

Mexican Chimera

Most Mexican long-distance passenger trains vanished during the 1990s, although one or two tourist operations remain – most famous is the Copper Canyon trip over the former Chihuahua-Pacific Railway between Topolobampo and Chihuahua.

When President Peña Neto took office on 1 December 2012 he caused a sensation in transport circles by vowing to reintroduce passenger trains. One scheme is aimed at tourist travel across the Yucután Peninsula, but the star in the programme was a 40.8 billion pesos project for 300km/h services between Mexico City and the city of Querétaro.

Early in 2014 the Secretariat of Transport & Communications published details of a 212km double-track electrified line through Huehuetoca and San Juan del Rio, plus an environmental impact report. On 15 August 2014 tendering documentation for a turnkey contract was signed off by Secretary of Transport & Communications Gerardo Ruiz. On 3 November 2014 the contract was awarded to a Chinese consortium, but this was promptly cancelled just three days later. A new competition was announced on 14 January 2015, but on 30 January the government decided that the project was suspended 'indefinitely' owing to its impact on the public finances in 2015–16.

the Pennsylvania Railroad set out to launch trains running at 258km/h (160mph) without building new tracks. A fleet of fifty high-powered *Metroliner* EMU cars was ordered from the legendary Budd Company that had built many of the famous streamliners of the 1930s when US passenger trains were in their heyday. The *Metroliners* were heavy and trouble-prone, and the problems were made worse by politicians insisting that they be rushed into service quickly. Not only that, but the NEC tracks were simply not up to the standard needed for high-speed running.

In 1979 Amtrak introduced the first of a fleet of Swedish-designed AEM-7 locomotives, which were matched with new Amfleet coaches that had the same distinctive stainless steel bodyshell as the *Metroliners*. Built to share premium 200km/h services with the EMUs, which they eventually replaced, they retained the *Metroliner* name.

However, it was clear that the NEC, which had passed into Amtrak ownership in 1976, would need massive upgrading if the desired speeds and shorter journey times were to be attained. Hefty doses of federal money were ploughed into the elderly infrastructure, which had three different electrification systems (11kV 25Hz, 12.5kV 60Hz, 25kV 60Hz) and was shared with a mix of commuter and heavy freight trains. Electrification was extended north from New Haven to Boston in the 1990s, and much of the corridor was eventually made fit for 200km/h. Some short segments have since been upgraded to permit 240km/h, and even 255km/h on a section of the modernised line to Boston thanks to a new transponder-based speed-enforcement system.

During the 1980s the success of high-speed services in Europe prompted Amtrak to test a Swedish X2000 tilting train and a German ICE 1 train set on US tracks. Both trains ran in regular service in 1992–93, quickly proving popular with

ICE bound for America. Amtrak's search for high-speed rolling stock extended to Europe. Modified to suit US conditions, a Swedish X2000 tilting train and an eight-car ICE 1 formation from Germany crossed the Atlantic. The ICE power car was prepared for shipment from Bremerhaven to Baltimore in June 1993. (Siemens)

the clientele, and Amtrak resolved to acquire something similar for the NEC. Its NEC strategy of upgraded tracks and faster trains was by now paying off, and in 1989 the NEC carried more passengers between Washington DC and New York than all the airlines combined.

In 1996 Amtrak ordered eighteen (later twenty) high-performance tilting train sets, each formed of two electric power cars and six trailers, from an Alstom-Bombardier partnership, together with fifteen matching locomotives for long-distance trains. The first 240km/h *Acela Express* entered service on 11 December 2000, taking over the

premium duties from the loco-hauled *Metroliners*. The New York–Boston timing was cut from about 5 hours to around 3 hours 30 minutes, quickly attracting new business. In January 2002 Amtrak launched a 2-hour-28-minute non-stop service between New York and Washington DC, 2 minutes faster than the original *Metroliner* timing on 2 April 1969. The trains were an instant hit with Amtrak's customers.

The operator, however, was not happy. A series of mechanical faults led to a bitter dispute with the train's builders, made worse on 13 August 2002 when Amtrak pulled the entire fleet out of service for checks following the discovery of cracks in brackets on the power car yaw dampers. The problems were eventually ironed out, and Amtrak settled down to try and build its ridership. In this endeavour it had some success, achieving 50 per cent growth in ten years, with record numbers in ten out of the eleven years to 2013. In that year it carried 31.5 million passengers, 11.4 million of them in the NEC.

The positive trend, plus capacity problems along the NEC, prompted Amtrak to think deeply about the future. The outcome of its deliberations was published on 28 September 2010, when it unveiled a 'concept plan' proposing construction by 2040 of a 680km high-speed line from Washington DC to Boston. Designed for 355km/h, this would allow a 3-hour timing compared with the present 6 hour 30 minutes, attracting five times the present *Acela* traffic. This bold proposal carries a price tag

Northeast Corridor. Amtrak's 240km/h Acela Express fleet handles premium traffic between Boston, New York and Washington. The New York skyline at Moynihan frames Set 2005 on 13 August 2013. (Amtrak/Chuck Gomez)

Boston fireworks. Amtrak's *Acela* Express entered service in 2000. An Amtrak photographer captured the extravagant display laid on to mark the arrival of the first train at Boston South after its 3-hour-10-minute sprint from New York on 11 December. (Amtrak/*Railway Gazette* collection)

of $117 billion, but Amtrak predicts an annual operating surplus of $990 million.

In the short term Amtrak needed to update its ageing NEC traction fleet. In October 2010 it ordered seventy ACS-64 'Amtrak Cities Sprinter' locomotives from Siemens to replace the AEM-7s on 200km/h *Northeast Regional* trains on the Washington DC–Boston route and 177km/h *Keystone Service* trains between Philadelphia and Harrisburg. It also contemplated adding two extra cars to each *Acela Express*, but decided in 2012 to order new trains instead. Joining forces with CHSRA, Amtrak issued a Request for Information on 17 January 2013 with a view to procuring a common fleet. This led to the publication on 24 January 2014 of a formal Request for Proposals for forty-three trains. The fifteen trains for CHSRA were to have a 320km/h maximum speed, and the twenty-eight for Amtrak were for a more stately 257km/h (160mph).

The joint procurement exercise was intended to keep down the costs, but after meeting suppliers, the two operators announced on 23 June 2014 that they had abandoned the joint purchase plan as the requirements for the two fleets were too diverse. Amtrak expected to start procurement before the end of 2014 and, on 22 October 2014,

CHSRA said it had received ten responses to a request for expressions of interest for 'a base order plus options for up to ninety-five trainsets' able to run at 354km/h (220mph).

So far, President Obama's hoped-for rail legacy is a tiny dot on the US transport landscape, although the Californian scheme has better prospects than any of its predecessors. Its future, and that of the Texan and the NEC projects, depends on several factors specific to North America:

- many Americans have little or no concept of inter-city rail travel;
- there is deep hostility to inter-city passenger trains at all political levels;
- the privately owned US freight railroads generally regard passenger trains as a nuisance;
- the powerful airline lobby may fight any high-speed rail project threatening its business;
- public transport needed to feed inter-city rail services, with some exceptions, does not exist;
- any project that is not privately funded is often dismissed out of hand.

If these formidable obstacles can be overcome, the fictional paragraph at the start of this chapter could just come true.

13

High Hopes in the Low Countries

Whoever chose to brand the Dutch high-speed trains as *Albatros* was presumably not familiar with *The Rime of the Ancyent Marinere* by Samuel Taylor Coleridge, a poem in which an albatross shot by a sailor appears to bring ill fortune to the ship and the crew. Welcome to the history of the Dutch high-speed line, *Hogesnelheidslijn-Zuid* (HSL-Zuid).

HSL-Zuid connects directly with the Belgian high-speed network, which has three lines radiating from Brussels. One runs west to meet LGV Nord-Europe near Antoing, around 30km east of Lille. This opened in stages in 1996–97, making Belgium the third country in the world to attain 300km/h in commercial service. In technical terms, the line is similar to the French LGVs with 25kV 50Hz electrification and TVM430 cab signalling.

An initial high-speed Paris–Brussels service taking 2 hours 3 minutes with a reversal at Lille was launched in January 1995 using TGV Réseau trains. These were soon replaced by PBA and PBKA train sets in their distinctive red livery, and on 2 June 1996 services were diverted over the cross-border section of the high-speed line as far as Antoing. From there they ran over conventional tracks to Brussels-Midi, with some continuing to Amsterdam.

Paris–Brussels services were in the hands of Westrail International, set up in 1995 as a subsidiary of SNCF and Belgian Railways (SNCB), with the Dutch and German national railways also represented. Westrail changed its name in May 1999 to Thalys International to reflect the *Thalys* brand name chosen for high-speed services from Paris to Brussels, Amsterdam and Cologne.

Completion of the main section of Belgium's first high-speed line was commemorated on 10 December 1997 when a special train conveyed King Albert II and Queen Paola from Brussels to Paris and back. 'For the first time in the history of international rail transport, two capitals are directly linked by services running at 300km/h from end to end', intoned Managing Director of Belgian National Railways Etienne Schouppe at Brussels-Midi before departure, which was 8 minutes late. Just 78 minutes and 46 seconds later, the flag-adorned PBKA set drew punctually to a halt at Paris Nord, where the grinning driver maintained that the train had run at 'strictly no more than 300km/h'. With a timing of 1 hour 25 minutes between Paris and Brussels, regular Thalys trains quickly boosted rail's market share, and from 14 December 1997 they were extended to Cologne.

Lady in red. A Thalys PBA train arrives at Amsterdam Centraal from Paris on 1 October 2013. Running over high-speed lines in France, Belgium and the Netherlands, these services cover the 541km in 3 hours 17 minutes, including intermediate calls at Brussels, Antwerp, Rotterdam and Schiphol Airport. (Quintus Vosman)

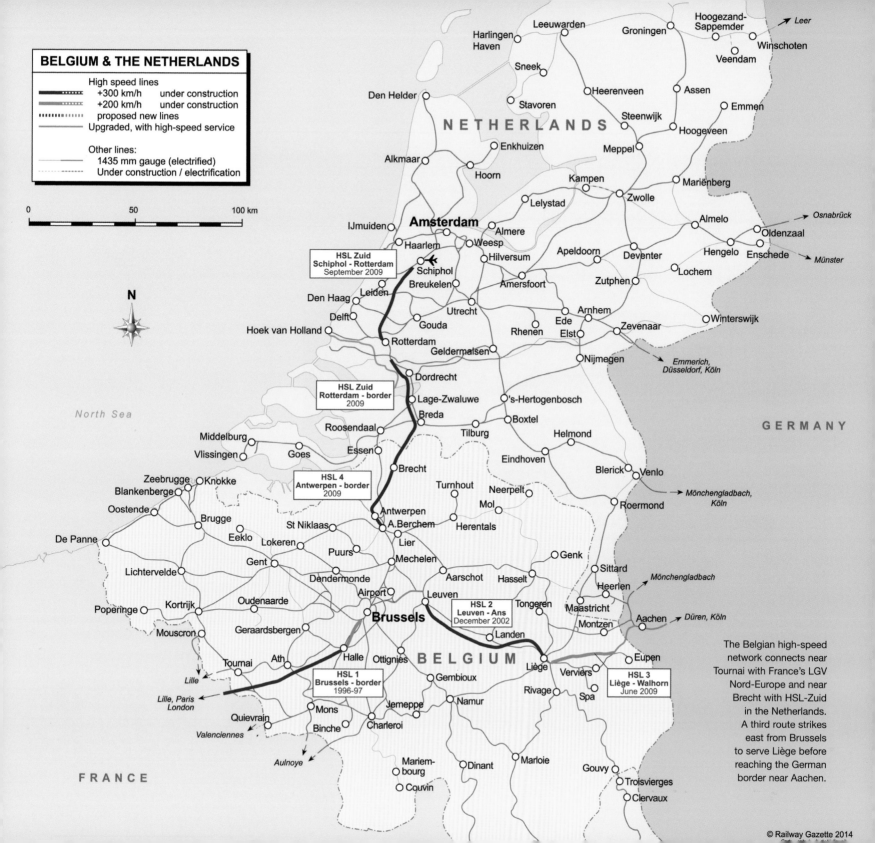

BELGIUM & THE NETHERLANDS

High speed lines

+300 km/h   under construction
+200 km/h   under construction
proposed new lines
Upgraded, with high-speed service

Other lines:
1435 mm gauge (electrified)
Under construction / electrification

0   50   100 km

N

North Sea

NETHERLANDS

Leer

Hoogezand-Sappemder
Leeuwarden   Groningen   Winschoten
Harlingen   Veendam
Haven   Sneek   Heerenveen   Assen
Den Helder   Stavoren   Emmen
                    Steenwijk   Hoogeveen
                         Meppel   Mariënberg
          Enkhuizen   Kampen
Alkmaar   Zwolle   Almelo   Osnabrück
Hoorn   Lelystad   Oldenzaal
                    Almere   Hengelo   Enschede   Münster
Amsterdam   Weesp   Apeldoorn   Deventer
IJmuiden   Haarlem   Hilversum   Lochem
HSL Zuid   Schiphol Breukelen Amersfoort Zutphen
Schiphol - Rotterdam   Amersfoort
September 2009   Utrecht   Ede   Arnhem
Den Haag   Leiden   Rhenen Elst   Zevenaar   Winterswijk
Delft   Gouda   Emmerich,
Hoek van Holland   Rotterdam   Nijmegen   Düsseldorf, Köln
               Geldermalsen
HSL Zuid   Dordrecht
Rotterdam - border   Lage-Zwaluwe   's-Hertogenbosch   GERMANY
2009   Breda   Boxtel
Roosendaal   Tilburg   Helmond
Middelburg   Goes   Essen   Eindhoven   Blerick Venlo
Vlissingen   Brecht   Mönchengladbach,
HSL 4   Turnhout   Neerpelt   Köln
Zeebrugge Knokke Antwerpen - border   Mol   Roermond
Blankenberge   2009   Antwerpen   Herentals
Oostende   Brugge   St Niklaas A.Berchem
          Eeklo   Lier   Genk   Sittard   Mönchengladbach
De Panne   Lokeren Puurs Mechelen   Heerlen
Lichtervelde   Gent   Dendermonde   Aarschot Hasselt   Maastricht
                    Airport   Leuven   Tongeren   Aachen   Düren, Köln
Poperinge Kortrijk Oudenaarde   HSL 2   Montzen
                    Geraardsbergen   Leuven - Ans Landen   Eupen
Mouscron   Ath   Halle Ottignies December 2002 Liège Verviers   HSL 3
Tournai   BELGIUM   Rivage Spa   Liège - Walhorn
Lille   HSL 1   Gembloux   June 2009
Lille, Paris   Brussels - border   Namur
London   Quiévrain 1996-97 Mons Jemeppe
               Binche Charleroi   The Belgian high-speed
Valenciennes   Mariem-   network connects near
               Aulnoye   bourg Dinant Marloie   Tournai with France's LGV
                         Couvin   Gouvy   Nord-Europe and near
                              Troisvierges   Brecht with HSL-Zuid
                              Clervaux   in the Netherlands.
                                        A third route strikes
FRANCE   east from Brussels
                                        to serve Liège before
                                        reaching the German
                                        border near Aachen.

© Railway Gazette 2014

By 2000 Thalys had reached agreement with Air France that its trains would replace short-haul flights between Paris and Brussels.

Belgium's two other high-speed lines run north and east from Brussels towards the Dutch and German frontiers respectively. In commercial terms these were less attractive than the western route, which was destined to carry both Paris and London traffic. The Belgian government nevertheless committed to complete high-speed routes from border to border, as it rightly saw them as international corridors.

The northern route begins in the Brussels suburb of Schaerbeek and relies on upgraded tracks – plus a short new section – for much of the first 50km to Antwerp. Here a new cross-city tunnel was needed, and the opportunity was taken to build new underground platform tracks below the majestic Central terminus, which was restored to its former glory.

From Antwerp a new alignment was required to reach the Dutch border. Unfortunately, the Dutch and Belgians had different views about the site of the border crossing as they each wanted the shortest (cheapest) alignment on their territory. The ensuing squabble was eventually resolved without resorting to arms, and the Belgian part of the line ran from Antwerp to a parkway station at Noorderkempen near Brecht before crossing the frontier at Hazeldonk. Signalling consisted of ETCS Level 2.

The eastern route also diverges at Schaerbeek, from where extra tracks for 220km/h were created by quadrupling the old route to Louvain (Leuven). From there a new 300km/h alignment was built alongside the E40 motorway to the outskirts of Liège, with the railway protected from intruding road vehicles by 'green walls'. At Liège, trains call at a magnificent new station designed by Spanish architect Santiago Calatrava. From here to Walhorn, just short of the German border at Aachen, a new 260km/h alignment includes the 6.5km Soumagne Tunnel. In Germany, DB undertook to upgrade the route to Cologne for 220km/h.

Tests over the Louvain–Liège section started in August 2002, with Thalys trains running at up to 330km/h before commercial services began on 15 December. The line is equipped with a modified version of SNCB's standard TBL (Transmission Beacon Locomotive) automatic train protection as it is shared by domestic inter-city trains.

The section between Liège and Aachen is fitted with ETCS Level 2, but this did not open until 12 June 2009. Apart from the Thalys PBKA trains, the line carries several daily return ICE workings operated by DB between Cologne and Frankfurt-am-Main – these compete with Thalys on the Cologne–Brussels leg.

DUTCH DECISION

The Dutch government began planning a high-speed line from the border to Amsterdam in 1991, but it could not decide how to proceed. Only in 1997 did Parliament endorse the scheme, and on 15 January 1999 Prime Minister Wim Kok informed

Brief encounter. A Deutsche Bahn ICE 3 from Frankfurt-am-Main and Cologne meets a Thalys PBA train at Brussels-Midi on 25 September 2010. DB is relinquishing its small stake in the Thalys business, which from 2015 will be entirely in the hands of Belgian and French national operators SNCB and SNCF. (Author)

Dutch MPs how the line would be built – it was to be a PPP in three parts.

First, the state would procure the substructure through a project management company, *Projectorganisatie HSL-Zuid*. Second, a private-sector consortium would design, build and maintain the track, signalling and 25kV 50Hz power supply under a thirty-year concession. In return it would be paid a fee by government, with penalties incurred should availability fall short of the 99 per cent target. Third, operators would be contracted to run the trains, paying fees to government for use of the line. At the time, it was the largest PPP awarded by the Dutch government. In geographical terms, the line is divided by a gap through Rotterdam, which means that all trains must run over old tracks for part of the journey, requiring them to operate with the standard Dutch 1.5kV DC power supply and ATB train protection – which they also need for the final leg from Schiphol Airport to Amsterdam.

Consortia bidding for the six main civil engineering lots, each worth around €400 million, were shortlisted in May 1999, and a ceremony on 27 March 2000 near Breda marked the start of work. Hosting the event was Dutch Transport Minister Tineke Netelenbos, who was joined by her Belgian counterpart Isabelle Durant to emphasise the project's international nature.

The civil works included structures to pass over or under several of the country's main waterways: the 1.1km Hollandsch Diep bridge, a 2.5km tunnel below the Oude Maas and another of the same length under the Dordtsche Kil. Both relied on immersed tube techniques. A 7.2km tunnel was needed to avoid disturbing the 'Green Heart' nature reserve east of Leiden – a fen landscape formed in the Middle Ages by peat cutting. A tunnel boring machine with a huge 14.87m diameter cutting head was used, said to be the largest in the world.

A dividing wall separates the two tracks, with fire-resistant doors at 150m intervals. These are intended to withstand a temperature of 1,000°C for 1 hour, but the price per door was €30,000.

Much of the line runs across weak subsoil, so most of the alignment was built using concrete slabs mounted on deep piles to avoid the risk of subsidence. Another unusual feature is a concrete plinth between the rails along about half the route; this is designed to prevent a derailed train leaving the alignment.

The Infrastructure Provision concession was finally let in 2001 to the Infraspeed Consortium, which was given five years to design, finance and install the electrical and mechanical equipment and a further twenty-five years to maintain it using a 5-hour nightly slot. ETCS Level 2 would in theory match that between Antwerp and Hazeldonk in Belgium.

Bidding to pick an operator was under way by 1999, and in the following year Nederlandse Spoorwegen (NS) formed an alliance with national airline KLM to bid for access rights. Registration closed on 15 September 2000, but one of the four contenders was later suspended from bidding for telling local paper *de Volkskrant* that the access charges were too high and that one of its rivals had been set up to win. Netelenbos revealed on 15 June 2001 that the preferred bidder was NS-KLM, which subsequently traded as High Speed Alliance (HSA); NS had a 90 per cent stake and KLM 10 per cent.

HSA agreed to pay the government €148 million a year for exclusive use of HSL-Zuid for fifteen years. Opening was scheduled for December 2005, but planning delays meant that domestic high-speed services would not start until October 2006. From the same date Paris–Amsterdam trains were due to switch to the new line with HSA forming a joint venture with Thalys. HSA Managing Director

Nol Döbken noted in early 2002 that HSL-Zuid had the potential to compete with air over short distances, suggesting that KLM's barely profitable three flights a day from Schiphol to Antwerp and seven to Brussels could be replaced by trains with high-quality service – essential so that premium fares could be charged to pay off HSA's access fees.

New rolling stock was needed for domestic high-speed services from Amsterdam and Den Haag to Rotterdam and Breda and for a high-frequency Brussels–Amsterdam service to replace the conventional 'Benelux' trains that ran via Roosendaal and Den Haag. HSA and SNCB accordingly signed a contract with AnsaldoBreda of Italy on 24 May 2004 for twelve eight-car trains, with an option for fourteen more; the order was later increased to nineteen sets. Initially, nine would be owned by HSA and three by SNCB, with first delivery in April 2006 in time for the planned launch in October that year. With a power rating of 5.4MW, these V250 trains were an uprated version of a 220km/h design.

A RAILWAY IN SEARCH OF TRAINS

By early 2005 it was clear that the V250 fleet would not arrive until April 2007 at the earliest, and HSA admitted in August that there were problems with fitting Level 2 ETCS because the train control specification had not been received from the transport ministry. Use of Thalys PBKA train sets was also ruled out as a short-term fix as fitting them with Level 2 was a major exercise – they were already stuffed with seven different train control systems. SNCF confirmed that Level 2 would be installed during 2007 as part of a refurbishment programme, meaning that the trains would not be ready to run over HSL-Zuid until April 2008.

New Transport Minister Karla Peijs conveyed news of the delays to the Dutch Parliament. The ministry nevertheless wanted HSA to pay its monthly access fee from the agreed date of April 2007, but HSA countered with a claim for €22 million a month from the ministry for failing to specify the train control equipment. HSA then asked the ministry to install back-up signalling on HSL-Zuid, but this request was rejected.

Faced with having no trains with which to earn revenue, HSA opted to make a start with temporary rolling stock running at 160km/h. Two days before Christmas in 2005 it agreed to lease twelve electric locomotives that would be paired with coaches hired from NS. The dispute with government was meanwhile placed with an independent referee.

Another year passed, and Peijs announced that even the interim HSL-Zuid services would not start before December 2007 because of delays with the wayside ETCS equipment. This prompted the Dutch Parliament to order an enquiry by the National Audit Office. Delivery of the V250 trains from Italy had in the meantime slipped to the end of 2008.

In March 2007 *NS Hispeed* was chosen as the marketing name for services between Amsterdam and the Belgian border – and indeed for other high-speed services such as the ICE trains that ran from Amsterdam into Germany. It was at this point that the name *Albatros* was picked for the V250 trains, which were now a year past their original delivery date. Not that the railway was ready for them, as it turned out that different versions of ETCS Level 2 had been installed on the Dutch and Belgian sides of the border. Upgrading to match the Belgian equipment was put in hand.

In May 2007 the transport ministry said that HSA's planned interim service would run only over the northern half of HSL-Zuid to allow the ETCS to be upgraded on the southern section, but a month later it admitted that even this was optimistic. The National Audit Office then

weighed in with its report, blaming the transport ministry for a lack of co-ordinated leadership and suggesting that the delays had cost €222 million in lost access charges. The 1990s capital cost of €3.5 billion for HSL-Zuid had meanwhile rocketed up to €6.3 billion in 2006.

Next, investigations revealed that HSA's €148 million annual access fee was spectacularly higher than rival bids of around €100 million and even way above the €120 million that the government had considered viable. No wonder that by autumn 2007 HSA was seeking a cut in its fees to compensate for underestimating journey times in Belgium, while it also became concerned over sharing tracks with ordinary trains between the north end of HSL-Zuid at Hoofddorp and Amsterdam.

To compound all these issues, Belgian infrastructure manager Infrabel, split from SNCB in January 2005, was reported to be pursuing a claim against the Dutch transport ministry for delaying the start of HSL-Zuid services and hence losing track access fees over the Belgian part of the route.

Hopes rose briefly when a trial run for the interim passenger service on the northern section of HSL-Zuid was made in September, but in October the next Transport Minister Camiel Eurlings conceded that commercial operations had been postponed indefinitely, the latest delay being attributed to problems with certification of the leased locomotives to operate on HSL-Zuid.

Expectations that HSL-Zuid could be shown off to the professionals in the business had led to Amsterdam being chosen to host an international conference on high-speed railways in March 2008. Embarrassingly, at the opening session Eurlings was only able to tell delegates that he expected to announce a date for the start of services 'shortly'.

In Italy, progress was at last being made with the *Albatros* fleet. The first train arrived at the rolling-stock test centre in Velim in the Czech

Republic in early 2008, but insiders reported that it was far from complete. Several months elapsed while it was fitted out for testing – entry into service seemed as far away as ever.

Still without an income stream, the hapless HSA was now on the brink of bankruptcy, forcing Eurlings to mount a rescue. Announcing this in early 2009, the minister confirmed that HSA had already received one payment to compensate for the delay in opening HSL-Zuid, while a second had been agreed to cover the period up to the latest projected opening date of July 2009. In return, HSA would drop its claim against the government over delays in preparing the ETCS specification. The start of the concession would be switched to July with operating rights extended to 2024, while HSA would be temporarily exempt from access charges for three or four years, although this would have to be made good later.

On 7 July 2009 NS Hispeed and SNCB took advantage of the delivery of the prototype V250 train, painted in a red, white and pink livery, to announce that Amsterdam–Brussels services would be branded as *Fyra*. NS Hispeed said that the brand name was 'short, international and powerful, providing an interesting visual combination that projects stateliness, strength and self-confidence', while the logo was 'red, which evokes sparks, fire and speed'.

LOW-KEY LAUNCH

Final preparations were meanwhile in hand for the interim service on the northern part of HSL-Zuid using ETCS Level 1. A low-key ceremony attended by Eurlings and the mayors of Amsterdam and Rotterdam was held on 6 September 2009 before NS Hispeed launched a supplementary fare Amsterdam–Rotterdam service on the following day with seventeen return trips taking 43 minutes to cover the 72km at no more than 160km/h.

Thalys trains fitted with ETCS Level 2 were diverted over HSL-Zuid from 13 December 2009, finally putting the Netherlands into the 300km/h club, although the maximum speed from Rotterdam to Schiphol remained at 160km/h pending the upgrade from ETCS Level 1 to Level 2. Although the cross-border ETCS transition problems had in theory been solved, further issues quickly became evident. These were temporarily dealt with by imposing a speed reduction.

Unbelievably, the litany of trouble with the V250 trains continued. Eurlings admitted to Parliament in mid-2010 that they would not carry passengers before December 2011, four years later than envisaged when NS-KLM was awarded the operating contract. Four were undergoing tests on Dutch tracks, but at least six were required to run a commercial service.

From October 2010 HSA stepped up its interim Fyra service between Amsterdam and Rotterdam from one to two trains an hour, but speed remained limited to 160km/h pending certification to use Level 2 ETCS. This was finally achieved in 2011, allowing the service to be extended in April over the southern part of HSL-Zuid to Breda. It also cleared the way for the upgrade to Level 2 on the northern half, allowing Thalys to run at 300km/h on both sections.

The temporary arrangements were a far cry from HSA's original expectations, and traffic fell short of budget, forcing HSA to cut its premium fares. The alliance hoped that its fortunes would change in July 2012 when the V250 trains were finally certified to run in the Netherlands. They were hurriedly pressed into service between Amsterdam and Rotterdam. More good news arrived in September when the Belgian authorities signed off the V250 to run there too. NS Hispeed immediately filed an application to launch cross-border services from December.

However, another obstacle arose. NS and SNCB planned to withdraw the Benelux service when the cross-border Fyra trains were launched. Although the railways saw this as a replacement, passengers did not, as Fyra used HSL-Zuid and did not serve Roosendaal or Den Haag. Not only that, but Fyra attracted a premium fare and reservations were compulsory. Regular cross-border travellers were not amused.

Nor was the city council in Den Haag, which appealed to the Dutch Parliament to retain the Benelux trains. Although an Antwerp–Breda–Den Haag Fyra service was planned, with SNCB sharing the cost and expected to purchase an extra V250, the money was not forthcoming, and Dutch Infrastructure Minister Melanie Schultz van Haegen told Parliament that a meeting with her Belgian opposite number was 'not substantively satisfactory'. Legal action against Belgium was in prospect.

On 9 December 2012, six years and three months late, V250 trains started to shuttle between Brussels and Amsterdam with fare-paying passengers on board. At least, they were supposed to. The new trains quickly gained a reputation for unreliability, with numerous services cancelled and only half achieving arrivals within 5 minutes of the timetable, although this later improved to 71 per cent following attention to maintenance routines. NS Hispeed Managing Director Jan-Willem Siebers explained that the trains had experienced 'electronic communications failures', causing emergency brake applications. But worse was to come.

Laid up. Three of the V250 'Albatros' train sets await their fate at the Nedtrain yard at Amsterdam Watergraafsmeer on 1 October 2013. (Quintus Vosman)

Winter in northern Europe is not a good time to introduce a novel type of train, let alone one originating in the sunnier climes of Italy, and on 17 January 2013 all Fyra services were suspended. Three of the V250 fleet had been damaged by snow and ice, and Belgian safety authority DVIS immediately withdrew permission for the V250 fleet to carry passengers after a component was found on the track north of Antwerp. CEO of SNCB Marc Descheemaecker declared that he was 'truly disgusted' and vowed to propose 'brutal measures' when seeking reparation for the business and its passengers. An emergency board meeting next day resolved to give AnsaldoBreda three months to sort out the issues or SNCB would refuse delivery of its three trains and seek return of the €35 million it had paid towards the €63 million cost.

Although the V250s were still permitted to run in the Netherlands, NS pulled them out of service and halted the acceptance process. AnsaldoBreda issued a formal apology on 19 January, attributing the problems to an 'undue accumulation of snow, that turning into ice and detaching during the train running, damaged some parts of the underframe'. This despite tests in a climate chamber that could simulate winter conditions.

NS and SNCB rushed to cobble together some replacement services. NS used the loco-hauled Fyra trains between Amsterdam and Breda and shuttled passengers by bus between Breda and Antwerp, while SNCB extended some of its Brussels–Antwerp trains to Roosendaal. A service of eight (later ten) return trains a day was introduced between Brussels and Den Haag, no doubt to rejoicing on the part of passengers who had come to regard Fyra as a very bad joke.

NS set up a task force to investigate the debacle and SNCB commissioned consultants to do the same. The consultants reported back in May 2013, and Descheemaecker promptly made the findings public. 'Fundamental gaps and deficiencies in terms of reliability and safety in design and production' had been identified, he said, and apart from the problems with snow and ice, doors had fallen off, water had leaked, sections of roof had broken off and electrical fires had been caused by overheating batteries. Taking into account the likely time and cost needed to rectify all this, SNCB decided to cancel its order and seek to reclaim the money it had paid.

The findings of the Dutch review were presented to the government on 7 June. They included a recommendation that NS cancel its €336 million contract and seek to recoup more than €180 million that it had paid for nine out of the sixteen train sets that had been delivered. The government concurred.

In Naples, AnsaldoBreda swiftly called a press conference at which Director Maurizio Manfellotto said that the company had received the news with 'dismay and disappointment' and described the allegations as 'baseless and unfounded'.

NS Financial Services notified the Italian supplier of the contract cancellation in August, but Manfellotto announced on 16 September that AnsaldoBreda was 'capable of finding a solution'

Low country link. It was party time at Lille on 12 April 2014 when Thalys launched a service of two trains a day between the French city and Amsterdam. A PBKA four-system train set formed the first service, arriving at Lille-Europe at 9.52 a.m. (Thalys, Maxime Dufour)

Dutch destination. Eurostar's ten-strong e320 Velaro fleet is equipped to run from London to Amsterdam via the Belgian and Dutch high-speed lines. Eurostar plans to launch this service in partnership with Netherlands Railways in 2015–16. Set 4005 eclipses an easyJet Airbus as it speeds past Roissy-Charles de Gaulle Airport on an endurance run in June 2014. (Christophe Masse)

to the faults. The company tried to obtain the independent technical reports commissioned by NS and SNCB, but the Court of Justice in Utrecht ruled that they should not be released. AnsaldoBreda refused to accept the trains back as they had been 'fully approved' for commercial service, and Manfellotto insisted that his company's interests were in line with those of Dutch and Belgian citizens who 'wanted to ride on high-speed trains', remarking that they would be rightfully asking where their taxes had been spent.

Back in the Netherlands, NS declared in November 2013 that the Fyra name would be replaced from the 15 December timetable change by 'Intercity Direct'. Supplementary fares on the Rotterdam–Breda trains would be dropped, and hourly trains would be introduced between Brussels and Den Haag, while more Thalys services would be added, including two daily trains between Amsterdam and Lille that started in April 2014.

The row with AnsaldoBreda rumbled on until 17 March 2014, when NS announced that it had reached an agreement with the supplier and its parent Finmeccanica. This provided for AnsaldoBreda to take back all sixteen V250 trains ordered by NS and to return €125 million to the operator. The three trains for SNCB had never been delivered. Very sensibly, the parties agreed that a compromise was better than a long legal battle. They both agreed that the V250 fleet

Fallback fleet. In the wake of the V250 debacle Netherlands Railways is procuring nineteen of its own locomotives to run with refurbished inter-city coaches over HSL-Zuid between Amsterdam, Rotterdam and Eindhoven from late 2015. The 160km/h Traxx F160MS locomotives are being built in the Bombardier factory at Kassel in Germany. (Christoph Müller)

could have been repaired and returned to service. AnsaldoBreda was free to modify the trains to suit another operator, and in the event of selling them, it would make additional payments to NS of up to €21 million.

Since then the Dutch government has abolished the HSL-Zuid operating concession, while NS is buying locomotives to replace those leased by NS Hispeed. The Benelux service will in due course resume running to Amsterdam.

14

Britain on a Branch Line?

Just by the entrance to the Underground at London's magnificently restored St Pancras station is a large plaque set into the wall. At the top in bright yellow lettering is 'HIGH SPEED 1', and below that in red is 'BRITAIN'S FIRST HIGH-SPEED RAILWAY'. This commemorates the opening of High Speed 1 and St Pancras International station on 6 November 2007 by 'Her Majesty the Queen accompanied by His Royal Highness the Duke of Edinburgh'.

On 14 November the second stage of the 109km new railway from St Pancras to the British portal of the Channel Tunnel was opened for business.

Precisely thirteen years had elapsed since the first commercial train ran from London through the Channel Tunnel to Paris. The London terminus was then at Waterloo, and the train did not travel at high speed until it reached French soil, where it sped away over LGV Nord-Europe to Paris.

Britain had been a reluctant partner in joining Europe's high-speed network. When a high-speed link from the Channel Tunnel to a London terminal at White City was proposed in 1973, the project aroused the fury of many of the inhabitants of Kent, the 'Garden of England'. British Rail officers given the job of selling the scheme to the public

Monument to speed. The commemorative plaque at St Pancras International marking completion of Britain's first high-speed line. (Author)

were not all equal to the task, which sometimes meant dealing with hordes of vociferous protesters. The line was at that time inextricably linked to the equally controversial Channel Tunnel, which was cancelled, along with the high-speed railway, by Environment Secretary Anthony Crosland on 20 January 1975.

Both projects went back to the drawing board. Plans for a Channel 'fixed link' were revived in the 1980s and, after proposals for gigantic bridges with artificial islands and other unlikely schemes lost out in a competition for the best project, the Tunnel eventually went ahead. At Prime Minister Mrs Thatcher's insistence, the Tunnel had to be privately financed, and Section 42 of the Channel Tunnel Act expressly forbade subsidy to public operators of international rail services – although private operators could be subsidised. Doubtless mindful of the earlier problems, British Rail insisted that international trains could be accommodated on the existing network. No serious discussion about a high-speed line was to be entertained until construction of the Tunnel had reached the point of no return.

Predictably, the difference in speed between travel on LGV Nord-Europe and the gentle trundle past Kent's orchards and oast houses, to say nothing of the long crawl through the London suburbs where Eurostars shared tracks with loitering commuter trains, had highlighted the absurdity of not having a dedicated link. It was some compensation to arrive at the elegant Grimshaw-designed international terminus erected alongside the domestic platforms at Waterloo, but this did not disguise the fact that

London was on the end of a branch line. Apart from anything else, the 300km/h Eurostar trains (p184) derived from the French TGV were condemned to travel over historic tracks electrified at 750V DC third rail – much to the horror of French rolling-stock engineers who could not believe that ordinary British trains actually ran at 160km/h using such quaint technology.

In 1990 the engineering consultancy Arup came up with a fresh route from the capital to the Tunnel calculated to minimise the impact in Kent and to avoid disruption in the London suburbs thanks to a long approach tunnel. The plan included a 3km tunnel through water-bearing chalk under the tidal River Thames near Dartford. Much discussion followed before the route was settled in 1993 (the year when the Railways Act initiated the break-up and sale of British Rail into around 100 private companies), and The Channel Tunnel Rail Link Act received Royal Assent on 18 December 1996.

In February 1996 the Department of Transport chose London & Continental Railways (LCR) to build the line and to run European Passenger Services (EPS), the British arm of the Eurostar business that had been set up by the national railways of France, Britain and Belgium to operate passenger trains through the Channel Tunnel; EPS was renamed Eurostar (UK) Ltd in October 1996. LCR's original shareholders were Arup, Bechtel, Halcrow, Systra, National Express, SNCF, electricity supplier EDF and investment bank UBS.

LCR sought to raise money from private investors on the back of future revenue from Eurostar, but in practice the revenue fell far short of the forecasts – in 1997 there were only 6 million passengers compared with the predicted 9 million. In January 1998 LCR sought an additional £1.2 billion from government, prompting Deputy Prime Minister John Prescott to make an Emergency Statement to the House of Commons.

The government contemplated dropping the entire scheme but gave LCR until 31 March to come up with a rescue package, although the deadline was later extended to May. At this point proposals emerged for splitting the project into two. The 70km Section 1 was to be completed by October 2003 from the Channel Tunnel to Fawkham Junction near Longfield, from where trains would continue over existing tracks to Waterloo. Section 2 would run from Southfleet Junction to St Pancras.

On 3 June 1998 Prescott announced that the project would be restructured. Apart from being divided into two, the main difference was that the government was willing to guarantee £3.7 billion of LCR bonds in addition to promising further funds if LCR's cash dried up. Prescott turned the first sod at Cuxton close to the River Medway on 15 October 1998.

On 24 February 1999 LCR completed the issue of government bonds worth £2.65 billion to fund construction. Financial close also allowed the establishment of two LCR subsidiaries, Union Railways (South) for Section 1 and Union Railways (North) for Section 2. Design and construction management was placed with Rail Link Engineering, a consortium of four LCR shareholders, while Bechtel and rail infrastructure owner Railtrack were handed the job of project management.

Railtrack agreed to buy Section 1 at cost when it was completed. It also held an option to buy or lease Section 2, but its collapse after the Hatfield derailment in 2000 obliged it to surrender the option before it entered administration in October 2001. Network Rail succeeded Railtrack in 2002 and paid Railtrack £375 million for Section 1. It also agreed to pay LCR a one-off fee of £80 million for the right to operate the line for the duration of LCR's lease, which ran to 2086.

Earth work. Former Deputy Prime Minister John Prescott kicks off construction of the Channel Tunnel Rail Link, now HS1, in the traditional way on 15 October 1998. In the background is the M2 viaduct over the River Medway. (*Railway Gazette* collection)

The first track was laid in May 2001, and on 2 July that year Transport Minister John Spellar launched work on Section 2 at the site of the future Stratford International station in East London. With 25kV 50Hz electrification and TVM430 signalling, both sections used equipment and techniques derived from France's TGV lines, so much so that project staff referred to the alignment as the 'trace', from the French *tracé*. Much of Section 1 was engineered for 300km/h, with long sections following the M20 and M2 corridors. Historically, Britain's railways have a smaller loading gauge than their counterparts in mainland Europe, so the dimensions of bridges and other structures were specified to allow standard European trains to reach London.

Section 1 finally opened on 16 September 2003, twenty-two years after the first part of LGV Sud-Est in France and thirty-nine years after the launch of the Tokaido Shinkansen. Prime Minister Tony Blair made a token speech at Waterloo and Transport Secretary Alistair Darling rode the inaugural train to officiate at a ceremony at Sandling near Folkestone.

Section 2 proceeded on schedule, but the engineering complexity and the high proportion of tunnel drove the cost up to £84 million/km compared with £26 million/km for Section 1. In November 2006, with an eye to the high-speed network expanding north of London, the Channel Tunnel Rail Link was renamed High Speed 1.

During 2006 there was speculation about LCR's future, and in November 2007 the government confirmed its intention to sell off LCR's three business elements: the infrastructure, including track and stations, its property interests and the UK stake in Eurostar. On 8 June 2009 Transport Secretary Lord Adonis confirmed that LCR had been restructured and that the government had acquired it for a nominal price. This paved the way for sale of a long-term concession to manage and market HS1, which had an outturn cost of £5.8 billion – the sale was seen as a way of offsetting public investment in its construction. Among parties expressing interest were Deutsche Bahn and Air France.

Although the Labour government was replaced by a coalition of the Conservative and Liberal Democrat parties in May 2010, bids to run HS1 were invited on 21 June. On 5 November 2010 the government announced that a thirty-year concession to manage HS1 had been let to a

consortium of Borealis Infrastructure and the Ontario Teachers' Pension Plan for £2.1 billion.

In December 2013 the government confirmed that it was contemplating the sale of LCR's property interests, which included the former Eurostar platforms at Waterloo, and its stake in Eurostar International Ltd, the former Eurostar (UK) Ltd having been transformed into a 40 per cent shareholding when the tri-national joint venture completed its legal transformation into a unified company on 1 September 2010. SNCF holds the majority share at 55 per cent and SNCB just 5 per cent.

MAKING HISTORY

Looking back, it seems remarkable that HS1 was built at all. So it was especially interesting to experience travel over the entire route shortly before it opened. Join me in Brussels, then, for a quick dash to St Pancras.

On the morning of 20 September 2007 champagne glasses were clinking on Platform 2 at Brussels-Midi as passengers boarded Train 9125 for the non-stop run to London St Pancras. Among them was Eurostar Chief Executive Richard Brown, who declared that we were about to 'make a small piece of history' as 'we are firmly putting

Access denied. Eurostar is obliged by the British government to operate with stringent security precautions. These include gates enclosing the two tracks serving platforms 1 and 2 at Brussels-Midi.

Brussels–London into the two-hour club'. Around 700 guests were on board the twenty-car train which slid out of Midi at 11.05 a.m. Driver Luc Stockx opened up as soon as the opportunity arose, and the train was soon racing through the fields of western Belgium under a pale sun. The French border was crossed at 300km/h before Stockx eased off for the junction at Fretin that routed the train towards the English Channel.

The Eurostar stormed through the gloomy barn of Lille-Europe at 11.34 a.m. and headed for Calais-Fréthun and the Channel Tunnel, although its passage was slowed by a speed restriction where First World War trenches had been unexpectedly located beneath the tracks. At 11.59 a.m. the train plunged into the Channel Tunnel. The supposedly rare commodity of English sunshine brightened our exit at Cheriton near Folkestone at 11.18 a.m. local time as we accelerated to full line speed. Here, HS1 runs parallel to the existing railway from Folkestone to Ashford, where grade-separated spurs link two platforms used by international trains.

Stockx has meanwhile handed the controls to his British colleague David Green, and the train soars past Ashford on a viaduct. Attractive wood-fringed fields and orchards flit by as the Eurostar approaches Boxley, site of the British rail speed record. It was here that sister Eurostar 373 313/14 – one of seven built with fourteen rather than eighteen intermediate cars – notched up 334.7km/h at 11.35 a.m. on 30 July 2003. The view vanishes as the train burrows under the North Downs in a 3km tunnel, emerging on to a downhill grade in the Nashenden Valley. Immediately ahead lies the 1.2km viaduct taking HS1 across the River Medway.

Only 90 minutes after leaving Brussels Train 9125 rolls imperceptibly on to the pristine tracks of Section 2 and races through the parkway station at Ebbsfleet at 230km/h before diving into the 2.5km tunnel under the River Thames. The Queen Elizabeth II road bridge over the Thames is briefly glimpsed on the left as the train powers across Rainham Marshes. Sweeping past Dagenham and Barking, where a terminal receives freight trains from mainland Europe that began using HS1 in 2011, the train slows for the 18km of tunnels that take HS1 under the densely populated suburbs of East London. The tracks and the tunnel structure here are cleverly designed to avoid transmitting noise and vibration into the surrounding ground.

Daylight appears briefly as the concrete box of the unfinished Stratford International station flashes by, but now the brakes are squealing and we emerge from the last tunnel to make the final approach. Sharp curves lead the long train over the Grand Union Canal, and we come to a stand beneath William Barlow's superbly restored train shed at London St Pancras. A band on the platform strikes up as the doors slide open – our time from Brussels–Midi was just 103 minutes. A similar train had made the trip from Paris on 4 September, completing the 491.1km in 123 minutes at an average speed of 239.5km/h.

St Pancras was an inspired choice to replace Waterloo as Britain's gateway to the Continent. There are connections to the Midlands, to the north-east from adjacent King's Cross, while Euston and its panoply of services to the West Midlands and the north-west is 10 minutes' walk away. Underneath the surface station are six Underground lines and new platforms for trains on the north–south Thameslink artery, destined for massive expansion by 2018.

Record number. Celebrations at Waterloo after Eurostar set 373 313/14 broke the British speed record on 30 July 2003. In the picture are Rob Holden (second from left), Chris Jago of Union Railways South (holding the 0) and Walt Bell of Union Railways North (on Jago's left). The figure translates to 334.7km/h. (Author)

River running. On 10 August 2007 a canoeist paddles downstream as a Eurostar speeds across the 1.2km-long Medway viaduct. The structure matches the parallel M2 viaduct visible in the picture on p176. (Eurostar)

DOMESTIC BLISS

St Pancras is also the terminus for domestic high-speed services from Kent. Launched on 29 June 2009 by train operator Southeastern using six-car Class 395 trains imported from Japan by Hitachi Rail Europe, they offer the residents of Thanet, Canterbury and the Medway Towns more time at home thanks to dramatically shorter journey times to London, admittedly for a premium fare. The trains have third-rail power collection to operate on conventional tracks and join HS1 at either Ashford or Ebbsfleet for a quick sprint to the capital under 25kV at up to 225km/h.

Inevitably described by the British media as 'bullet trains', they incorporate some high-speed technology, but their small-profile bodyshell is derived from Japanese narrow-gauge rolling stock. Adaptation to suit the conditions in Britain – which included meeting European crashworthiness standards – means that there is not much resemblance to anything on the Shinkansen. The twenty-nine trains played a starring role during the London Olympics in 2012, operating a frequent 'Javelin' shuttle between St Pancras and Ebbsfleet via Stratford, from where visitors had access to the main Olympic venues.

Arrival of Eurostars at St Pancras did much to enhance the image of high-speed rail travel in the UK, with the trip from the capital to Brussels taking just 1 hour 51 minutes (since relaxed to around 2 hours) and Paris just 2 hours 15 minutes away.

Other services (which had also run from Waterloo) ran to Disneyland Paris and, seasonally, Avignon and the French ski resort of Bourg-Saint-Maurice.

Of course, nothing is perfect, and Eurostar heaped a considerable amount of mud on its own reputation by messing up during bad weather. The worst of these events was a blizzard in December 2009 which led to five Eurostar trains breaking down in the Channel Tunnel – it was an expensive lesson as the collapse of the high-profile service generated a deluge of bad publicity and a very critical Independent Review.

In 2013, for the first time, Eurostar whisked more than 10 million passengers to and from mainland Europe – still below the original forecasts. The Eurostar network is set to expand in 2015–16 to destinations such as Amsterdam and Marseille, although the British government's security and immigration strictures will require the inbound Marseille service to decant its passengers at Lille to pass through the checks before regaining the train.

Some of Eurostar's planned services will be allocated to a fleet of ten e320 Velaro train sets ordered in 2010 from Siemens, much to the concern of Alstom, the traditional supplier of high-speed rolling stock to SNCF, the majority owner of Eurostar. The first train was hauled through the Channel Tunnel during the night of 29–30 January 2014 for delivery to Eurostar's London depot at Temple Mills from the Wildenrath test centre in Germany.

Ironically, the trains will be sixteen-car sisters to the eight-car ICE 3s that Deutsche Bahn hopes to run on the Frankfurt–London route – if its plan is ever implemented. The 320km/h fleet incorporates all the requirements for passage through the Channel Tunnel such as fire-resistant inter-car doors and the ability to continue operating for 30 minutes even after a fire breaks out. Each set has 222 first-class and 672 standard-class seats.

High-speed commuters. One of Southeastern's fleet of twenty-nine Hitachi-built Class 395 EMUs streaks away from the M20 near Charing on 20 April 2010 with a service from London St Pancras to Dover Priory. (Christophe Masse)

High-speed icon. Refurbished, re-engined and repainted, British Rail's diesel high-speed trains, dating from the 1970s, soldier on in 200km/h front-line service in 2015. Sporting temporary Virgin Trains East Coast branding, following the takeover of the InterCity East Coast franchise on 1 March 2015 by a Stagecoach–Virgin joint venture, a power car rests at London's King's Cross. (Author)

HERITAGE OF SPEED

To put Eurostar into context, Britain enjoys a magnificent history of designing and operating trains at 200km/h over existing tracks. It should never be forgotten that British Rail launched the world's first diesel-powered services at 200km/h as long ago as 1976 between London Paddington, Bristol and South Wales. Marketed as InterCity 125, these High Speed Trains (HSTs), re-engined and refurbished, continued to form the mainstay of inter-city services on the UK's Great Western Main Line in 2014.

On the East Coast Main Line to York, Newcastle and Edinburgh, they took over the *Flying Scotsman* duty in 1977, and on both routes these remarkable trains are subjected to some of the most demanding duty cycles for diesel traction anywhere in the world. On the East Coast route they share tracks with the IC225 push-pull electric fleet that emerged from British builders GEC and Metro Cammell in the late 1980s. These were designed with tilting coaches for 225km/h, but never tilted or ran at that speed in public service, although on 26 September 1991 a shortened formation sprinted over the 633km from London to Edinburgh in just 3 hours 29 minutes to mark completion of the East Coast electrification project.

On the Midland Main Line from St Pancras to Nottingham and Sheffield, HSTs are the train of choice for the cognoscenti travelling to and from Derby, where some of the UK's railway manufacturing resides. The alternative are the more recent and equally fast Meridian underfloor-engined diesel sets, sister trains to the Voyager and Super-Voyager diesel-electric multiple-units that operate many long-distance services on cross-country routes such as Bristol to Newcastle, as well as Virgin's services to Chester and North Wales. The forty-four-strong Super-Voyager fleet was built to tilt, but in 2008 the tilting gear on some of the fleet was isolated as the operator felt the journey time gains were not worth the extra cost and complexity. Both Voyagers and Meridians were built by Bombardier, initially at Bruges in Belgium and later in Wakefield.

Nor should the tragic saga of the Advanced Passenger Train (APT) be erased from memory. This was a bold but unsuccessful attempt in the early 1970s to develop a high-speed train using aerospace engineering. The idea was to achieve Shinkansen speeds on historic tracks, so avoiding the cost of new

ones, but the project was controversial and plagued by ill luck. The APT is remembered mainly because of its body tilting, and the Pendolinos that hum effortlessly up and down the sinuous West Coast Main Line suggest that the tilting strategy of the 1970s was actually correct.

Tilting perfection. The 200km/h Virgin Pendolinos are probably the world's most intensively used tilting trains. Maintained for Virgin by manufacturer Alstom, the trains link London Euston with Birmingham, Manchester, Liverpool and Glasgow over the busy and sinuous West Coast Main Line. (Alstom Transport)

The days of the HST are inevitably numbered, but some will survive for a few more years. Many will be replaced by another generation of inter-city trains developed under the government-driven Intercity Express Project (IEP). The IEPs will be supplied in two batches for the Great Western and East Coast main lines by Agility Trains, a consortium of Hitachi Rail Europe and John Laing Investments, which secured the contract in July 2012. This is a train service provision contract with the Department for Transport that looks to be rather more expensive than some of the alternatives that were put forward while the deal was being negotiated after bids were called in 2007.

Classes 800 and 801 are a Hitachi design that appears closely related to Class 395. The first of three pre-production trains began low-speed trials at Hitachi's Kasado factory in Japan in September 2014 for delivery in early 2015. Designed for 200km/h, the production build of ninety-two five-car and nine-car trains will be manufactured in Britain at a new factory at Newton Aycliffe in County Durham. The trains are distinguished by having underfloor diesel engines, both to provide auxiliary back-up power and to allow operation over non-electrified routes. This incurs a weight and cost penalty compared with a straight electric, but a comparable electro-diesel concept was chosen in 2013 for a fleet of thirty-four 'Coradia Liner' long-distance inter-city trains to be built by Alstom for SNCF.

SECOND HIGH-SPEED LINE

The IEP is certain to make headlines when it is launched, but media coverage has devoted far more attention to plans for Britain's second high-speed line. The concept of a line running north from London to Birmingham and beyond took root in January 2006 when an organisation called Greengauge 21 published its *High Speed Rail Initiative* to 'research and develop the concept of a high-speed rail network and to promote its implementation as a national economic priority'.

The idea gained momentum in October 2008 when newly appointed Labour Transport Secretary Geoff Hoon revealed that he had asked his Minister of Transport Lord Adonis to take a closer look at potential new rail routes. Remarkably, Shadow Transport Secretary Theresa Villiers had announced on 28 September that the opposition Conservative party favoured a north–south high-speed railway rather than a controversial third runway at London's Heathrow Airport, confirming that both major political parties were in favour.

On 15 January 2009 Hoon announced the establishment of High Speed Two Ltd (HS2 Ltd) to develop options for a new line from London to the West Midlands, as the West Coast Main Line was forecast to reach the limit of capacity by 2025. A decade-long £9 billion upgrading programme completed in 2008 had already lifted capacity, but the scheme was far more expensive than first envisaged. Nor did it achieve all its original objectives, with some of the planned improvements, particularly at the southern end of the line, left to be tackled at a later date – the money would arguably have been better spent on a new line right from the outset.

Favour returned? Japan's first railway was designed by Englishman Edmund Morel. Following in the footsteps of Japanese car manufacturers, Hitachi Rail Europe is setting up a European manufacturing base at Newton Aycliffe in County Durham to build trains for the British and European markets. One of three pre-production Intercity-Express trains destined for Britain's East Coast and Great Western main lines was unveiled in Japan in November 2014. (Nick Kingsley)

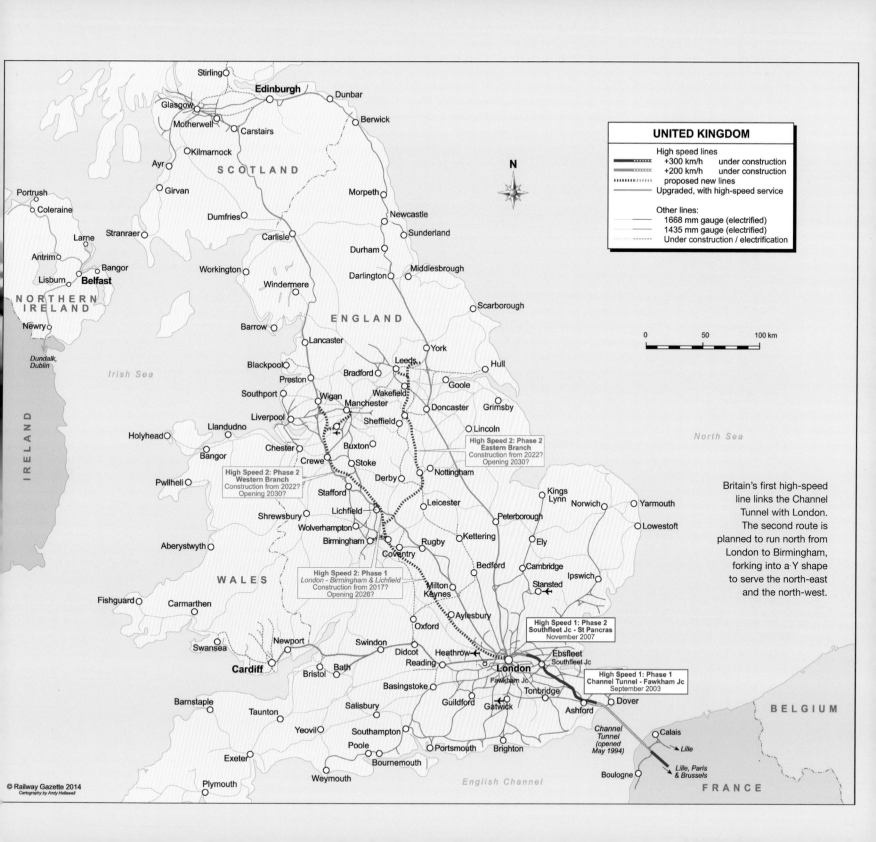

UNITED KINGDOM

High speed lines
+300 km/h   under construction
+200 km/h   under construction
proposed new lines
Upgraded, with high-speed service

Other lines:
1668 mm gauge (electrified)
1435 mm gauge (electrified)
Under construction / electrification

N

SCOTLAND

ENGLAND

WALES

NORTHERN
IRELAND

IRELAND

Irish Sea

North Sea

English Channel

BELGIUM

FRANCE

Stirling
Edinburgh
Glasgow
Motherwell
Carstairs
Kilmarnock
Ayr
Girvan
Dumfries
Carlisle
Dunbar
Berwick
Morpeth
Newcastle
Sunderland
Durham
Middlesbrough
Darlington
Scarborough

Portrush
Coleraine
Larne
Antrim
Stranraer
Bangor
Lisburn
Belfast
Newry

Dundalk,
Dublin

Workington
Windermere
Barrow
Lancaster
Blackpool
Preston
Southport
Wigan
Liverpool
Manchester
Bradford
Wakefield
Leeds
York
Hull
Goole
Doncaster
Grimsby
Sheffield
Lincoln
Buxton
Chester
Crewe
Stoke
Derby
Nottingham

Holyhead
Llandudno
Bangor
Pwllheli

Aberystwyth

Stafford
Lichfield
Shrewsbury
Wolverhampton
Birmingham
Coventry
Rugby
Leicester
Kettering
Peterborough
Kings
Lynn
Norwich
Yarmouth
Lowestoft
Ely
Cambridge
Ipswich
Stansted
Bedford
Milton
Keynes
Aylesbury
Oxford

Fishguard
Carmarthen
Swansea
Newport
Cardiff
Bristol
Bath
Swindon
Didcot
Reading
Heathrow
London
Fawkham Jc
Basingstoke
Guildford
Gatwick
Tonbridge
Ebsfleet
Southfleet Jc
Ashford
Dover

Barnstaple
Taunton
Salisbury
Yeovil
Southampton
Poole
Portsmouth
Brighton
Exeter
Bournemouth
Plymouth
Weymouth

Channel
Tunnel
(opened
May 1994)
Calais
Lille
Boulogne
Lille, Paris
& Brussels

High Speed 2: Phase 2
Eastern Branch
Construction from 2022?
Opening 2030?

High Speed 2: Phase 2
Western Branch
Construction from 2022?
Opening 2030?

High Speed 2: Phase 1
London - Birmingham & Lichfield
Construction from 2017?
Opening 2026?

High Speed 1: Phase 2
Southfleet Jc - St Pancras
November 2007

High Speed 1: Phase 1
Channel Tunnel - Fawkham Jc
September 2003

Britain's first high-speed
line links the Channel
Tunnel with London.
The second route is
planned to run north from
London to Birmingham,
forking into a Y shape
to serve the north-east
and the north-west.

0   50   100 km

© Railway Gazette 2014
Cartography by Andy Hellawell

HS2 Ltd duly produced a report with a preferred route, and in February 2011 the government issued a consultation document setting out its strategy. However, in terms of publicity, it appeared that no lessons had been learnt from the early years of HS1. HS2 had to pass through the Chiltern Hills, a favoured abode of the well-heeled and influential. The message came over that HS2 was merely about shaving a few minutes off the London–Birmingham trip. In fact, the main rationale was the need for more capacity on a crowded network where demand for rail travel was rising as the population expanded and road congestion made driving unattractive.

This message went largely unheard and unheeded, and the media went to town, aided and abetted by the swiftly constituted opposition focused around the Chilterns. 'Stop HS2' posters appeared across the countryside and anti-HS2 white elephant models could be spotted in unlikely places. More seriously, a series of legal challenges was drawn up.

Almost any worthy cause could be heard saying that it was better to spend money on its particular pet project than on HS2. A vocal campaign fronted by something called the HS2 Action Alliance fed a media that appeared astonishingly biased against the project. Many opponents claimed that the money would be better spent on other rail schemes – an argument that may have held water were it not for the fact that under the coalition government the level of investment in railway infrastructure such as electrification, station

From TGV Transmanche to Eurostar

The technical specification for the 300km/h Channel Tunnel trains that are universally known as Eurostars was drawn up by a team of engineers from British Rail, SNCF and SNCB in the late 1980s in conjunction with the Trans-Manche Super-Train Group, a consortium of British, French and Belgian suppliers formed in 1987 to build them. Described variously as Three Capitals trains and TGV Transmanche, they are part of the TGV family. Traction equipment was the responsibility of Britain's GEC, which helpfully signed a joint venture with France's Alsthom on 22 March 1989.

The specific requirements relating mainly to fires and safety for operation through the Channel Tunnel included the ability to split a train so that one half could be driven out of the Tunnel if the other half was damaged or on fire. Accordingly, the trains are built as two half sets, at the inner end of which is a 'secability box' housing a lever that can be used to disconnect all electrical and other links between the two sections.

Another constraint was the small British structure gauge on the historic tracks in southern England over which the trains would run before HS1 was built. Electrified at 750V DC with third-rail current collection, these routes featured high station platforms that obliged the design team to jiggle with the TGV bogie design to ensure that the yaw dampers did not foul the platforms and to come up with a novel type of retractable entrance steps. The trains also had to accept 25kV 50Hz for operation on LGV Nord-Europe in France

and Belgium and 3kV DC to run on conventional lines in Belgium. An array of signalling and train control equipment to match the different systems used in the three countries was also needed.

The initial contract was for thirty trains of two power and eighteen trailer cars, but variations changed the deal to cover thirty-one of these twenty-car sets plus another seven with only fourteen trailers for use north of London to fit Britain's short domestic platforms. As with the Paris–Sud-Est sets, the end trailers of both builds accommodate some of the traction equipment with drive to the bogie adjacent to the power car; each train thus has twelve powered axles. Asynchronous motors offer a continuous rating of 12.2MW when the train is drawing power at 25kV. In due course nine trains were modified for operation at 1.5kV DC in southern France to work the services to Avignon and Bourg-Saint-Maurice. Three were later transferred to SNCF ownership, leaving Eurostar International with twenty-eight 'Three Capitals' sets.

Partly because the British government would not allow international trains to carry domestic passengers, the north of London services never materialised as it was impossible to make a commercial case. Some of the 'short' fleet ran in 2000–05 on Britain's East Coast Main Line on Great North Eastern Railway's *White Rose* services to York and Leeds, while further use was found for some of them running domestic TGV services between Lille and Paris.

rebuilding, two cross-London railways and much more besides was far higher than at any time in living memory. Funding for HS2 is in addition to the considerable sums earmarked for improving the present network.

The promoters seemed barely able to make their voice heard. But the anti-HS2 campaign's strident calls to halt the plans were increasingly weakened as successive legal challenges were dismissed by judges.

In January 2012 the government announced that the project would go ahead in two phases. Opening in 2026, Phase 1 will run for 225km from a revamped London Euston to an interchange

at Old Oak Common and then north towards Birmingham. After another interchange close to Birmingham Airport and the National Exhibition Centre, the route will throw off a western spur to a new terminus at Birmingham Curzon Street. The main route will strike north towards Lichfield to rejoin the West Coast Main Line. Phase 2 will take the line further north in a Y shape to Leeds and Manchester, with intermediate stations serving the East Midlands, Sheffield Meadowhall and Manchester Airport. As with TGVs in France, trains will continue beyond the new line to reach many cities in northern England and Scotland.

Up to eighteen trains an hour are planned in each direction, with each service accommodating up to 1,100 passengers. Proposed journey times from Birmingham will see Manchester reached in 49 minutes, York in 63 minutes and Leeds in 57 minutes – more than halving the present timing. London to Manchester will take just 68 minutes and London to both Edinburgh and Glasgow 3 hours 38 minutes.

To reduce noise and other impacts, nearly one quarter of the line will run in tunnel and about one-third in cuttings. In 2012 the cost of the two phases was put at £28.2 billion, plus £14.4 billion for contingencies.

A Hybrid Bill, effectively a planning application, for Phase 1 was published on 25 November 2013, together with an environmental statement. The Bill had its Second Reading on 28 April 2014, and despite strong suggestions in the media that the project had lost the support of the Labour opposition, the Bill passed with a huge majority. The Second Reading firmly established the principle of the project, and a process of petitioning then began with the detail being scrutinised by a committee of MPs. Assuming that the project is not derailed by an incoming government after the general election in 2015, the Bill is likely to complete its passage through Parliament by the end of December 2016 so that work can start in late 2017.

On 1 January 2014 Network Rail Chief Executive Sir David Higgins took over as Chairman of HS2 Ltd – his track record included the role of Chief Executive at the Olympic Delivery Authority, whose work culminated in the immensely successful London 2012 Olympic and Paralympic Games. Higgins lost no time in producing his own report on HS2. Published in March 2014, this document recommended that 'the government should accelerate Phase 2 as soon

'No' campaign. Posters opposing HS2 appeared in villages close to the route soon after the plans were announced. Despite media suggestions to the contrary, both the coalition government and the Labour opposition remained firm supporters of the project during 2014.

Low impact. The HS2 design team plans a range of measures to ensure the line blends into the landscape.
Tunnels will have specially configured portals to dissipate the noise of trains passing through at high speed. (HS2 Ltd)

Royal Opening

On 6 May 1994 Waterloo was the starting point for the Royal Eurostar when HM Queen Elizabeth II travelled to Coquelles near Calais to inaugurate the Channel Tunnel. In a carefully staged extravaganza that will never be repeated, her train arrived at a red-carpeted platform in Eurotunnel's French shuttle train terminal at precisely the same moment that a Eurostar conveying President Mitterrand from Paris drew to a halt at the same platform — but arriving from the opposite direction. The nose of the train with Union Jacks emblazoned on it was just metres away from the one decorated with the red, white and blue *Tricolore*.

Royal occasion. The Eurostar conveying HM Queen Elizabeth II from London Waterloo halts at a red-carpeted platform in the Eurotunnel shuttle terminal at Coquelles, nose-to-nose with the train that has carried President Mitterrand from Paris. The date is 6 May 1994. (Author)

as possible' to take the line 69km further north than planned in Phase 1 'to a new transport hub at Crewe which could be completed by 2027, six years earlier than planned'. Higgins also believed that more work on Phase 2 was needed to give better connectivity with the conventional network in northern England.

Apart from recommending completion of Phase 2 in 2030, Higgins believed that a proposed link to HS1 should be 'reconsidered' as the plan was 'sub-optimal'. The HS2-HS1 link was subsequently dropped from the Bill for Phase 1, and given the security and immigration concerns that wrecked plans for North of London Eurostar services, there seems little prospect of direct high-speed trains linking cities north of London with mainland Europe in the foreseeable future.

In parallel with the Parliamentary process, HS2 Ltd forged ahead to develop the technical specifications so that all was ready to start as soon as the political process was complete. In September 2014 Technical Director Professor Andrew McNaughton said that many 'big decisions' had still to be taken. These included choices between slab and ballasted track and whether to have one or two types of train in the 180-strong fleet – there could be a 'captive' design for the London–Birmingham/Manchester/Leeds services, which will generate the bulk of the revenue, and a 'classic-compatible' variant for trains running beyond the core infrastructure.

All equipment will meet the latest European technical standards, but much of the design effort is focused on finding a good balance between the trains and the infrastructure. Noise, for example, can be controlled by special features on the trains and by lineside mitigation, and McNaughton was considering how to incentivise suppliers to offer quieter trains.

In line with aspirations in Japan and elsewhere, maximum speed will be 360km/h, although the alignment will be designed for 400km/h. HS2 Ltd has received help and advice from France, Germany and Japan, and JR East has been consulted on specific topics. Spain has provided valuable knowledge of integrating ETCS Level 2 equipment from different suppliers – HS2 will have Level 2 with Automatic Train Operation. Italy's NTV offered an excellent model for train maintenance, and McNaughton sees that operator's *italo* fleet as a reference for high-speed train design. Of particular interest is HS2's aspiration to achieve Shinkansen reliability: the target is an average delay of 'less than 30 seconds per service'.

McNaughton was clear about HS2's objectives: 'it's about emptying the motorways and getting people to travel who don't travel now – the more people travel, the more prosperous the country gets'. A 'passenger panel' has been set up to obtain input from the public, and McNaughton insists that there will be a 'wow factor' about the design of trains and stations. Apart from the obvious benefits of shorter journey times, HS2 will generate a much-needed pool of railway engineering expertise thanks to the establishment of a National College for High Speed Rail with headquarters in Birmingham and another site in Doncaster. The HS2 project promises to be a testament to the best of high-speed railway engineering in the 2020s, offering fast, safe and reliable travel between the north and south of Britain for generations to come.

Man with a mission. Sir David Higgins, former Chief Executive of the Olympic Delivery Authority, was appointed Chairman of HS2 Ltd in January 2014. Publishing his report 'HS2 Plus' on 17 March 2014 in Manchester after an eight-week review, Higgins said that, 'I firmly believe that HS2 is essential for the future of this country.' (HS2 Ltd)

Details of Selected High-Speed Trains

	TGV-Duplex	ICE 3 (Class 407)	S-112	N700	CRH380D
Country	France	Germany	Spain	Japan	China
Operator	SNCF	DB	Renfe Operadora	JR Central	CRC
Length *m*	200.19	200.0	200.0	404.7	215.3
Cars	2+8	8	2+12	16	8
Powered axles	8	16	8	56	16
Power supply	various[1]	4 systems[2]	25kV 50Hz	25kV 60Hz	25kV 50Hz
Power rating *kW*	8,800	8,000	8,000	17,080	10,000
Maximum speed *km/h*	320	320	330	300[3]	380
Seating capacity	512/509/634[4]	460	353	1,323	569
Weight *tonnes*[5]	380	454	322	715[6]	458
Highest axle load	17	17	17	11.4[7]	17

1 25kV 50Hz/1.5kV DC; some sets also 15kV 16.7Hz
2 25kV 50Hz/15kV 16.7Hz/1.5kV DC/3kV DC
3 270km/h on Tokaido Shinkansen; 300km/h on Sanyo Shinkansen
4 Ouigo sets
5 Weight in working order or empty weight
6 Loaded weight
7 Series 700

Selected Rail Speed Records

Date	Speed *km/h*	Country	Location	Vehicle
27 Oct 1903	210.2	Germany	Marienfelde–Zossen	AEG electric railcar
9 May 1904	164.6	UK	Exeter–Taunton	City of Truro steam loco
21 June 1931	230.2	Germany	Ludwigslust–Wittenberge	Schienenzeppelin
19 Dec 1932	165.0	Germany	Berlin–Hamburg	VT877 diesel railcar
11 May 1936	201	Germany	Hamburg–Berlin	05-002 steam loco
3 July 1938	203	UK	Grantham–Peterborough	A4 Mallard steam loco
20 July 1939	203	Italy	Bologna–Milan	ETR232
28 Mar 1955	331*	France	Lamothe–Morcenx	CC7107
29 Mar 1955	331	France	Lamothe–Morcenx	BB9004
23/24 July 1966	295.8	USA	Bryan, Ohio	M–497 railcar
4 May 1978	230.0	Spain	Alcázar de San Juan–Rio Záncara	Class 353 Talgo loco
20 Dec 1979	257.5	UK	Beattock–Lockerbie	APT-P
26 Feb 1981	380.4	France	Moulins-en-Tonnerrois	TGV Set 16
1 May 1988	406.9	Germany	Hohe Wart–Mottgers	IC-Experimental
18 May 1990	515.3	France	Courtalain–Tours	TGV Set 325
24 May 1991	319.0	Italy	Rome–Florence	ETR500X
8 Aug 1992	350.4	Japan	Ogori–Shin Shimonoseki	WIN350
23 Apr 1993	356.8	Spain	Mora–Urda	S-100
3 June1993	220.0	Portugal	Espinho–Avanca	LE56 electric loco
21 July 1993	276.0	Sweden	Falkenberg–Varberg	X2000
5 Oct 1993	271.0	Russia	Shluze–Doroshikha	TEP80 diesel loco
21 Dec 1993	425	Japan	Tsubame-Sanjo–Niigata	STAR21
11 May 1994	251	Poland	Warsaw–Kattowice	ETR460
12 Nov 1995	360	Germany	Hannover–Göttingen	ICE power cars+Talgo set
26 July 1996	443.0	Japan	Kyoto–Maibara	JR Central 300X
6 Nov 1997	354	Belgium	Brussels–Antoing	PBKA set

24 June 1998	239.7	China	Zhengzhou–Wuhan	SS8 electric loco
9 July 2002	254	Spain	Bujaraloz–Vallmanya	Talgo XXI diesel
27 Nov 2002	321.5	China	Shenyang–Qinhuangdao	China Star
6 Apr 2003	362	Japan	Urasa–Niigata	E2-1000
20 Aug 2004	305	Austria	Vienna–Linz	ICE-S
2 Mar 2006	336.2	Netherlands	Hazeldonk–Rotterdam	PBKA set
2 July 2006	390	Spain	Alcalá de Henares–Calatayud	S-103
30 July 2003	334.7	UK	Ashford–Ebbsfleet	Eurostar 373-313/14
16 July 2006	404	Spain	Madrid–Lleida	S-103
2 Sep 2006	357	Germany	Kinding–Allersberg	'Taurus' electric loco
3 Apr 2007	574.8	France	Vaires–Baudrecourt	V150
26 July 2007	281	Sweden	Stockholm–Göteborg	Regina EMU
14 Sep 2007	303	Turkey	Beylikova–Esenkt	ETR500Y2
8 Nov 2007	288	Switzerland	Ferden–Lötschen	ICE
1 Mar 2008	355	Italy	Milan–Bologna	ETR500Y1
24 June 2008	394.3	China	Tianjin–Beijing	CRH3
3 Feb 2009	362	Italy	Florence–Bologna	ETR500Y1
2 May 2009	281	Russia	Okulovka–Mstinskiy Most	Sapsan
29 May 2009	235	Poland	Psary–Gora Wlodowska	'Taurus' electric loco
28 Sep 2010	416.6	China	Shanghai–Hangzhou	CRH380A
3 Dec 2010	486.1	China	Beijing–Shanghai	CRH380A
10 Jan 2011	487.3	China	Beijing–Shanghai	CRH380BL
31 Mar 2013	421.4	South Korea	Seoul–Busan	HEMU-430X
2 Dec 2013	293	Poland	Gora Wlodowska–Psary	Pendolino

★ Official recorded figure, subsequently revealed to be 326km/h

Index